A POLICY OF

KENNETH CRAGG

AND

ISLAM

Christopher A Lamb

Islam in Christian minds must always be the object of a policy of hope
Kenneth Cragg

MELISENDE

A POLICY OF HOPE

Kenneth Cragg and Islam

First published 2014 by Melisende
London
ISBN 9781901764 71 0

Published in association with the HRH Prince Alwaleed bin Talal Centre for the Study of Islam in the Contemporary World, University of Edinburgh.
For further details of the Centre, see www.alwaleed.ed.ac.uk.

www.melisende.com

Printed and bound in England by 4Edge

In grateful memory of
David Kerr
Scholar, Teacher and Friend

CONTENTS

Note

Every effort has been made for consistency in the transliteration of Arabic words, but the original authors' usage has been retained in direct quotations, and they have not always been consistent.

INTRODUCTION

Some of the most interesting theologians are those who seem to be perpetually talking with themselves—and I don't mean talking to themselves, the mark of a depressing number of religious professionals. A theologian who talks with himself or herself is one on whose inner questioning and self-challenge we are privileged to eavesdrop. We see or hear them testing their best insights and most eloquent formulations, risking some bold or wild or over-complex statement so as to get the sense of how it will 'sit' in an argument. They will not satisfy those who want systems; but there will be no sustainable systems without their voice.

Augustine is the most famous, of course; but Kenneth Cragg is surely another. Reading Kenneth Cragg, you don't feel he is out to persuade you of his case so much as that he is out to walk you through a sometimes vastly complex internal conversation, so that you can see where the final proposals and expression come from. In his last years—unusually—the inner conversation grew more and more intense and the reflections more and more many-layered and sometimes tangled, yet always (the word can't be avoided) beautiful—crafted with immense care, evocative of an unmanageable range of allusion and feeling. Reading his work, there is an awareness of rare transparency. But it is not an easy journey, and the reader is bound to ask repeatedly how such an unusual mind is formed.

Christopher Lamb charts that formation with clarity and insight. He does not shy away from the hard questions or deny the frustration that sometimes overtakes the reader. He depicts very lucidly how Bishop Kenneth comes to identify his focal question to the Muslim interlocutors he so loved and respected: can the Islamic vision, with all its overwhelming awareness of the divine liberty and sovereign otherness, cope with the self-humbling of such a liberty in the remaking of the human world through mortal fragility? It is a question of fundamental importance and one that is not easy for a Muslim to hear. Yet the love and respect he felt was amply returned, and very few Muslims wanted to deny him the right to ask such a question. Not only was his intellectual integrity respected; he was readily recognized as a person of spiritual authority and depth. Not long ago, I met a Muslim scholar who had not yet heard of Bishop Kenneth's death; when I told him, his reaction was one of instant and manifestly deep grief, and he spread his hands immediately in prayer.

This is the thinker—and the believer—whom this book so ably and sympathetically portrays. The many people for whom he was a touchstone of theological insight especially in interfaith matters will be glad of such a comprehensive and careful guide to his thought and its evolution. And they will all share the hope that it will also inspire a new generation to wrestle with this long and intense 'inner conversation'—remembering that, for Augustine, the honest setting-out of such a conversation was in itself an invitation to converse with the eternal Word. Bishop Kenneth's friends and pupils would say no less of him.

+*Rowan Williams*

1

THE MAKING OF A PIONEER THINKER

1 Outlines of his Career

Too bright for our infirm Delight
The Truth's superb surprise.

These favourite lines from Emily Dickinson are some of the verses prefacing Kenneth Cragg's autobiographical *Faith and Life Negotiate: a Christian Story-Study.*[1] The sketch of his life which follows here is hugely amplified in that book, together with much reflection on the surprises of its twists and turns. The titles especially of his later books do not always fall easily on the ear, but like the texts they introduce they reflect the rich hinterland of his mind. His long career of study, travel, speaking and writing began on 8 March 1913, born Albert Kenneth, the younger son of Albert and Emily Cragg, a devout couple of evangelical Anglican conviction. He was educated at Blackpool Grammar School, and Jesus College, Oxford, where he read Modern History, narrowly missing first class honours. His elder brother Herbert had already preceded him to Tyndale Hall, Bristol, and into the ministry of the Church of England, and in 1936 Kenneth was ordained to serve in the parish of St Catherine's, Higher Tranmere, Birkenhead, in the diocese of Chester, where he met Theodora Melita Arnold. They married in Beirut in 1940. Cragg's first professional role was as a pastor, but he did not neglect study during his curacy, and in 1936 successfully submitted an essay for the Ellerton Theological Prize at Oxford University on the subject of 'The Place of Authority in Matters of Religious Belief'. In 1939 he fulfilled long-cherished hopes by beginning his missionary service in Lebanon under the auspices of the British Syria Mission, soon to be joined by Melita. After initial language study and teaching in a Bible college he became attached

1 The Canterbury Press, Norwich 1994. References to Cragg's books in the text that follows is by abbreviated title and page number. Only occasional reference will be made to *Negotiate.*

to the American University of Beirut, and founded and ran a hostel for Arab students. The university was seriously short of staff in wartime conditions, so Charles Malik, the head of the Department of Philosophy, invited Cragg to teach in the department. He became the acting head of the department on the departure of Malik to be Lebanese ambassador in Washington, and proved his philosophical competence by winning a further prize at Oxford University in 1947 with an essay for the T H Green Moral Philosophy Prize on 'Morality and Religion'.

In 1947 the couple returned to England so that Cragg could pursue doctoral studies in Islam. In order to help him find sufficient income for his growing family (there were eventually three sons), his old Oxford college presented him to the recently vacated living of Longworth in Berkshire, where he lived while completing his D.Phil. His subject was 'Islam in the Twentieth Century: The Relevance of Christian Theology and the Relation of the Christian Mission to its Problems'. It was presented not to the Faculty of Oriental Studies but to the Faculty of Theology, so his primary academic qualification was not as an orientalist but as a theologian. His supervisor was Dr Ernest Payne, who was learned in Hinduism rather than Islam, and his examiners were H A R Gibb, the Islamicist, and Herbert Danby, the translator of the Talmud. The dissertation was a massive work of some 300,000 words, far longer than universities would allow today. On its successful completion he was appointed to the chair of Arabic and Islamics at the Hartford Seminary Foundation, Connecticut, USA, where he remained from 1951-1956. Hartford was the home of the journal *The Muslim World*, founded by Samuel Zwemer in 1911 in the wake of the Edinburgh Conference of 1910. It was to be a focus of Christian missionary thought about Islam, and remains today one of the major English-language periodicals on Islam. From 1952-1960 Cragg jointly edited the journal with Edwin Calverley, his predecessor in the chair of Islamics. Cragg contributed most of the editorials.

In 1956 he published his classic work *The Call of the Minaret* (revised and reissued in 1986 and again in 2000), and left Hartford to be a residentiary canon of St George's Cathedral, Jerusalem, at that time part of Jordan. 'Residential' he was not, however. Two years earlier he had been awarded a Rockefeller Travelling Scholarship (at the suggestion of Wilfred Cantwell Smith), and this had taken him on extensive journeys through the Middle East from Tangier to Baghdad. This experience helped to develop the idea of a Study Programme, which, with the encouragement of the International Missionary Council and Bishop Stewart of Jerusalem took shape in 1956 as 'Operation Reach'. From 1956 to 1959 he was constantly on the move alerting Christian groups throughout the Middle East and beyond to the issues of Christian engagement with Islam and with Muslims, and holding Summer Schools on Islam at St George's College, Jerusalem.

This period of intense travel ended with the appointment of Cragg, now known internationally as a Christian interpreter of Islam, to St Augustine's College, Canterbury. He was a Fellow from 1959, and Warden from 1961. The missionary scholar had moved into a position of ecclesiastical leadership. His colleague and predecessor as Warden was Kenneth Sansbury, subsequently Bishop of Singapore and then General Secretary of the British Council of Churches. The intention had been that St Augustine's should serve as a Central College for the Anglican Communion, providing a variety of courses, for older ordination candidates, for those with considerable ministerial experience, and for potential church leaders. The institution lacked, however, a historic constituency among the different ecclesiastical parties of the Church of England, and was not adequately supported either by the General Assembly or by the rest of the Anglican Communion. To Cragg's lasting regret it closed in 1967, leaving him with no clear future. At this time Campbell McInnes, Anglican Archbishop in Jerusalem, renewed a suggestion made previously that Cragg should become his Assistant Bishop, but proposed a year's 'breathing space'. Before the end of that year, however, McInnes had resigned through ill health, and extensive discussions about the nature of Anglican leadership in the Middle East meant that George Appleton, his successor, was not appointed till 1969. Cragg in consequence became a Visiting Professor in the University of Ibadan, Nigeria, one of the leading universities in West Africa, before taking up a temporary appointment as a Bye-Fellow at Gonville and Caius College, Cambridge.

Cragg was consecrated Assistant Bishop in the Jerusalem Archbishopric in February 1970, and lived in Cairo for some two and a half years. He resigned in 1973 to allow an Egyptian Arab, Ishaq Musa'ad, to become bishop of the revived Anglican diocese of Egypt, which had been suspended since 1958. He had collaborated with Musa'ad on a translation of 'Abduh's *Theology of Unity* when they had both been at Canterbury in 1964. Cragg's book *Paul and Peter* (1980) is dedicated to Musa'ad and two others. Cragg, now again redundant, moved to Sussex University, where he was Reader in Religious Studies until obliged to retire in 1978, at the age of 65. He was also honorary Assistant Bishop in the diocese of Chichester. From 1978 to 1981 he returned to parochial life as Vicar of Helme, just outside Huddersfield, in the diocese of Wakefield, where he was also an Assistant Bishop. In 1981 he retired to a village near Oxford (again becoming an Assistant Bishop in the diocese), but continued to write and lecture extensively for another 30 years, publishing his sixtieth and last book, *Bent to Literary Event. Masters in their Masterpieces*[2] in 2011, at the age of 98. He died in November 2012, just four months short of his century.

The bare bones of his career give some idea of the sustained commitment to study, to the Muslim world, and to the Christian Church which marked his life. Pastoral, missionary, academic and literary concerns were its keynotes. It is also abundantly clear, especially from what happened to Cragg in the late sixties and early seventies, that his Church was not well organised to make maximum use of the particular combination of gifts that he possessed. No way could be found of employing him adequately in the Church of England in 1967, or in the Episcopal Church in Jerusalem and the Middle East (the new title of the Jerusalem Archbishopric) in 1973. Nor, after his departure from Sussex University in 1978, did the Church of England seem to be really alert to the possibilities of using so gifted and experienced a man in ministry to the growing number of Muslims in Britain, though his move to Huddersfield was an attempt to meet that concern. The verdict may be that he was too much of a pioneer to fit easily into Anglican structures still geared to a mono-religious society.

Cragg's career might be seen as an indication of the marginal status which has sometimes been the reward of British people deeply involved with other faiths and cultures. At the height of Empire in 1884, the great Persian scholar Edward Granville Browne was warned at the outset of his career by the Cambridge Arabist William Wright that

> The posts for which such knowledge will fit you are few, and, for the most part, poorly endowed, neither can you hope to obtain them till you have worked and waited for many years. And from the Government you must look for nothing, for it has long shown, and still continues to show, an increasing indisposition to offer the slightest encouragement to the study of Eastern languages.[3]

Not until the mid-1970s did Islam and other faiths begin to become significant issues for the Churches of Britain. Ecclesiastical debates centred on quite other matters. But some of Cragg's own contemporaries with extensive involvement in the world of Islam were not so marginalized in the life of the Church. David Brown and Sir Norman Anderson, both at one time missionaries in the Middle East, became respectively Bishop of Guildford and Chairman of the House of Laity in the Church of England's General Synod.

2 Melisende, London, 2011.

3 Browne, E G, *A Year among the Persians 1887-1888*, Century, London, 1984, p. 3.

Was it then a question of personality? Some might suppose that Cragg's intellectual powers meant that he lacked the common touch, but this is not supported by his parishioners at Helme, who witness to a pastor eager to communicate with every sort of person at all ages in the village. It seems that through a combination of circumstances Cragg became one of those extremely able people who are almost exclusively identified with their field of specialism in spite of real interests and ability outside it, and consequently do not win general confidence as a Church leader.

There is no doubt about the tributes paid to Cragg's importance as a highly-skilled interpreter of Islam for Christians and as a missionary to Islam. Among English-speaking interpreters of Islam he is in the general tradition, and of the stature of men like Samuel Zwemer, Duncan Black Macdonald and Temple Gairdner. A garland of praise can easily be put together for him from his contemporaries. For the historian of Western attitudes to Islam, Norman Daniel: 'Bishop Cragg is the most perceptive and authoritative interpreter of Islam in English (or, in my view, in any language) to Christian readers.'[4] For the Indian Muslim diplomat and scholar Asaf Fyzee (commenting on Cragg's contribution to a series of books on other faiths): 'No better man could be selected to deal with Islam in the English speaking world.'[5] For the Oxford historian of the Middle East, Albert Hourani, Cragg 'is one of our finest Islamic scholars.'[6] Wilfred Cantwell Smith called Cragg 'the eloquent conscience of the Protestant missionary movement',[7] and Max Warren, the General-Secretary of the Anglican Church Missionary Society, called him 'my revered and beloved teacher'.[8] The biographer of Warren, one of the most significant of post-war missionary thinkers, reckons that 'The Call of the Minaret ... made an indelible impression upon Max's whole philosophy of mission.'[9]

What sort of person earned such accolades? The career outlined above reveals a man at home in three continents, tireless in travel, closely

4 Daniel, Norman, review of *Muhammad and the Christian* and *Jesus and the Muslim* in *The Tablet,* 16 August 1986.

5 Fyzee, Asaf A A, review of *The House of Islam* in *Islamic Culture* (January 1976, pp. 48-9).

6 Hourani, Albert, art. 'Christians and Muslims' in *Frontier* 3:2 (Summer 1960), p 128 [reprinted in Hourani: *Europe and the Middle East*, Macmillan, London, 1980, chapter 3].

7 Smith, Wilfred Cantwell, review of *Christianity in World Perspective* in *Journal of American Academy of Religion* 37 (Summer 1969), p. 306.

8 Warren, Max, *A Theology of Attention*, CLS/ISPCK, Madras, 1971, p. 12.

9 Dillistone, F W, *Into All the World. A Biography of Max Warren*, Hodder and Stoughton, London, 1980, p. 200.

associated with half a dozen universities, deeply involved in the task of Christian ministry at several different levels, and perhaps above all gifted with a desire and ability to communicate in the spoken and written word whether in the parish magazine or the learned journal. His output was immense; the sixty books included four full-length translations from Arabic. There were also contributions to twenty-one other books, and over eighty major articles, as well as four series of lengthy pamphlets and the editorship of *The Muslim World* for eight years. This gives some clue to the fascination with words which marks Cragg most as a scholar and thinker. For he not only produces words but plays with them, feeling for their richness and their ambiguity. A typical passage begins with a favourite quotation:

> 'Rescue a word … discover a universe … Can we bury ourselves in a lexicon and arise in the presence of God?' … Words are the highways of the traffic of ideas, sentiments, emotions, and relationships, and the work of the world is done by them … (In translation) the word is the point of exchange. [*Call*, pp. 243, 244]

Here Cragg opens his theme of 'the Call to Interpretation' by reminding us of the power and flexibility of words. The same idea begins the book itself. And not content with other people's words, Cragg continually coins new ones of his own: 'scriptuary', 'Arabicity', 'dissession', 'equijacent', 'paradoxiality', 'illude'. There is always the chance that such inventions may puzzle, or irritate, or confuse the reader. But words inspire him with a sense of adventure, and a desire to be bold and creative with them. The alternative, he feels, is a smaller and poorer world. 'Unrisking minds mean cautious trusts and so, in turn, diminished meanings. The claims of communication ought always to be paramount.' [*World*, p. 74]

The range of his quotations reveals a mind with broad sympathies, and a highly developed skill for making connections between apparently unrelated topics. The next chapter reviews his specific books on literary topics. Here we note the quotations he makes in his specialist books on Islam and world religions. Among novelists he quotes from Americans in particular—from Hemingway, Faulkner, Melville, Steinbeck and Henry Thoreau, but also from George Eliot, D H Lawrence, John Cowper Powys, E M Forster, Somerset Maugham, and Laurens van der Post; from Proust, Camus, Sartre, Thomas Mann, Kafka and Dostoevsky; from James Joyce, Samuel Beckett and Chinua Achebe. With poets the list grows even longer: from Chaucer, Langland, Shakespeare, Donne, Herbert, Milton, Vaughan,

Traherne, Blake, Wordsworth and Browning: from Hardy, Burns, Kipling and de la Mare; from Wilfred Owen, Arthur Clough, T S Eliot, George Macdonald, Rainer Maria Rilke, R S Thomas and especially Robert Frost.

Such a random recital by no means exhausts his repertoire. Nor are such quotations restricted to his more general and discursive works, like *The Privilege of Man* and *Christianity in World Perspective*, where one might anticipate some broader brush-strokes. A chapter in *The Mind of the Qur'an* begins with a passage from a letter of Van Gogh [*Mind*, p. 146], and a chapter on Buddhism with one of the reflections of Dag Hammarskjöld in his *Markings*. [*Christ*, p. 245] The reader may suddenly turn the page to seven verses of a poem from Pushkin, entitled 'The Prophet' [*Event*, p. 85], or find himself following the association of ideas in Pasternak's Russian translation from *Hamlet*, put back into English. [*Christ*, p. 11f] Cragg has a particular fondness for beginning chapters or sections of chapters with some apparently remote quotation which turns out on closer examination to be remarkably apt. The most sustained example of this comes at the opening of *The Privilege of Man*, which begins with Hemingway's *The Old Man and the Sea*, and passes in rapid succession to the opening words of John Cowper Powys's *A Glastonbury Romance*, Samuel Beckett's *Malone Dies* and Herman Melville's *Moby Dick*, before settling on the curtain-raising words of *Hamlet* as the right beginning. [*Privilege*, pp. 1, 2]

Virtuoso catenas of quotation like this may irritate some readers, but they illustrate the capacity of a mind searching the ranges of literature for clues about how to begin communicating with the bewildering variety of human experience. When that mind also possesses a keen sense of the nuances of words, the search for an appropriate title to a book can be prolonged, and the result more awkward than arresting. The sure touch sometimes falters, especially in his final book *Bent to Literary Event,* a title he does not even explain. Cragg reveals that he 'toyed' with several titles like 'In Stead of God' and 'In Lieu of God' for what became *The Privilege of Man*, only to discover it had also become the title of a popular film, with a rather different meaning. [*Privilege*, p. vii] The introduction to *The Christian and Other Religion*, so often misquoted with a final '*s*' to *Religion*, also hints at a problematic choice of title. [*Other*, p. xiii] Gillian Paterson, who was the Cassells book editor responsible for his *Palestine. The Prize and Price of Zion* reports that she had a hard task to dissuade him from entitling the book 'Palestine Agonistes'. Few, she thought, would understand the reference to Milton's Samson Agonistes, 'eyeless in Gaza'.

These literary skills and considerations raise the question at the outset of whether Cragg's is not a rather 'literary', in the sense of unreal and artificial, approach to the subject of religion. There is perhaps a conflict within him between a deep love of literature of all kinds, and an equally deep conviction that where faith is concerned it is better to meet the faithful than to turn to books to understand them. Should he open the dictionary or go to the mosque? But Cragg is very critical of any 'spectator attitude' on the part of writers, any attitude to human experience which treats it primarily as raw material for literature. He twice attacks the novelist Somerset Maugham for suggesting that 'Nothing befalls (the artist) that he cannot transmute into a stanza, a song or a story and having done this to be rid of it.' [*Passage*, p. xiv and *Other*, p. 128] All his books urge a personal engagement with the people of other faiths, and not merely with their thought or their history.

How successful and complete has his own engagement been? We shall want to examine later what gaps are evident in Cragg's account of Islam, but it seems wise to concentrate our main efforts on establishing the essential theological convictions from which Cragg works as an interpreter of Islamic literature and life, in terms of his doctrines of God and humanity, of his understanding of the nature of religion, and of the central question (for Cragg) of the manner in which those truths are guarded and promoted, of their political custody. Having examined his theological 'method' in this way, we then need to identify his theological goal, the task of mission, before coming to the crucial question of the adequacy of his criteria of interpretation.

The question which needs to be borne in mind throughout is whether, despite Cragg's great reputation in certain circles, his view of Islam and other faiths, and the view of Christianity on which it is ultimately based, turns out finally to be a rather idiosyncratic and personal view, not easily shared or expounded by others, or recognised as having much degree of plausibility by Muslims themselves. Alternatively, can it be said that Cragg's theme and the techniques he proposes of 'retrieval' offer a theological method with profound evangelical and ethical implications? That his work has significance for relations between different faith communities which are of critical contemporary importance?

The initial task must be to investigate further his personal and religious background in order to discover in more detail what has shaped him as a thinker, and whom it is he has in mind when writing.

2 His Intellectual Formation

> It was a life of unrelieved repetition, with never a new thing, from the time the study year began until it was over … Throughout these studies it was all merely a case of hearing re-iterated words and traditional talk which aroused no

> chord in my heart, nor taste in my appetite ... I had become competent to understand what the shaikhs repeated. But all to no point. [*Passage*, pp. 1, 2]

Cragg does not suggest that his motive for translating the final volume of Taha Husain's autobiography was anything other than his admiration for the tenacity of the blind scholar, his defiance of his handicap. The translation was done in Cairo at a time of 'considerable personal difficulty' connected with his resignation as Bishop in 1973, and this must have impressed meaning on the message of courage and hope implicit in the book. But there is another significance in Husain's story for understanding the mind of Cragg. The passage quoted above reflects Husain's experience of the Azhar, the great bastion of traditional Sunni Muslim learning in Cairo, and the book goes on to recount the stages of his intellectual liberation, culminating in his achievement of a doctorate at the Sorbonne. Cragg too passed from an Azhar to a Sorbonne, and the experience marked his life and shaped his thinking permanently.

As already noted, Cragg was reared in a devout evangelical family, supporters like their parish church, of the Bible Churchmen's Missionary Society (BCMS, now renamed 'Crosslinks'). Cragg's brother Herbert (1910-1980) remained all his life in this conservative evangelical Anglican tradition, and was for many years Chairman of the Keswick Convention, a yearly focus since 1875 for studies on what its Handbook calls 'practical scriptural holiness'. Kenneth sent Herbert a copy of *The Call of the Minaret* on its publication in 1956, but was convinced that the book had remained unread because of its 'unsound' views. It was only many years later that he was moved to discover his brother quoting from it in his very last address at Keswick.

The move to a more liberal interpretation of Christian faith did not happen rapidly. 'Looking back (he wrote in 1994) I find myself intrigued by the things I never questioned yet ardently loved and I am tempted to wonder now whether fervour always means a certain imperception.' [*Negotiate*, p. 21] At Jesus College, Oxford, where he was an undergraduate from 1931-1934, Cragg studied Modern History, but was already thinking of working overseas as a BCMS missionary. On the completion of his degree he wanted to do his ordination training and theological studies at Wycliffe Hall, Oxford, which was also an evangelical college but with a more open tradition. But his narrow failure to obtain a first class degree deprived him of his college's financial support to remain in Oxford, so he went to the college founded by BCMS for missionary and ordination training, Tyndale Hall in Bristol, where his brother had also studied. [*Negotiate*, p. 44] There he found few satisfactory answers to his growing theological questioning. Critical studies of the Bible were treated as material to be learnt for the Church of England's General Ordination Examination and then forgotten as quickly as possible. Cragg found that his attempts to discuss theological questions with the teaching staff were dealt with only by handing out a series of cyclostyled notes. These gave the interpretation of the issue concerned which was acceptable within the college and the BCMS tradition. He found himself wearying of the insistent question asked about any prominent churchman, potential speaker or colleague: 'Where does he stand?' A man's theological position seemed to have overtaken his importance as a person. It was when Cragg went to his first parish appointment as curate that he began to find freedom from these attitudes. The vicar of the parish was Henry Hill, to whom, with Francis Graham Brown, the Anglican Bishop in Jerusalem, Cragg later dedicated *The Call of the Minaret.* Hill was himself conservative in theology, but held that 'you cannot repudiate relationships in the name of dogma', and sought to remain on close personal terms with those of very different persuasion in the locality.

The complex history behind an ecclesiastical tradition characterised by such apparently closed minds needs to be carefully understood. Ten years of Cragg's youth, from 1918 to 1928, were years of continual theological conflict within the Church of England. In 1917 Hensley Henson (Bishop of Hereford 1918-1920, Bishop of Durham 1920-1939) was nominated to the see of Hereford amid intense controversy over his theological views.[10] Owen Chadwick has compared the affair with the earlier *cause célèbre* over the appointment of Frederick Temple to Exeter in 1869, and noted how much more radical the theological issues involved had become by the time of the second dispute.[11] At the time many conservative minds were convinced of a menacing increase in theological liberalism within the Church of England. The Modern Churchmen's Union held a conference in 1921 at Girton College, Cambridge, which confirmed that impression. This provoked the setting up in 1922 of a Commission to examine the existing agreement on doctrinal questions within the Church of England, 'with a view to investigating how far it is possible to remove or diminish existing differences.'[12] It is significant that the Commission did not report until 1938, and meanwhile many other theological storms swept over the Church of England, not least the Prayer Book controversy

10 Chadwick, Owen, *Hensley Henson. A Study in the Friction between Church and State*, Clarendon, Oxford, 1983, Chapter 6.

11 Chadwick, Owen, *The Victorian Church* (Part Two), Black, London, 1970, p. 146.

12 Vidler, Alec, *The Church in an Age of Revolution: 1789 to the Present Day*, Penguin, London, 1961, p. 200.

of 1927 and 1928. Cragg notes how Parliament's rejection of the proposed new book, widely suspect to Evangelicals, was greeted in his home parish 'with great acclaim'. [*Negotiate*, p. 24]

The most pertinent of these storms to the present discussion was the dispute within the Church Missionary Society (founded 1799) which led in 1922 to the breakaway of a substantial minority of its members to form the Bible Churchmen's Missionary Society (BCMS), the society supported by Cragg's family and his parish church. The issues of this dispute again focussed on the interpretation of the Bible, and also on the extent to which the Church Missionary Society (CMS, now renamed the Church Mission Society) should demand conservative theological orthodoxy from its missionaries and other bodies with which it co-operated. How comprehensive of doctrinal variation was the Society to be? In the tangled web of resolution, amendment and counter-resolution which marked the public counsels of CMS in 1922 it became clear that the conservative party was determined to maintain official recognition of the authenticity of the Bible as they understood it, and that the 'utterances' of Jesus, which included his references to Noah, David and Jonah, were as significant as his ethical and spiritual teaching. It had long been customary for conservative scholars to defend the literal historic truth of the Old Testament by citing the references of Jesus to the Flood, the Davidic authorship of Psalm 110 and the reality of Jonah's whale. H P Liddon's Bampton lectures of 1866, for example, 'the finest Bampton lectures of the century', had based the infallibility of the Old Testament on the infallibility of Christ.[13] At a critical point in the CMS debates the resolution under discussion stated that 'we believe in the absolute truth of his (Jesus') teaching.' The conservative party wanted the addition of the two words 'and utterances', but this was defeated, and the issue, says the historian of CMS, 'proved decisive for the formation of the BCMS.'[14] When the BCMS drew up its doctrinal Basis article 2 referred to: 'Belief in the essential Deity of our Lord Jesus Christ; His Incarnation and Virgin Birth; the truthfulness of all His utterances …'

Bishop Stephen Neill, whose own family was split over the CMS/BCMS issue, wrote that the result of the events of 1922 was that 'for the moment Evangelicalism was reduced to a level of less repute and less influence in the Anglican world than at any time in the preceding hundred and fifty years.'[15] If the issues had been clearly and unambiguously

---

13 Chadwick 1970, *op. cit.*, pp. 75, 101.

14 Hewitt, Gordon, *The Problems of Success. A History of the CMS 1910-1942*, vol. 1, SCM, London, 1971, p. 471.

15 Neill, S C, *Anglicanism*, Penguin, London, 3rd edition 1965, p. 400.

theological, Evangelical morale might not have been so adversely affected, but as so often this was not the case. Another historian of the Church of England has written that

> it would be facile and irresponsible to think that the formation of BCMS represented an exact split between conservative and liberal Evangelicals since it was much more difficult to define the exact casus belli, for its seeds were sown in seemingly minor issues and flowered in outwardly unimportant clusters of words.[16]

The same writer entitled his chapter on the post-First World War period, 'The Defensive Years', and suggested that the first stage of BCMS' existence was marked by being 'much misunderstood' and 'developing a kind of siege mentality'.[17]

'Outwardly unimportant clusters of words' suggests precisely the sort of theological shibboleth against which Cragg rebelled. Like others who had much earlier ceased supporting both CMS and BCMS after 1922, Cragg severed his formal connections with BCMS during the years of his curacy, and paid back the money which had been spent on his theological training by the Society. When he came to the time for missionary service, he went abroad neither with BCMS nor with CMS, but with the British Syria Mission, a small interdenominational society which had a strongly evangelistic concern but had originated in welfare and educational work.

We must leave for the next section the influences of Lebanon, of Islam, Arab Christianity and philosophy upon Cragg's intellectual development, and ask what influences from the British theological tradition were available to fill the vacuum caused by abandoning evangelical conservatism. His own writings give only scattered hints of his specifically theological debts, but his thesis of 1950, and especially its fourth chapter, offers several clues. Cragg wrote that 'Historic Christianity has persisted into the middle of the 20th century by virtue of a painful exposure to every form of scrutiny and testing.'[18] This had admittedly been carried out by a minority, but it was

16 Manwaring, Randle, *From Controversy to Co-existence. Evangelicals in the Church of England 1914-1980*, CUP, Cambridge, 1985, p. 26.

17 *Ibid.*, p. 28.

18 'Islam in the 20th Century', unpublished D.Phil. thesis, Oxford University, 1950, pt 2, p. 1.

> a creative minority whose influence and achievement have permeated and infected the whole, even if its undoubted excesses have sometimes been no less guilty than the inertia of the masses.[19]

We shall have cause to note again the reliance of Cragg on the concept of 'a creative minority' in relation to Muslim understanding of Islam. Here it is important to realise that Cragg's abandonment of conservative evangelicalism did not entail contempt for the school of thought which had first nurtured him. He writes sensitively about 'the mutual debt of critic and devotee', and, speaking perhaps from experience within his own family, reckons that 'the reactions of the devout... supplied the inertia which had to be soundly overcome—the corrective which saints often administer to scholars.'[20] He is aware of 'the inglorious quality of many controversies', but sees in them the necessity for mutual admonition. He concludes that, judging from Christian experience, 'it might almost be right to say that Islam is in dire need of heretics and of a conservatism capable of giving them an honest reckoning.'[21] Here is an early sign of the fruitfulness of theological controversy in his own thinking, which is determined to promote a dynamic and dialogical mode of mutual correction between conservative and radical rather than the dogged but static defence of a single viewpoint met with impatient demands for change.

Cragg has considerable confidence in the long-term value of the debates in which Christians have historically been engaged, and entitled one of the sections of his thesis 'The Alert Frankness of Christian Self-Criticism'.[22] In this section he illustrates his argument by fixing on the contributors to *Lux Mundi*, a volume of essays produced by a group of Anglican theologians of Catholic tradition in 1889, and particularly on their editor and most famous member, Charles Gore (1853-1932, Bishop successively of Worcester, Birmingham and Oxford).[23] With the ten pages of Gore on the Scriptures, comments Stephen Neill, 'Anglo-Catholicism had moved out of the obscurantist fundamentalism in which Dr Pusey would gladly have imprisoned it. Liberal Catholicism had been born.'[24] But Gore did not merely, as Neill says, allow as valid the 'reasonable

19 *Ibid.*, p. 4f.
20 *Ibid.*, p. 7.
21 *Ibid.*, p. 8, 9.
22 *Ibid.*, p. 3.
23 Ed. Gore, Charles, *Lux Mundi. A Series of Studies in the Religion of the Incarnation*, John Murray, London, 1889.
24 Neill, S C, *Anglicanism*, p. 272f.

results of scientific criticism of the Scriptures'. He offered the doctrine of *kenosis*, or Christ's voluntary self-limitation, based on Philippians 2:7 and 2 Corinthians 8:9. The late nineteenth-century Christian mind found itself in a dilemma because the findings of scholars on the dating and authorship of the psalms and prophetic writings seemed to run counter to Jesus' own words from the Gospels. Liddon, as we have seen, had defended the Old Testament, as he thought, by the New. Cragg identified Gore's theory as a historic solution to the dilemma.[25] If Christ's words seemed contrary to the results of critical scholarship it was because as a genuine human being he knew no more on such questions than others in his day, or perhaps because he spoke in controversy *ad hominem*, citing the Jonah story as parable but not necessarily as history. It will be noted that it was precisely this issue of Jesus' validation of the Old Testament which was at the heart of the CMS/BCMS controversy in 1922.

Cragg clearly appreciated the emphasis in *Lux Mundi* on the Incarnation rather than the Atonement in the life of Christ as a timely move, which set the Atonement in a broader theological context than had been customary, particularly in his own evangelical tradition. The stress on the work of God in and through the genuine humanity of Jesus also assisted an engagement with contemporary secular thought. For many had been troubled by the impact of Darwinian work on evolution and were tempted to suppose God ousted from his world by new scientific discoveries.[26] Cragg returns to the *Lux Mundi* school of writers in an appendix designed to illustrate for Muslim readers

> something of the spirit and form of the Christian 'liberalism', as a measure of what awaits Islam and what Islam owes itself ... *(Lux Mundi)* was a plain example of the constructive influence that could be exerted by a band of colleagues, responding to the vocation to intellectual trusteeship in religion, alert to contemporary thought and conceiving of all truth as capable of inward harmony.[27]

Cragg, like most readers of *Lux Mundi*, fastened on the essay of Gore on the Holy Spirit and Inspiration as particularly significant. Gore had affirmed a form of the doctrine of the humanity of Jesus which no Anglican theologian had previously approved, and offered a way

25 'Islam in the 20th Century', pt 2, p. 6.

26 Mozley, J K, *Some Tendencies in British Theology. From the Publication of Lux Mundi to the Present Day*, SPCK, London, 1952, p. 18.

27 'Islam in the 20th Century', pt 2, pp. 263, 264.

of releasing what had become a logjam of inconclusive discussion on the authority of the Bible and contemporary critical research. By 1950 his proposals had become conventional. But this general movement of Christian thought could easily be seen to validate Muslim strictures on Christian orthodoxy by emphasizing the humanity of Christ at the expense of his (previously supposed) divine omniscience, and Cragg has some difficulty in conveying the significance of *Lux Mundi* without allowing this. In consequence, as he attempts to indicate the spirit and manner of its treatment of 'a domestic issue within Christian Theology' without going into the precise details of its proposals, his writing becomes rather cloudy. Referring to critical questions about literary form and date in Old Testament literature he paraphrases Gore as saying that

> The truth of the Incarnation, so often earlier regarded as closing all questions, in fact left them open, and their being open rather than closed was more congruent with the nature of the Incarnation.[28]

Here is a characteristic of Cragg's thought we shall meet with again, an unwillingness to have anything too tightly defined, often expressing itself in rather elliptical language. But it is particularly the idea of divine self-limitation in Gore's essay which Cragg valued, even though the clearest expression of the 'Kenotic Theory' was limited to a footnote.[29] Gore later wrote in his Bampton Lectures that

> The method of God in history, like the method of God in nature, is to an astonishing degree self-restraining ... It is physical power which makes itself felt only in self-assertion and pressure: it is the higher power of love which is shewn in self-effacement.[30]

Cragg, however, refers only to *Lux Mundi* among Gore's writings, and this raises the suspicion that, moving by the instincts of a mind which is eclectic rather than systematic, his encounter with the thought of Gore was influenced by the accident of residence rather than a methodical search for ideas congruent with his own. For from 1947-1951, the years of his thesis research, Cragg lived as Rector in Longworth Rectory, the

---

28 *Ibid.*, appendix 3, pp. 12, 11.

29 Gore, *op. cit.*, p. 360, cf. Ramsey, A Michael, *From Gore to Temple*, Longmans, London, 1960, p. 6.

30 Ramsey, *op. cit.*, p. 34f.

very place where the original papers for *Lux Mundi* were first delivered, and where their authors and their successors used to meet annually for 25 years. The Rector of Longworth in the years from 1889 to his death in 1915 had been J R Illingworth (1848-1915), a contributor of two of the *Lux Mundi* essays, who invited 'The Holy Party', as they became known, for summer exchanges of theological reflection.[31] Behind the 'Holy Party' too was the influential figure of the philosopher T H Green, never an orthodox Christian but extremely congenial intellectually to the idealism of the *Lux Mundi* authors, especially Illingworth and Scott Holland, who was a personal friend.[32] We shall meet T H Green again in connection with Cragg's encounter with philosophy.

It is not then to the Liberal Catholic and (in later years) rather authoritarian Bishop Gore that Cragg turns for the development of these kenotic ideas but to the Baptist scholar H Wheeler Robinson. In his book *Redemption and Revelation in the Actuality of History* Wheeler Robinson has a passage entitled 'The Kenosis of the Spirit', saying that

> the phrase is meant to suggest that God as Holy Spirit enters into a relation to human nature which is comparable with that of the Incarnation ... There is a far wider activity of the Spirit, which would, if we could conceive it clearly, bring all existence into unity, and show us the divine self-emptying from the foundation of the world. Through this long and patient kenosis, God has carried the burden of all humanity, the humanity which it is His purpose to redeem. The believer is simply entering into a new and greatly deepened experience through Christ of what God has been doing all the time by His 'prevenient' grace.[33]

Cragg twice quotes from this section of Wheeler Robinson's book. [*Sandals*, p. 86f and *Other*, p. 119] He is also clearly moved by a quotation of Wheeler Robinson's from the American theologian Horace Bushnell (1802-1876) to the effect that if we could see the suffering of the Spirit within humanity it would 'make the world itself a kind of Calvary from age to age.' [*Sandals*, p. 87, *Christ*, p. 278]

---

31 'Islam in the 20th Century', appendix 3, p. 9f.

32 Reardon, B M G, *From Coleridge to Gore. A Century of Religious Thought in Britain*, Longman, London, 1971, p. 434.

33 Wheeler Robinson, H, *Redemption and Revelation in the Actuality of History*, Nisbet, London, 1942, pp. 290, 295.

We have suggested that Cragg's theology is eclectic rather than systematic, and moves in part at least by the prompting of location. Bushnell may serve as a second example. He was a New England Congregational minister who served as pastor of North Church, Hartford, Connecticut from 1833-1859, in the very town where Cragg served as Professor of Arabic and Islamics. Bushnell's book *Vicarious Sacrifice* (1866) was a reaction against the modified Calvinism of N W Taylor's so-called 'New Haven Theology', and was criticised by F W Robertson for being 'shadowy' and vague, and by R W Dale for lacking an objective understanding of the Atonement.[34] Cragg has written, in connection with Bushnell and the Atonement, of his own reaction, 'partly in response to Islamic pressures about divine "effortless" forgiveness', against

> those 'forensic' interpretations which somehow involve a 'change' in the divine posture brought about, from outside, by the afflicting of Jesus ... I suppose a register of Bushnell's feel for kenosis and his finding it in creation per se and certainly in the 'grievings' of the ever-patient Holy Spirit, far outweighed what may, or may not, be proper by way of strictures on his 'vagueness'.[35]

There is no doubt that Cragg seems drawn to writers who might be criticised for blurring the distinction between the revelation of God and the general experience, intellectual and emotional, of humanity. The late nineteenth-century theologians were concerned to claim evolution and progress and contemporary science for Christ. Illingworth actually saw the Incarnation as giving rise to a new species of human being.[36] Behind much of their thought lay that of F D Maurice (1805-1872), for whom 'every child that is born is born into a world already redeemed, and in Baptism this truth is proclaimed and the child is put into relation to it.'[37] Cragg uses Maurice in another of the appendices to his thesis as an illustration for Muslim readers of significant Christian thinkers. There, however, he treats Maurice only as a Christian Socialist, emphasizing the unity of his religious and social thought, and the courage which enabled

34 Douglas, J D, *New International Dictionary of the Christian Church*, Zondervan, Grand Rapids, 1974, articles on 'Bushnell' and 'New Haven Theology'. Also Reardon, *op. cit.*, pp. 219, 464.

35 Letter to the present author, 17.10.86

36 Ramsey, *op. cit.*, p. 4.

37 Ramsey, A Michael, *F D Maurice and Modern Theology*, CUP, Cambridge, 1951, p. 35.

him to sustain attacks from both political and ecclesiastical sources. He saw in him a precursor of William Temple.[38]

There are, however, at least two respects in which Cragg's thought is reminiscent of that of Maurice. Maurice's writings provoked quite contradictory estimates from his contemporaries, according to whether his hearers found his language cloudy or illuminating. One historian's judgement is that 'he exalted his hearers, but he could not make them understand what he said.'[39] The reason probably lay in Maurice's principle of the complementarity of apparently opposed truths, and his related opposition to theological system-building of all kinds. Stephen Sykes has criticised Maurice's influence on twentieth-century Anglicanism for just these features.[40] As we shall see in chapter 3, Cragg's early exposure to a rigidly doctrinaire understanding of theology engendered a comparable suspicion of theological systems and a particular dislike of handling questions of the status in Christian eyes of other religions or religious ideas.

The second respect in which Cragg resembles Maurice is related. Maurice lectured in 1845-6 on the religions of the world, contending that in Christ is the wholeness of truth of which other faiths reveal only partial expressions.[41] In his lectures on world religions, however, he charges the Muslim with being

> the worshipper of a dead necessity ... Because he does not acknowledge a loving Will acting upon men's wills, to humble them in themselves, and to raise them to God, therefore he becomes the enslaver of his fellows ... Because he will not acknowledge that the highest and divinest unity is that of love, but rests all upon the mere unity of sovereignty, he has never been able to establish one complete government upon the earth.[42]

Maurice argued that the Muslim concept of the absolute power of God had a strong tendency to be reflected in political autocracy. Cragg agreed in his thesis of 1950 that when law and religion are identified

38 'Islam in the 20th Century', appendix 2.

39 Chadwick, Owen, *The Victorian Church* (2 parts), Black, London, 1966, 1970. This ref. pt 1, p. 349.

40 Sykes, Stephen W, *The Integrity of Anglicanism*, Mowbray, London, 1978, p. 19.

41 Reardon, *op. cit.*, p. 194.

42 Maurice, F D, *The Religions of the World and their Relations to Christianity*, 6th edition, Macmillan, London, 1886, p. 152.

> this sets the whole course and tone for the relationship of society to God, stereotypes the social order, externalises devotion, discourages necessary social change and keeps religion static.[43]

Thirty years later his views had not changed: 'If we have an ultimately repressive theism, we shall have repressive society.'[44] This, and the allied self-justifying stance of those who govern in the name of God, proves to be Cragg's major 'dissuasive' from Islam.

We shall see whether this theological inheritance has proved adequate to cope with the demands Cragg has made upon it.

3 The Importance of Lebanon

The British Syria Mission had been founded in 1860 by Mrs Bowen Thompson, the widow of a British engineer who had lived for some years with her husband in Turkey, and felt a keen desire to help the widows and orphans of the Lebanese massacres of 1860. Her work was first known as 'The Ladies Association for the Moral and Religious Improvement of Syrian Females', and later as 'British Syrian Schools'.[45] It began in Beirut but soon extended its work to education and evangelism in the mountain villages, working among boys as well as girls, and among the crippled and the blind. It was an interdenominational society with ecclesiastical links to what became the National Evangelical Synod of Syria and Lebanon, with a Presbyterian church order. It declined to join other missionary groups in their representations against religious persecution, preferring to extend its educational work without political involvement. At an early stage it challenged American supremacy in the education of girls, and by its heyday in the late 1890s had fifty schools. In 1960, after the Mission's withdrawal from Syria, it became the Lebanon Evangelical Mission, and merged with the Middle East General Mission in 1976 to become Middle East Christian Outreach (MECO), an international body with its British headquarters in Tunbridge Wells.

Cragg entered then into a tradition of evangelistic and educational concern in the Middle East which compelled him to face the issues

---

43 'Islam in the 20th Century', pt 1, p. 96.

44 Art. 'Being Christian and Being Muslim. A Personal Debate' in *Religion* 10 (Autumn 1980), p. 206.

45 Scott, Frances E, *Dare and Persevere. The Story of 100 years of Evangelism in Syria and Lebanon, from 1860 to 1960*, Lebanon Evangelical Mission, London, 1960, p. 30.

confronting Islam in adjusting to a modern world dominated by European science, technology, and commerce. The Mission's magazine *Under Syrian Skies* records his arrival in April 1939 as only the second male ever to serve with the British Syria Mission. He was assigned initially to the Lebanon Bible Institute at Shimlan close to Beirut, and later issues of the magazine saw him involved in leading groups of students on evangelistic tours. [*Negotiate*, ch. 4] Soon after his arrival Lebanon, as a French mandate, passed under the suzerainty of the Vichy Government in France, and Cragg and his new wife were evacuated to Jerusalem and then worked for a time at the CMS Hospital in Gaza, where their first child was born. Francis Graham Brown, the Anglican bishop in Jerusalem in whom Cragg found a real father-in-God, wanted a residential hostel in Beirut for the many Palestinian students drawn there by the American University. So after his spell at the Lebanon Bible Institute, and in addition to work in the Anglican chaplaincy at Beirut Cragg found himself creating St Justin's House, named after the Palestinian Christian martyr of the second century who had worn the philosopher's robe. [*Negotiate*, p. 97] From the beginning Cragg's vocation among Muslims was involved with education, scholarship and philosophy.

The hostel was affiliated to the university, and in order to have some status in it and also to help the hostel finances, Cragg at first taught English classes, while he himself learnt much about Islam informally from his students. The American University of Beirut (AUB) was founded in 1866 as the Syrian Protestant College, and took its present name in 1920. The particular tradition of its American Presbyterian founders emphasized ethics and good citizenship rather than a dogmatic Christianity, and Cragg describes the Principal of his days there, Bayard Dodge (who had married into the family of the founder, Daniel Bliss), as a 'virtual Unitarian'.[46] Compulsory chapel for students on Mondays, Wednesdays and Fridays avoided explicitly Christian themes, but was supplemented by a series of house study groups where Christianity could be seriously discussed. In these Cragg recalls using a book entitled *Types of Philosophy* by the liberal American thinker, W E Hocking, who is also well known as the chairman of the group which produced the controversial report *Rethinking Missions. A Laymen's Inquiry after One Hundred Years*. It was partly Hocking's report which provoked Hendrik Kraemer into writing *The Christian Message in a non-Christian World* by way of refutation.[47]

---

46 Dodge, Bayard, *The American University of Beirut*, AUB, Beirut, 1958.

47 Hocking, William E, *Rethinking Missions. A Laymen's Inquiry after One Hundred Years*, New York, 1932. Kraemer, Hendrik, *The Christian Message in a Non-Christian World*, Edinburgh House Press, London, 1938.

The country of Cragg's initial encounter with Islam is also of great significance. Lebanon in the early 1940s was emerging from French tutelage to a fragile independence. With its distinctive confessional polity whereby power was divided by custom between a Maronite President, a Sunni Prime Minister, a Shi'ite Speaker of Parliament and an Orthodox First Deputy, the Lebanese National Pact of 1943 inspired hope that Muslim and Christian together could secure the future of an independent Lebanese nation. Economically dependent, as it proved, on being Europe's gateway to the Muslim world, and always subject to the changing policies of great powers, Lebanon was for some a symbol of the precarious possibilities of reconciliation among peoples and confessional groups long at odds with one another. Cragg was resident in Lebanon as the National Pact was hammered out, and as Lebanese Christians and Muslims weathered the early storms of independence and extensive political in-fighting.

Charles Malik, head of the Department of Philosophy and a member of the (Chalcedonian or 'Greek') Orthodox Church in Lebanon, became Cragg's mentor and colleague in the American University of Beirut, though his *Negotiate* has curiously little to say about him. (Some pages in *Hands* and a detailed tribute in 2011 rectify the omission.)[48] Later Malik was to be Lebanese Ambassador in Washington and Minister of Foreign Affairs in Lebanon from 1956-1958, closely identified with President Chamoun's pro-Western policy. His great achievement was to be the main architect of the United Nations' Declaration of Human Rights. At this time he held particular hopes that Lebanon could be a great place of meeting. In 1952 he wrote:

> The Lebanon has a positive vocation in the international field. It is not political. It is spiritual and intellectual. It consists in being true to the best and truest in East and West alike. This burden of mediation and understanding she is uniquely called to bear ... Lebanon—little and fragile as she is—is the only country, not only in existence today but perhaps throughout history, where East and West meet and mingle on a footing of equality. The vigorous Moslem citizens of Lebanon bring in the integral contribution of the East, while the Christian citizens are in deepest spiritual and historical communion with the West. If this

48 Cragg, Kenneth, *The Order of the Wounded Hands. Schooled in the East*, pp. 6-10, Melisende, London, and art. 'Charles Malik and the Meaning of Lebanon. In Medias Res' in *Journal of Eastern Christian Studies* 63 (1-2), pp. 221-232, 2011.

> situation can endure, there is a wonderful possibility of creative confrontation.[49]

'Creative confrontation' might be a phrase straight out of Cragg's own writing, but the development of Nasserite Arab nationalism, its growing conflict with Israel and the bitter Lebanese civil war was to threaten Malik's vision of Lebanese mediation and ultimately to make it look 'desperately tarnished and compromised'. [*Hands*, p. 6]

During Cragg's years in Lebanon, however, it seemed that the AUB, as a powerful intellectual centre in the Arab world, and Malik as a powerful force within it, might bring about the reality of the vision. It is significant that it should have been an Orthodox Christian, and not, for example, a Francophile Maronite who shaped Cragg's career at this point. For the Maronites tended to claim a Phoenician rather than an Arab identity, and to have fought on the side of the Crusaders. Malik, in contrast, judged that the Orthodox had 'worked more closely with their Muslim compatriots on civic, social, cultural and national problems than any other Christian group,' and were the best suited to undertake dialogue with Islam. Malik's Christianity was far from being a Crusader outpost from Europe. He might at times have described it as a 'Christian Hellenism' in deference to its Byzantine links, but the cultural roots of his Church lie in the eastern Mediterranean. The Patriarchates of Antioch and Jerusalem have fought extended battles with the Greeks to establish their Arab identity in leadership and liturgy. Malik's spiritual ancestors suffered as much from the Crusades as any Muslims, and their representative figure could well be the theologian John of Damascus, protosymboulos to the Umayyad dynasty, though Malik, at least, would not have subscribed to John's very negative views of Islam as a Christian heresy. Malik had few illusions about the four historic sees of his Church: 'You cannot expect great spiritual heights from four orphans quarrelling miserably like children in a totally alien world.' At the same time he wrote about Orthodoxy in the Middle East that: 'The Muslim spirit encompasses it. It is free only within this spirit.'[50]

There are obvious connections here with Cragg's search for what he later described as 'Islamic reasons for being Christian'.[51] If, as Cragg

49 Malik, Charles, art. 'The Near East. The Search for Truth' in ed. Sylvia G Haim, *Arab Nationalism. An Anthology*, University of California Press, Berkeley, 1964, pp. 197, 198.

50 Malik, Charles, art. 'The Orthodox Church' in ed. A J Arberry: *Religion in the Middle East*, vol. 1, Cambridge University Press, Cambridge, 1969, pp. 297-346.

51 Kenneth Cragg, art. 'Temple Gairdner's Legacy' in *International Bulletin of Missionary Research*, 5:4, October 1981, p. 166.

wrote in his thesis, 'all truth (is) capable of inward harmony', and if the culture surrounding the Christian is shaped and permeated by Islam, then for his own soul's health and for the witness of the Church, he must find the true meaning of that culture, the answer to its deepest questions and concerns, in the untapped resources of his Christian faith. The alternative is emigration, physical or psychological, or perhaps a retreat into a cultural eccentricity unrelated to the public life of the nation. By moving to the AUB and becoming a colleague of Malik, Cragg had left the 'private' world of the evangelical mission, and associated himself decisively with the public life and culture of the nation.

Malik had grand, even grandiose, ideas about the significance of the Middle East. While (in Malik's rather eccentric judgement) it had shown no creativity in science or philosophy 'it has been reserved to it to storm heaven itself and open its doors.' Although 'the historical discontinuities are appalling … yet it is here that history started.' Western civilisation is only an offshoot of 'what was revealed, apprehended, loved, suffered and enacted' in the Middle East. He complained that people in the Middle East were interested in everything except propagating their faith yet 'man can regain his full stature as man … only in relation to, only as an outpouring from, the events of Bethlehem, Nazareth and Jerusalem.'[52]

The corollary of this is a willingness among Muslims also to think through the fundamentals of Islamic culture. Malik wrote that 'there is room for a hundred Muhammad 'Abduhs,' and room too for a serious Muslim consideration of Christianity. 'There isn't a single Moslem scholar in all history, as far as I know, who has written an authentic essay on Christianity.'[53] The hope for more 'Abduhs inspired Cragg's 1950 thesis, the journeys of Operation Reach and the translations (including one from 'Abduh) in particular, while he often pleads for a reciprocal attention by Muslims to Christianity. In particular Malik's bold grasp of the 'wonderful possibility of creative confrontation' has offered Cragg a vision of a Christian approach to Muslims which does not totally reject the work of controversialists like Pfander and Zwemer, but attempts to reorientate it in a completely new spirit of love, without the armour of political patronage, without the assumption of cultural superiority and without the expectation of destroying Islam by dialectical victory. In 1952 Malik wrote that Lebanon stood for existential freedom,

52 Ed. Charles Malik, *God and Man in Contemporary Christian Thought*, AUB, Beirut, 1970, and articles cited above.

53 Malik, article 1964, p. 215f.

> 'freedom of thought, choice, being, becoming … To be able to perform her moderating and mediating function between East and West, the Lebanon must be and feel secure in her existence … Thus the secure existence of Lebanon measures the degree of love abroad … The principle of international politics is power; but Lebanon's power is reason, truth, love, suffering, being.'[54]

We have seen the influence of a 'kenotic' and incarnational theology on Cragg, and it is easy to see how Malik's thinking would have fitted into this growing pattern. Even though Malik later abandoned his exalted conception of Lebanon for the 'realist' defensive policy of a Christian enclave, Cragg retained something of the original vision. He did not of course have the political responsibilities and experience of an ex-ambassador to Washington. Thirty years after Malik's 1952 essay Cragg mourned the ending of Lebanese stability and its rare intercommunal understanding:

> Lebanon, it is true to say, was martyred in the Arab confrontation with Israel … There is deep pathos here, as well as bitter irony. Lebanon was, in commendable measure, exemplifying what an inter-Arab experiment in cross-communal relationships might achieve. It could well have afforded a precedent for how such relationships might have availed for Jews themselves … It enjoyed a degree of intellectual liberty unique in the Arab world. [*Jerusalem*, p. 70f.]

We will see what solution Cragg sees for the Palestine/Israel problem and whether he or Malik is in the end the greater realist. It is clear at least that, whatever its subsequent history, the Lebanon of the 1940s was a seed-bed of hope for interfaith understanding.

We have seen how intellectual liberty was precious, because hardly won for Cragg. His sense of its value was undoubtedly fostered by the need to teach philosophy, which presumes it. Cragg acquired enough expertise in philosophy in the AUB to win an Oxford University prize in the subject, and gain the agreement of his old college for his doctoral studies. If Lebanon were to provide the physical environment for the meeting of faith communities, philosophy might provide the intellectual meeting-place. We have already seen how Cragg used Hocking's book *Types of Philosophy* with Muslim and Christian student groups working

---

54 *Ibid.*, p. 198, 199.

on religious issues. Hocking was a idealist philosopher who described philosophy as 'the resolute effort for integrity,' a search for wholeness which he expected that the world would before long find fulfilled in the Kingdom of God. For him the Kingdom of God meant the 'spiritual unity of all men and races'.[55] Hocking's idea was one of 'reconception', in which all faiths would undertake the rethinking of their basic convictions, preserving their cores of truth but expanding to include the insights of others. Cragg later criticised Hocking for this approach, but it clearly influenced his early thinking, and even in 1977 he admits that 'its spirit is admirable'. [*Other*, p. 76f.] It is interesting that philosophical idealism is also prominent among those that Cragg admired in the *Lux Mundi* movement of Liberal Catholicism, and above all in their philosophical mentor T H Green. Cragg's 1947 philosophical essay won a prize named after Green, and dealt with the issues of ethical theism that characterised the idealist tradition. But Cragg was in no sense a professional philosopher, or he would not have incurred some of the criticism that he does. When he taught in the Department of Philosophy at the AUB he had to read up the seventeenth-century writers at great speed to keep ahead of his students. Nevertheless the interest was significant, and to some degree sustained in the rest of his career.

Evangelical Christians are not commonly drawn to philosophical studies. The popular books of Francis Schaeffer in the 1960s and 1970s were significant for their advocacy of philosophy in the service of Christian faith, and together with the Christian rationalism of C S Lewis marked a turning point for British Evangelicals. Throughout Cragg's youth and early career professional British philosophy was typified by the atheism of Russell and Ayer, and this served to reinforce the suspicion of contemporary philosophy engendered by Biblical conservatism and, for the more widely read, the attacks on natural theology by the Barthian school, and those it influenced like Hendrik Kraemer. Cragg's interest therefore marked a further departure from his origins.

It also gave him a concern for those Muslim writers who were most alert to the broader intellectual implications of their faith, writers like Muhammad 'Abduh, Iqbal and Kamil Husain. Of his work in translation 'Abduh's *Theology of Unity* and Husain's *The Hallowed Valley* are notably speculative books. We shall see how this approach to Islam may be justified as an interpretation of the faith. Meanwhile we have to establish his basic theological presuppositions. In some ways these are revealed most clearly through his love of literature.

55 Sharpe, Eric J, *Faith Meets Faith. Some Christian Attitudes to Hinduism in the 19th and 20th Centuries*, SCM, London, 1977, p. 83, 84.

2
THE LOVE OF LITERATURE

1 The Cragg Literary Style

> Would the very art of poetry be possible were the earth that evokes it not itself a poem? [*Bent*, p. 6]

Some indication has been given in the previous chapter of Cragg's range of literary allusions and his evident fondness for calling upon them unexpectedly. Who else would have thought to include, in a book about Muslim suicide bombers, a chapter on writers who took their own lives? (Hemingway, Woolf, Plath and others in ch.9 of *Faith at Suicide,* 2005) Here we should pause to consider his own literary style and the influences upon it. Many have complained that his writing is dense and rich in meaning, and not easy to follow. Many sentences have to be read more than once, which slows and discourages the reader. Many have found that Cragg demands too much of his reader, and he presents non-native speakers of English with particular problems. The sentence quoted at the beginning of this chapter is characteristically compressed and demanding. The immediate reference is to Keats, of whom he says that 'The poet is exulting in the sublime poem that is divine creation and the affinity that binds them is unfailing. Would the very art of poetry be possible were the earth that evokes it not itself a poem?' He seems to mean that there is a unity between the poet and the natural world because the natural world is itself the work of an artist like the human poet. If this were not so, he asks, would there be any poetry? If Kepler described his scientific work as 'thinking God's thoughts after him', perhaps the poet can say the same.

It is often said that Cragg is himself a poet, and we shall shortly look at some of his verses. It is true that he gives close attention to the origins and nuances of words, delighting in their range of meaning as a poet will. He also has a fondness for complex sentences which begin with a word or phrase which is returned to at the end, as in the 'poetry… poem' sequence above. We have quoted here from Cragg's last book, but this is not just a feature of Cragg's later writing. The complexity, and the returning theme are also evident in his first book, as here:

> And in any event the story to be told is only safe in the custody of those for whom every antagonism is an opportunity. For that, precisely, is the heart of the story itself. [*Call*, p. 164]

His topic here is mission and telling the story of Jesus, but the reader wants to stop him and ask what he means by the story being 'safe', and in 'custody', and every 'antagonism' being an 'opportunity'. Cragg would no doubt respond that the answers to such questions are there in the rest of the book, and especially in the critique he makes of the 'custodians' of religious truth being often more concerned to safeguard it than to broadcast it. But the condensed style does not make for easy reading.

One wonders if his long absorption in the Arabic of the Qur'an has had an effect on his way of expressing himself in English. English versions of the Qur'an are full of bracketed words and phrases which the translators judge necessary to make sense of the text in English and to express some of its range of meaning, but which are missing in the Arabic. An extreme example is in Surah 82, verse 9:

> Nay, [O men,] but you [are lured away from God whenever you are tempted to] give the lie to [God's] Judgment! (Muhammad Asad's translation)

The Muslim reader is expected to understand a scripture which is often highly condensed and itself a form of poetry. Cragg speculates that the Arabic of the Qur'an, regarded as 'the speech of Allah' by Muslims, is a kind of sacrament for believers, in parallel with the Eucharist for Christians. Coining two words in one paragraph he suggests that the Qur'an's 'Arabicity' parallels the Christian doctrine of the Incarnation of Jesus in its 'inscriptation'. [*Inter-Text*, p. 62] He notes how the Qur'an insists on its character as an 'Arabic Qur'an' (12.2, 46.12), in contrast to the translated Greek of the New Testament. In an extended passage on the significance of Qur'anic Arabic for the theology of Islam, he notes that the absence in Arabic of a verb 'to be' implies that 'meaning could be simply declaratory rather than propositional and language thus somehow performative not discursive.' His examples are the simple nominal sentence *Allahu akbar*, literally 'God greater', and the absolute negation *la ikraha fi'l-Din* (2.256), 'No compulsion in religion'. 'God (is) greater' than what, is not stated, and the hearer is left to assume 'than anything one can name'. The comparative form requires this contribution from the listener or reader in a way that the expected superlative 'God is greatest' would not. Similarly with 'No compulsion in religion' the reader is required to think. Does the verse mean there ought to be no compulsion, or that there cannot be compulsion, because no-one can be compelled genuinely to believe? [*Inter-Text*, p. 67] The first interpretation is the more usual. The latter means that the text can actually be used to support rather than prohibit the enforcement of religious uniformity. Genuine faith indeed cannot be compelled, but outward observance can, and some would reckon this a proper way of promoting social cohesion. In this way compulsion may advance belief. The issue relates to Cragg's favourite distinction between *islam*, the personal surrender to God's will, and Islam, the religious institution. The distinction, as he notes, disappears in Arabic, which nowhere uses capital letters. Whether the distinction is then a strength or a weakness in Cragg's theology will engage us later.

This condensed and declaratory character of Qur'anic Arabic is also characteristic of much poetry, and—Cragg would claim—of the nature of prophecy.

> It may be doubted whether, in the last analysis, prophecy has ever been other than poetic and poetry, at its truest, ever other than prophetic ... Where prophecy is most authentic there is poetry, kindled and kindling in the heart—a poetry which is more than an artistry of words because its quality as language is enthused with a purpose and a power that require what they create. [*Event*, p. 45]

What do those final words 'that require what they create' mean? Has Cragg here been seduced by his own word-play? One is reminded of Owen Chadwick's remark about F D Maurice, quoted above, that 'he exalted his hearers, but he could not make them understand what he said.'

Does 'quality as language' serve as its own justification? Is Cragg more of a preacher than a theologian? Again the issue will occupy us later.

2 Cragg as Poet

There is no doubt that poetry and English literature has immense appeal for Cragg. His final publications are largely given to thoughts on English writers. His last book, *Bent to Literary Event. Masters in their Masterpieces* (2011), published when he was 98, has a characteristically tortuous title—perhaps his least felicitous—and contains a number of repetitions and some internal contradictions. It would not be surprising if his meticulous editorial eye had lost some of its vigilance. Nevertheless, the book is over 300 pages of quotation, insight and intriguing detail from Amos, St Paul, the Qur'an, Langland, Tyndale, Defoe, Gibbon, Wordsworth, Browning, Tennyson, Carlyle and Conrad. There are also extensive references to Shakespeare, Milton, Coleridge, Keats and the Egyptian novelist Najib Mahfuz. This volume followed the previous year's *Dying Daily. Quotidian Living* (2010), with chapters on Nicholas of Cusa, John Bunyan, John Clare, William Cowper, Edgar Allan Poe, Emily Dickinson, Gerard Manley Hopkins, Thomas Hardy, Virginia Woolf, Ezra Pound and Friedrich Nietzsche. In the same year *The Breaking of the Bread* contained extensive passages on John Donne, Richard Crashaw, George Herbert, Thomas Traherne, Walt Whitman, T S Eliot, Dylan Thomas, and R S Thomas, as well as other authors already mentioned. The year before that had seen an entire book on Shakespeare from his pen, *The Compass of the Globe. Shakespeare's Drama, Mind and Faith* (2009).

What drew this eminent student of religion to spend his last years writing about poets and novelists? He might have taken up his early interest in philosophy, or extended his religious studies into a deeper exploration of Hebrew literature, in the Talmud or contemporary Israeli novels. Hebrew is a cognate language with Arabic, and surely not difficult for this master of the latter. There was also an interest in Buddhism to develop, and areas of Islam he had not written about, *hadith* and *shari'ah*. But perhaps it was his desire and gift for writing his own English verse which provides the clue to these later works. We will come back to them.

Many of his friends received from him a hand-made card at Christmas which invariably included a poem of his own composition.

Many of these were collected and published in *Poetry of the Word at Christmas* (1987, revised and expanded 1996), and in a final version of the same material in *The Lowly Lintel* (2006). The latter took its title from the calculatedly low door of the main entrance to the Church of the Nativity at Bethlehem, which compels all visitors to stoop on entering. In self-deprecating vein he writes that he found Christmas 'somehow exciting a poetic strain, however fraught with what others might read as a strain to be poetic.' Drawing on Robert Herrick, Richard Crashaw, George MacDonald and others for inspiration, he noted how 'worthy poets may beget inferior ones.' [*Christmas*, pp. 12, 14] An example is his use of Robert Frost's poem 'Stopping by Woods on a Snowy Evening' with its final verse

> The woods are lovely, dark, and deep,
> But I have promises to keep,
> And miles to go before I sleep,
> And miles to go before I sleep.

Cragg borrows the second line as a refrain for his own stanzas, 'But I have promises to keep …'[1]

Many of the poems run counter to the usual Christmas festival joy and light-heartedness. The emphasis is rather on the Nativity as the prelude to suffering—of the mothers of Bethlehem, of Mary, of Jesus himself. The mothers of Bethlehem address the Magi in anger:

> Vain star-gazers, did you not know how wild
> And dire the tyrant's jealousy would be?
> Your feckless, futile, crass astronomy
> Indulging oriental mystery
> Extinguishes its signs in blood and misery.[2]

'This is the disconcerting truth'[3] could serve as another refrain to his writing.

He develops some borrowed images with remarkable skill. Seizing on Gerard Manley Hopkins' phrase 'Soft Sift in an Hour-glass', he finds in it an image of the Incarnation:

1 *Poetry of the Word at Christmas*, Worthing, Churchman Publishing 1987, 'A Body hast Thou prepared Me', p. 40f.

2 *Ibid.,* 'Magnificat: Maledicet', p. 47.

3 *Ibid.,* 'Why is incense brought to Me from Sheba?', p. 48.

Reversible spheres of an hour-glass
An apertured twain,
Emptying the higher's compass
Into the lower's gain.

And concludes:

In the turning glass of birth
Where God is Christly given
We measure in the flux of earth
The majesty of heaven.[4]

The Lowly Lintel (2006) includes all the earlier poems and adds 26 to the 1987 edition, ending with one to mark the 70th anniversary of his ordination as deacon in 1936. Otherwise Christmas and the Incarnation are again the themes, with the constant reminder that the Manger led to the Cross,

… the unison
Of birth and death, the seamless robe
That consummates the swaddling clothes,
The crown of thorns that mints the Magi's gold
And validates their frankincense and myrrh. [5]

The newcomers include an imaginative account of Joseph's thoughts on the journey from Nazareth to Bethlehem, passing by the landmarks of Israel's history, including 'a mound/Littered with bones—hence "Golgotha" named.' Joseph's thoughts rarely feature in popular versions of the Christmas story. Here Cragg has him begrudging the time spent on Augustus's census: 'I could ill afford uncertain weeks/Away from those tools at my bench.'[6]

The craftsman features again, indirectly, in a tour de force of imagery when Cragg takes the humble wheel-barrow to serve as metaphor for the ministry of Christ. His starting-point is the question of the 14 year-old

---

4 *Ibid.,* 'I am Soft Sift in an Hour-glass', pp. 62, 63, cf. also p. 13.

5 *The Lowly Lintel,* Melisende, London, 2006, 'In Bethlehem's Church of the Nativity', p. vii.

6 *Ibid.,* 'The Journey to Nativity', pp. 8, 6.

Thomas Carlyle, who asked his mother about the Incarnation, perhaps incredulously: 'Did God Almighty come down and make wheel-barrows in a shop?' Assuring Thomas that heaven was not empty when Christ was on earth, Cragg the poet notes

> How well endowed for burdens barrows are,
> Contrived for ready bearing,
> Devised to make the very burden serve
> Its carrying away …
> Matching hands between the shafts.
> These make momentum from the weight they hold
> With slant that tells the wheel its purpose,
> And what is borne is partner to the bearing.
> You have chanced unwittingly my son,
> Upon the secret of the Cross
> Whereon the very burden of the world's full sin
> Was His to bear and bear away.[7]

Cragg's long engagement with Islam is not altogether forgotten in these Nativity poems. 'A Muslim/Christian Reflection' takes its starting-point from the Qur'anic verse 'Say: Had there been angels in the earth going about in tranquillity, We would have sent an angel from heaven as a messenger.' (17.95) A variation on the sonnet forms Cragg's response, and with it an elegant yet passionate defence of the Incarnation:

> But we are men. An angel messenger
> Might fitly serve as heaven's harbinger
> For angel-kind. Our human case demands
> The voice of man, the living, working hands
> Of traffic in our world, bone of our bone,
> Flesh of our flesh, one known as we are known,
> Skilled in the truth of us. In peace to walk
> Is not our habit. Passions grimly stalk
> Through all our centuries. Our flesh is proud,
> Our structures harsh, our better reason cowed
> By fear or guile, our story marred and stained.
> The Word by God's initiative constrained

7 *Ibid.*, 'A Teenage Query', p. 57.

To seek our low estate must speak our mortal tongue,
In human travail take the human reach of wrong.[8]

Cragg's engagement with literature was founded on the conviction that 'our mortal tongue' was not only adequate for the expression of God's word, but everywhere already conveying it, if properly understood.

3 Poetry and Theology

As we will see in more detail later, Cragg's theological approach to Islam is to begin with the convictions that Christians and Muslims share about God as Creator, and to ask what they entail. What are the liabilities of God towards the creatures for which he has made himself responsible? Some Muslims would object to any line of thought which places moral responsibility on God, but Cragg would see it as a logical consequence of the act of creation. It is part of the engagement with humanity which is also seen in the Judaeo-Christian understanding that human beings are partners with God, sharing not only in that responsibility but in the very gift of creativity. These emphases appear throughout his writing on literature. He begins his last book with the chapter heading 'Let There Be—"Creativities"', and points out how the very terms 'poem' and 'poet' stem from the Latin *poema* and the Greek *poieio*, meaning to make or create. The poem is something created by one who thereby becomes a creator. The universe itself is the poem of the Creator poet, as celebrated in the passage praising Wisdom in *Proverbs* 8.22-31, especially its finale: 'then I was beside him, like a master worker; and I was daily his delight, rejoicing before him always, rejoicing in his inhabited world and delighting in the human race.'

So the created order is sacramental, a sign of the goodness and beauty of God. Gerard Manley Hopkins is perhaps the best-known celebrant of the hallowing of Nature. He writes that despite the generations that have despoiled the world, daily

the Holy Ghost over the bent
World broods with warm breast and with ah! bright wings.
[quoted in *Bread*, p. 155]

---

8 *Ibid.,* p. 53, also in *Lord*, p. 36f.

In his extended meditation on the Eucharist Cragg notes how Paul had to deal with Christians careless of the Sacrament and of each other. He reproved them for making the occasion one where 'each of you goes ahead with your own supper, and one goes hungry and another becomes drunk.' (1 Corinthians 11.21) Cragg comments that Paul had to teach them the distinction between normal bread and the bread of the Eucharist. 'Only then could the "sacramental" quality of the former be also understood. For unless all food was for hallowing, none could be.' [*Bread*, p. 30] In another place Cragg writes:

> In Christian terms, everything we handle is sacramental. We are *over* nature in order that we may be *under* God on behalf of nature.[9]

So Wordsworth was right to see man as the priest of nature, since 'the world was meant for celebration,' to be celebrated by the Creator and by the humans he had created. [*Bent*, p. 3] The human race is entrusted with the world as priest, celebrant and custodian. 'Man *(Cragg does not use inclusive vocabulary)* is the custodian within a natural order that invites, requires, awaits and rewards his custody. The poet re-creates the situation.' [*Bent*, p. 8] Of course the original harmony intended by God is broken by human sin and imperfection. This means that poetry takes on another role in partnership, recognised or not, with God. 'Poetry is indeed the searching of the soul.' [*Bent*, p. 16]

Despite disharmony the world is still sacramental and meant for celebration, and so it is still possible to find spiritual meaning in the everyday features of nature. 'Man is the custodian within a natural order that … rewards his custody.' Discussing William Tyndale as the Bible translator whose work was the foundation of the King James Version of 1611, Cragg goes to his 1528 book *The Parable of the Wicked Mammon*, on Luke 16.1-16 and its concern with the Reformation debate over faith and works. Cragg suggests that the image of a river with its two banks containing the flow can be an analogy for the proper place of faith and works. With his usual interest in the origins of words Cragg pauses to tell us that 'rivers and rivals are terms with the same etymology', and adds in a footnote: 'Rival—from the Latin *rivalis* ones on the opposite side of a

9 'Dum Spiro Spero', p. 8—Centre for Muslim-Christian Studies website, accessed 6.2.13. Emphasis original.

river or a stream so that they try to emulate or outdo each other over the thing between them.' [*Bent*, p. 144] It is a characteristic use of an obscure corner of the English language to demonstrate his conviction of the coherence of the whole creation.

4 Shakespeare and Religion

Shakespeare is the poet and dramatist who encompasses all of nature and human action. Cragg muses on the Globe Theatre on London's south bank, on Shakespeare's own reference to it in 'this wooden O', and on the recurring imagery of circles and wheels in his plays. All this suggests to him the need to invent a word. So he comes upon the word 'globetude', on the analogy of latitude and longitude. By this he intends to convey Shakespeare's reach of portrayal into every kind of human experience, including that called 'religious'. Overtly religious figures make few appearances in the plays, nor is it easy to be confident of Shakespeare's personal religious loyalties. 'Perhaps,' says Cragg, 'the vexed question of Shakespeare's religion is best resolved by saying that the theatre was his house of worship, the arena where he made a liturgy of his mind.' Some have discerned a Catholic emphasis in the plays, but Cragg does not see this as more than a 'bare conjecture'. [*Globe*, pp. 7, 88f.] What is certain is 'the deep moralism of Shakepeare's mind', especially evident in the tragedies.

> His is a world where crime meets its nemesis, where evil—however cunning its disguise—finds its reckoning. A moralism of this intensity assumes, by its very tenacity, a grounding in the sovereignty of God, its arbiter and guarantor. [*Globe*, p. 5]

Tragedy comes not by ill-fortune but 'in the workings of the human heart'. In *Macbeth* King Duncan comes as guest to Macbeth's house, but because of the workings of the witches' prophecies in the mind of Macbeth, he comes also and unwittingly as temptation. [*Globe*, p. 118] The prophecy says Macbeth will be king, but can he hasten and secure the fulfilment of the promise? It can only be by the murder of Duncan, a path of self-willed damnation. His tragedy is that he is keenly aware of what he is doing and where it leads. Macbeth thus illustrates the perversity in human nature which Cragg elsewhere insists cannot be met merely by education or enlightenment.

The answer to such 'disallowance' of morality is seen in the very different figure of the Earl of Kent in *King Lear*. Kent attempts to divert Lear from the disastrous decision of the King to divide his kingdom according to the love he perceives his daughters to have for him. Kent is banished from the court for his pains. Undaunted, he returns in disguise and remains loyally ready to serve and suffer with Lear. 'It is with him as if he had read in St Paul how "love bears all things and hopes all things"', comments Cragg. [*Globe*, p. 45] This is 'Shakespeare's sense of the sovereignty of love', which Cragg discerns throughout the plays, and which is most evident in such characters as Kent, who meets an evil situation by risking himself. [*Globe*, p. 73] For Cragg this links directly with his fundamental understanding of the nature of creation and of the God who makes himself responsible for it to the point of vicarious suffering. For Cragg doctrines of humanity and God are reciprocal, just as Creator and artist are partners in creation. 'Doctrines of God have always been answerable to measures of the human.' [*Globe*, p. 86] What human beings think, or imagine of God is directly linked to what they think about themselves, and vice-versa. Earlier he had written:

> Whenever we study or confess doctrines of God we proceed upon parallel affirmations about humanity. So inseparable are the two realms that every theology is inevitably also a view of the human. [*Call*, p. 38]

The reverse being also true, Cragg claims in a rather tortuous passage that the character of drama is essentially religious, with 'Shakespeare the playwright (as) Shakespeare the unintending theologian'. The theatre is incarnational.

> The theatre's perennial task giving of 'name and local habitation' to meanings in the soul of things is precisely kin to the enterprise whereby faith knows Christ in history, takes history into Christ. [*Globe*, p. 31f.]

The world is not an accident, or a joke, but has meanings which the dramatist and the theologian alike are there to elucidate. In the hands of

Shakespeare what is enacted in 'the wooden O' can delve into the deepest recesses of the human predicament, though drama can do no more than hint at its solution. Yet Cragg sees in figures such as Kent the self-risking love which attempts the rescue of another and so reflects the nature of the divine as inherent in creation.

> The tenacity of goodness is only the more evoked by the adversity it undergoes. Kent's vicarious devotion to Lear sustained to the end has Shakespeare close to the defining secret of Christianity as redeeming evil by the quality of love. [*Globe*, p. 45]

But Shakespeare does not preach. The message is latent. It is the task of the theologian and the missionary to make it explicit. The work of literature is what Hamlet ascribes to drama:

> 'the purpose of playing … was and is to hold as 'twere the mirror up to nature, to show virtue her own feature, scorn her own image and the very age and body of the time his form and pressure.'[10]

Philosophy, theology, faith must be 'circumspect and tentative', 'theology most of all'. That does not mean they cannot be discerned. [*Globe*, p. 5] Cragg's gift, and his intention, is to recruit all experience, and so all literature that reflects it, to the message of the God incarnate in Jesus Christ. We shall return to the question of how successful his interpretations are.

---

10 *Hamlet*, Act 3, scene 2.

3

THE THEOLOGIAN

1 The Reciprocity of God and Humanity

The writings of Kenneth Cragg return continually to one consistent theme which marks virtually all his work. It is the need for contact, for communication, for relationship, between human beings estranged from one another, and between humankind and God. He reflects the experience that many Christians concerned with other faiths have had that they cannot remain content to sit in a mental bunker and fire dogmatic missiles at strangers. Whatever their understanding of the beliefs of the others they feel the urge to be in personal contact with them, to speak and listen face to face. In a profounder but essentially similar way people have universally found themselves driven to seek personal knowledge of God, to know—at least in some degree—as they are known. 'God', says Cragg, 'cannot be greeted with a mere agreement to study Him.' [*Call*, p. 158] The note of salutation is characteristic, and focuses attention on the need for a relationship, an exchange, a two-way process of communication. Cragg's is, in perhaps a new sense, a theology of the word, a theory of relationships and of the inter-personal communication which is integral to them. 'All theology,' he says baldly, 'is about relationship.' [*Christ*, p. 75] 'A theory of relationships' may suggest undue abstraction, a reification of what is properly left un-analysed and un-dissected in the exchanges of personal engagement. Cragg is never guilty of such schematising. But 'theory' in its original sense of contemplative wonder *(theoria)* is an appropriate term for his thought, which is always characterised by a fundamental concern for spirituality, prayer and worship. The underlying theological issue for him is 'what sort of God is worthy of our worship? What understanding of God makes him worshippable?' To bow down, literally or metaphorically, before a dictatorial or capricious or merely tribal god, is to demean ourselves as human beings. The question to be asked then is not whether Cragg's thought is too philosophical and rarefied to be easily translated into daily life. It is whether his appreciation of the spiritual dimension in faiths other than his own does not lead him into a highly idiosyncratic understanding of them, and ultimately into a certain evasiveness where the harder issues of theology are concerned. We shall see that he is aware of the danger of appearing to do without a theology of religion, but we shall also have to ask whether his interpretive techniques are adequate for the material he is handling. Here we aim to set out the basic theological tools he works with, and to test their adequacy for the task he undertakes. As his life's work was a profound engagement with Islam, that is the area to be examined most carefully, though he wrote frequently on Judaism, and to some extent on Buddhism.

The concern for relationships leads Cragg to propose as the foundation of his thought about all religion the 'reciprocity' of the doctrines of God and humanity. As noted in the last chapter, this was a theme throughout his writing. 'Whenever we study or confess doctrines of God we proceed upon parallel affirmations about humanity. So inseparable are the two realms that every theology is inevitably also a view of the human.' [*Call*, p. 38] So he writes in his first book in 1956, and similarly in one of his last in 2009: 'Doctrines of God have always been answerable to measures of the human.' [*Globe*, p. 86] This reciprocity, or 'interpenetration' of God and humanity, is constantly argued by Cragg whenever the doctrine of God is under scrutiny, and his typical course is to plead that the act of creation itself opens God to a kind of vulnerability to his creatures. How well-grounded is such an argument in an inter-faith debate? Christians (and perhaps Jews) rely essentially on the Biblical text that God created men and women in his own image (Genesis 1:26). Christians may even speak of coming to share the nature of God (2 Peter 1.4), language which Muslims would find uncomfortably close to the sin of *shirk*, literally 'association' or 'partnership', associating created beings with God. Muslims believe profoundly in creation, but the Qur'an has no exact parallel to the Genesis 1.26 text and of course roundly condemns the idea of Jesus as the Son of God. It does, however, speak of Allah giving Adam life and spirit by breathing into him with his own breath (15:29, 38:72), and of entrusting him as his vicegerent or deputy on earth (2:30).

This would not be an adequate Islamic foundation for Cragg's theological assumption of divine-human reciprocity. But the *hadith*, the sayings of Muhammad recorded and passed down from his Companions, open up a little more theological space, or perhaps confusion. Here a somewhat technical discussion is in order.

There is an important tradition passed down from Abu Huraira, a companion and close friend of the Prophet. Some of the great volume of traditions attributed to him or foisted on him must be late and spurious, but the highly-regarded ninth-century *hadith* compilers Muslim and Bukhari both record on Abu Huraira's authority that Muhammad said: 'Allah, the Exalted and Glorious, created Adam in His own image with His length of 60 cubits.'[1] Ghazzali (d. 1111) expresses the key idea of the image of God in a different way, saying in one place that Bukhari records the words: 'Allah created Adam in the form of Al-Rahman' (one of the names of God), a version with which the jurist Ibn Hanbal (d. 855) evidently agreed.[2]

Many writers, especially from the Sufi and esoteric schools of Islamic thought have made use of this tradition, especially in their enthusiasm for the idea of *al-insan al-kamil*, the 'perfect one', often identified with Muhammad. Al-Muhasibi, the Shafi'i legist (d. 857), employs the tradition in his mystical meditation on the letter *alif*. He says that all other letters were first made in that shape, but became corrupted, just as Adam, formed in God's image, lost God's shape by disobedience.[3] Al-Ghazzali and his critic Ibn Rushd (known in the West as Averroes, d. 1198) both refer to the tradition.[4] Ibn Qutayba (d. 889) defends its authenticity against the Mu'tazilite *mutakallimun*, the Muslim dialecticians or rationalists, and the accusation they made of anthropomorphism. The contemporary Shi'ite scholar S H Nasr (b. 1933) links the tradition with the Qur'anic text of God's breathing his spirit into humanity, and continues 'There is therefore, something of a "divine nature" *(malakuti)* in man', though he omits to note that the word *malakuti* would signify something angelic rather than something divine.[5]

Elsewhere, however, Nasr speaks of our nature as both *nasut* (human) and *lahut* (divine) in an apparent echo of the mystics al-Hallaj (d. 922) and Ibn 'Arabi (d. 1240).[6] (Al-Hallaj has been regarded, probably incorrectly,

---

1 Muslim, Imam, *Sahih Muslim. Being Traditions of the Sayings and Doings of the Prophet Muhammad*, 4 vols., Ashraf, Lahore, 1976, IV: 1481; al-Bukhari: *al-Jam' al-Sahih*, 4 vols (ed. Juynboll), 1908, 79:1.

2 Gairdner, W H T tr., al-Ghazzali's *Mishkat al-Anwar*, Royal Asiatic Society, London, 1924 s. 34, 35.

3 Schimmel, Annemarie, *Mystical Dimensions of Islam*, University of North Carolina Press, Chapel Hill, 1975, pp. 188, 417.

4 al-Ghazzali, *Ihya Ulum id-Din*, 4 vols, Sind Sagar Academy, Lahore, 1971, IV: 6; Gairdner, *op. cit.*, s. 7, 24, 34, 35.

5 Nasr, Seyedd Hossein, *Ideals and Realities of Islam*, 2nd ed., Allen & Unwin, London, 1975, p. 18.

6 *Ibid.*, p. 90; Schimmel, *op. cit.*, p. 270.

as influenced by the Christian doctrine of the Incarnation because of his use of these originally Christian terms.)[7] Nasr, however, seems to be following Frithjof Schuon (d. 1998) in making of humanity a 'theomorphic being', denoted by his three faculties of intelligence, free will and the gift of speech. Schuon calls these faculties 'deiform'.[8] In some Muslim authors, therefore, both classical and contemporary, humanity has been characterised as in some sense sharing the divine nature.

Other Muslims, however, are much more reticent about the tradition quoted above from Abu Huraira. Perhaps they were alarmed by the implications of its reference to God's 'sixty cubits'. Nasr omits that part of the tradition altogether. The curious sixty cubits may refer to a discussion about the nature of Adam's body as it existed in Paradise, and the extent of the change he suffered in expulsion. Some argued that the tradition could mean that Adam was made in his own proper form (i.e. not God's) of sixty cubits.[9] Alternatively, the sixty cubits could refer to God's form, as an example of the grosser types of anthropomorphic conception of God.[10] One senses the reticence about the tradition even in Schuon, who manages to speak with two voices on the subject, saying that 'Islam is far from relying explicitly and generally on man's quality of being a divine image, although the Quran bears testimony to it … (in 15:29 and 38:72) … and although the anthropomorphism of God in the Quran implies the theomorphism of man.'[11]

There may indeed have been no general and explicit reliance in Islam on humanity being made in the divine image. But the CMS missionary in Egypt, Temple Gairdner (d. 1928), whose life so inspired Cragg, felt the Muslim fascination with this tradition. He suggested that it was this tradition 'that above all else led Moslem thinkers into temptation.' He meant the temptation for Muslims of trespassing on the uniqueness of Allah. He thought that 'its very riskiness seems … to have fascinated them supremely from the very outset. Not one of them could let it alone.'[12]

7 Schimmel, p. 72.

8 Schuon, Frithjof, *Understanding Islam*, Allen & Unwin, London, 1963, p. 15.

9 Massignon, Louis, *Kitab al-Tawasin par Hallaj*, Guenther, Paris, 1913, p. 129, n. 2; Brewster, D P, *al-Hallaj, Muslim Mystic and Martyr*, University of Canterbury, Christchurch, 1976, p. 37.

10 Wensinck, A J, *The Muslim Creed. Its Genesis and Historical Development*, CUP, Cambridge, 1932, pp. 67f., 148.

11 Schuon, *op. cit.*, p. 16.

12 Gairdner, *op. cit.*, p. 31.

Gairdner was particularly concerned with mystical Islam, and Nasr and Schuon represent Shi'ite and Sufi interpretations of Islam. For most Sunnis it is not the tradition of humanity being made in God's image, however reliably recorded, but the correct exegesis of the more authoritative texts from the Qur'an which occupies their mind, especially the verses where the Qur'an speaks of God breathing into the mortal 'of My spirit'.(15:29, 38:72) This action of God immediately precedes an order to the angels that they should 'fall down in obeisance unto him'. This might be understood to imply that it is the divine spirit in the mortal that the angels are to honour. But Muslim interpretation does not in fact dare to make that connection. Modern exegetes interpret the breath of God's spirit as the faculty of God-like knowledge and will, as in Yusuf Ali, or as 'man's inborn faculty for conceptual thinking' (Asad).[13] It is noticeable that most authors derive no general permission from this passage or from other parallel ones to argue by analogy from human nature to the character of God, in the fashion that Christian authors have done, taking their authority from passages like Luke 11:11-13. There is indeed one passage in al-Ash'ari (d. 935) where he reasons from the action of Joseph to the actions of God. He cites Joseph's willingness to face imprisonment rather than agree to adultery with his master's wife (based on Sura 12:33). So Joseph in a sense wills injustice for himself, yet cannot be considered sinful. Similarly, runs al-Ash'ari's argument, God may will acts of human evil without sinning himself. Watt's judgement, however, is that this line of thought may have been suggested by Christian writers and, perhaps for that very reason, was not much used by later Muslim authors.[14]

Here then we encounter a problem for Cragg at the very outset of his interpretation of religious issues between Christians and Muslims. If the key doctrine is that of the reciprocity of God and humanity, where is the common ground between Christians and Muslims? Since the doctrine concerned is the doctrine of God, the question could hardly be more acute. What does Cragg do in such a case? It is notable that he does not attempt a frontal assault on Islam by arguing the essential likeness of God and humanity, although that is certainly his own conviction. He might have been tempted to quote Schuon that 'the anthropomorphism of God

13 Yusuf 'Ali, A, *The Glorious Qur'an. Translation and Commentary*, the Islamic Foundation, Leicester, 1975, *ad. loc.*; Asad, Muhammad, *The Message of the Qur'an*, al-Andalus, Gibraltar, 1980, *ad. loc.*

14 Watt, W Montgomery, *The Formative Period of Islamic Thought*, Edinburgh University Press, Edinburgh, 1973, p. 310.

in the Qur'an implies the theomorphism of man.' (see above) He does not quote Genesis 1:26, though it is no doubt in his mind, or argue the authenticity of the tradition which echoes it. His preference is to focus on the meaning of the work rather than the character of the nature of God, and to explore the significance of the situation brought about by the very fact of God having created humanity. Instead of entering the well-trodden territory of the comparative natures of God and humanity he wants to use the common ground of Christians and Muslims in the doctrine of creation to suggest that in the very nature and fact of creation God has initiated a relationship with the human race, and this is a two-way thing. Here perhaps we see the influence of Gore and Bushnell.

Nevertheless it must be questioned how far this fundamental category of 'relationship' is appropriate here. To what extent do Muslims naturally use such a term to describe the debt of appropriate living owed by human beings to their creator? The modern sense of 'relationship', with its personal and emotional content, is naturally hard to find in classical texts. But, to take one example of a detailed Hanafite statement of Muslim belief, we find nothing in the tenth-century *Fiqh Akbar* II of any language which approximates to this meaning. Even where we do seem to read such language, its appearance is misleading. Article 25 gives a sense of the extreme care with which classical Muslim theologians handle the 'meeting' (*liqa'*, itself a Qur'anic term) of God with human beings:

> Allah's being near or far is not to be understood in the sense of a shorter or longer distance, but in the sense of man's being honoured or slighted. The obedient is near to Him, *without how*, and the disobedient is far from Him, *without how*. Nearness, distance and approach are applied to man in his intimate relation with Allah, and so it is with Allah's neighbourhood in Paradise, and with man's standing before Him, *without modality*.[15] (emphasis added)

Here indeed the term 'intimate relation' *(munajah)* is used, and believers are assured that they will meet God in Paradise. For the Sufis *munajah* meant the 'intimate conversation' with God in prayer.[16] But in the *Fiqh Akbar* II text what is given with one hand seems to be taken away with

15 Wensinck, *op. cit.*, p. 196; cf. *Inter-Text*, p. 72.
16 Schimmel, *op. cit.*, p. 155; cf. Wensinck, *op. cit.*, p. 238.

the other in the constant repetition of the formula 'without how', that is without demanding or giving an explanation as to how the term applies to God. We shall return to this issue in discussing Ghazzali's language about God in the next section. Among modern writers, where some use of a term equivalent to 'relationship' might be expected, the situation varies. In the case of an influential writer like the Pakistani Abu'l-A'la Mawdudi (d. 1979) it is noticeable that he reserves the term 'relationship' or 'relations' (Urdu: *ta'aluqat*) for the subject of human relatives, friends and acquaintances. Where God is concerned his vocabulary is different. God is the Master (Urdu: *malik*) to whom the only 'relation' is that of obligation and obedience:

> If you incur a loss by acting according to the wish of the Master, let it be so. You should never mind if life is lost, hands and feet are broken, children are lost and if money and property are destroyed. Why should you be grieved at all? If the owner himself desires loss of his things, it is perfectly within his right ... You are not the master of your soul. If you give your life according to the Master's wish you will only be fulfilling your obligation towards Him.[17]

Here it seems clear that the use of the term 'relationship' as applied between God and his creatures, or servants, feels inappropriate to Mawdudi, and it is avoided. The servant may indeed have a relationship with his master, but it is not the same kind of relationship that he will have with his equals and his kin, and so the use of a different word is preferred. The quotation here is from a Friday sermon, and seems to reflect the anxiety we have already noted among Muslims about speaking anthropomorphically of God.

However, a Pakistani contemporary of Mawdudi, Fazlur Rahman (d. 1988), speaking in an analytical rather than a devotional context, gives voice to a different understanding of Islam. He points out that the characteristic terms associated with God in the Qur'an are 'orderly creativity, sustenance, guidance, justice and mercy', and that 'all these are relational ideas.'[18] But

---

17 Maududi, S Abul A'la, *Fundamentals of Islam*, Islamic Publications, Lahore, 1975, p. 30.

18 Fazlur Rahman, *Major Themes of the Qur'an*, Bibliotheca Islamica, Minneapolis, 1980, p. 1.

this in no way implies anthropomorphism or theomorphism. The gulf between God and humanity is preserved because God in his essential nature is unknowable. His transcendence remains unaffected by his activity in revelation. Writing about al-Ghazzali, Fazlur Rahman claims that he

> affirmed an agnosticism about the ultimate and absolute nature of God and maintained that He was knowable only in so far as He was related to and revealed Himself to man. This revealed and relational nature of God is constituted by the Divine Names and Attributes.[19]

Though Fazlur Rahman elsewhere questions the value of the 'medieval theological heritage' represented by Ghazzali for today, he employs this idea of God's 'relatedness' extensively in his description of the world the Qur'an addresses. Humanity and nature are entirely dependent upon God and his mercy, and this 'necessarily entails a proper relationship between God and Man—a relationship of the served and the servant—and consequently also a proper relationship between man and man.' These relationships are 'normative' for all human conduct, and Fazlur Rahman can even speak of humanity becoming a 'friend' of God.[20] Fazlur Rahman is not alone in using such language. The Egyptian scholar Muhammad al-Nuwaihi (d. 1980) addressed Christians in Cairo Cathedral with the words:

> Islam is based on the direct and intimate relationship between God and man; a relationship so direct and so intimate as to cancel all need for any mediation between them.[21]

Has Cragg then found an adequate common language in which to pursue with Muslims his conviction of the reciprocity of God and humanity? A cluster of questions arises here, some of which must be pursued at a later point. How far are either Mawdudi or Fazlur Rahman typical of the broad range of Muslim opinion? Does Cragg, who has published little about the classical writers or about Mawdudi [*Counsels*, pp.

---

19 Fazlur Rahman, *Islam*, 2nd ed., University of Chicago Press, Chicago, 1979, p. 95.
20 Fazlur Rahman, 1980, *op. cit.*, pp. 2, 3, 12.
21 Al-Nuwaihi, Muhammad: art. 'The Religion of Islam. A Presentation to Christians' in *The International Review of Mission* 65:258 (April 1976), p. 221.

120-4], but with some enthusiasm about Fazlur Rahman [*Pen*, ch. 6], and who was a personal friend of Nuwaihi, interpret any of them correctly? Cragg suggests that Fazlur Rahman, in his 'scant appreciation of Sufism and Sufis' has settled for too 'functional' an understanding of God in the Qur'an, making of the Book a mere 'repository of answers ... to virtually all questions' rather than a meeting-place with God. [*Pen*, pp. 94, 93] We shall note later the significance of worship for Cragg, and the way in which in devotion, and particularly among the Sufis

> the humble of the Orders did not stay to debate with the scholastic theologians how such relationality, if real, could square with divine self-sufficiency. They simply took it to be the life-line of their own souls. [*Troubled*, p. 62]

Despite all Fazlur Rahman's talk about relationships in the divine/human encounter, Cragg perceives that in Fazlur Rahman's understanding humanity does not encounter God himself in the Qur'an, but rather the demands of his will for humanity. But in fastening critically upon this alleged 'programmatic character of the Qur'an' in Fazlur Rahman's writing [*Troubled*, p. 102], is Cragg pursuing an old Christian prejudice about the 'unknowable God of Islam'? Does he subscribe to the view that Christianity claims to reveal the nature of God, whereas Islam claims to reveal only his will? Does he recognise that, for example, the description of Ghazzali's thought given by Fazlur Rahman above, would also be affirmed by many Christians, particularly of the Orthodox Church? This discussion makes urgent for us the question of the knowability of God.

2 The Knowability of God

The question of whether or in what sense God can be known is clearly critical for Cragg's basic assumption of the reciprocity of God and humanity. The 'formative period of Islamic thought' (to borrow the title of Watt's book on the subject)[22] was marked by tremendous theological struggles between the traditionalists, above all Ibn Hanbal (780-855), and the Mu'tazilite rationalists or dialecticians. The orthodoxy which eventually emerged from generations of dispute was essentially a

22 See n. 14.

middle way formulated by al-Ash'ari (873-935), himself a convert from Mu'tazilism.[23] For the traditionalists all possible knowledge of God was contained in the Qur'an and *sunna*, and only there. God speaks to human beings in the recitation of the Qur'an, and in that process they come into personal contact with his living word. But as the Hanbalite theologian Barbahari (d. 940) wrote 'Religion is nothing but imitation, imitation of the companions of the Prophet of God.' There can be no place for any attempt to explain or question what God reveals and commands. Theology is doing, not thinking, for, to quote Barbahari again, 'knowledge does not consist in the abundance of *hadith* and books: the possessor of knowledge is the one who puts into practice knowledge and the *sunna*.'[24]

The difficulty was that the very attempt to put into practice the Qur'an and the *sunna* involved the use of reasoning, for not every human situation was explicitly covered by those sources. From the use of reasoning in jurisprudence, and perhaps from the experience of argument with non-Muslims, some passed to more inquisitive and subtle forms of reasoning about the meaning of the word of God, and *kalam* or Muslim speculative theology was born.[25] In the context of our present discussion on the knowability of God the significance of this movement was its interest in the correct use of language about God, and its strong tendency to regard descriptive terms for him, or *sifat* (attributes), even those found in the Qur'an, as metaphors belonging to the created order. Since they belonged to the created order they could not adequately describe the eternal nature of God. Here we see in operation the Mu'tazilite concern for the unity of God. For if God's knowledge, for example, were regarded as eternal, it would be thought of as itself divine, and a second god. This kind of thinking led the Mu'tazilites to the dissident doctrine that the Qur'an was created and not itself eternal. Its apparent anthropomorphisms were therefore merely metaphor, though admittedly metaphor given by God.[26] For the traditionalists, who observed that Mu'tazilite writers like al-Jubba'i (d. 915) rarely quoted the Qur'an and never the *hadith*, this threatened the heart of faith. Eventually, however, some of the traditionalists

23 Allard, Michel, *Le Problème des Atributs Divins dans la doctrine d'al-Ash'ari et de ses premiers grands disciples*, Éditions de l'Imprimerie Catholique, Beirut, 1965, p. 104.
24 *Ibid.*, pp. 104, 108, 109.
25 Watt, *op. cit.*, p. 180ff.
26 *Ibid.*, p. 246.

were compelled to adopt the vocabulary and ways of reasoning of the rationalists, if only to refute them.

By the time of Ghazzali (1058-1111), Sunni orthodoxy on the subject of the attributes of God had been largely established through the work of al-Ash'ari, and it was within al-Ash'ari's system of *kalam* (literally 'speech' and so 'theology') that Ghazzali worked. An examination of Ghazzali's thought opens up important perspectives on Cragg. Fadlou Shehadi, in an extensive philosophical analysis of it, has investigated the apparent contradiction between Ghazzali's consistent emphasis on the utter uniqueness and unknowability of God, as noted by Fazlur Rahman, and his parallel concern that Muslims should follow the path to mystical union with God.[27]

Gairdner's study of Ghazzali brought him to complain of what he called the 'hypertranscendence of the Allah of his theology': 'Of this Absolute Being nothing is, because nothing can be, predicated.'[28] Shehadi, however, insists that the problem is not simply one for Islam, but affects all those whose theism makes God 'above relation', and a radically different being from ourselves. His own conclusion of the problem as it appears in Ghazzali is that for Ghazzali statements which appear to be descriptive of God are not in fact so, for all such 'attribution' is inadequate and fails to define God. Nevertheless such statements have the valuable function of being vehicles for praise. 'Attribution makes religion possible.'[29]

Here are echoes of a long-running debate. For it is interesting to note that Shehadi's understanding of Ghazzali was also broadly the position of the nineteenth-century Christian philosopher Henry Mansel (1820-1871), with whom F D Maurice conducted a fierce pamphlet war on the whole issue of the knowability of God.[30] For Mansel's *The Limitations of Religious Knowledge Examined*, the Bampton Lectures of 1858, in some respects anticipated the dialectical theology of the twentieth century which rejected any metaphysical foundation for theology. Mansel argued that a transcendent God must by virtue of that transcendence be unknown and

27 Shehadi, Fadlou, *Ghazzali's Unique Unknowable God; A Philosophical Critical Analysis of some of the Problems raised by Ghazzali's view of God as utterly unique and unknowable*, Brill, Leiden, 1964.

28 Gairdner, W H T: art. 'al-Ghazzali's Mishkat al-Anwar and the Ghazzali-Problem' in *Der Islam* 5, 1914, pp. 144, 128.

29 Shehadi, *op. cit.*, pp. 62, 109.

30 Smart, Ninian et al, *Nineteenth Century Religious Thought in the West*, vol. 2, CUP, Cambridge, p. 240, and Chadwick, Owen, *The Victorian Church*, Black, London, 1966, p. 588.

unknowable, for human beings conditioned by the limitations of physical existence cannot have knowledge of the unconditioned. Mansel distrusted the powers of human reason adequately to describe God, and emphasized the self-contradictory character of much religious language. The infinite can only be known through negative concepts.[31] He was much influenced by the thought of the Scottish philosopher William Hamilton (1788-1856) who said that 'A God understood would be no God at all.' In answer to those who regarded this as the destruction of religion Mansel argued that 'a conception which is speculatively untrue may be regulatively true.'[32] In other words God has given us revelation so that we can worship him. But this did not satisfy those like F D Maurice who reckoned that Mansel had substituted the dry bones of theology for the living God. For Maurice divine revelation was not the unveiling of a set of propositions but the meeting of a person, 'and that Person the ground and Archetype of men, the source of all life and goodness in men.'[33] To suggest that revelation was the imparting of concepts that could be used but never really understood was a travesty of God's encounter with humanity. Later Gore also joined in the attack on Mansel in the interests of the Incarnation as the crown, and not the antithesis, of what may be known through nature and reason.[34] We have already seen the significance of Maurice and Gore for the thought of Cragg, and it is clear that he would share their criticisms of Mansel.

When we return to Ghazzali the parallels with Mansel are immediately obvious. As Shehadi understands Ghazzali, *Allahu akbar* means that God is greater, not than any other god or being, but greater than can be known by humanity.[35] Armed with such Qur'anic texts and phrases the Muslim can be sure that he is worshipping God in the language God himself has supplied, without having to suppose that such words give him any power of stating adequately what God is. If this is so, Gairdner was mistaken when he wrote, rather in the vein of Maurice: 'How Ghazzali the orthodox was able to keep in view so definite an attribution as that of Creatorhood amid the Stygian darkness of his hyperagnosticism, is a question that can

31 Reardon, B M G, *From Coleridge to Gore. A Century of Religious Thought in Britain*, Longman, London, 1971, pp. 223, 226f.

32 Smart, *op. cit.*, p. 239, 240.

33 Reardon, *op. cit.*, p. 239.

34 Gore, Charles, *The Incarnation of the Son of God*, London, John Murray, 1891, p. 116f.

35 Shehadi, *op. cit.*, p. 48.

be asked but not answered.'[36] There is an answer and it lies in the two roles of Ghazzali, as philosopher (however much he disavowed that role), and as spiritual director. Shehadi does not make the point, but it may well be that a religious as much as a philosophical reason lies behind Ghazzali's anxiety to exclude the possibility of knowing God: namely that knowledge always gives power, and in the traditional world of the Semites to know a person's name gives one power over him. In the same way Adam acquired power in the world because he was taught by God the names of all things, though these were unknown to the angels. (Qur'an 2:31, 32) But where God is concerned it is simply inconceivable to have power over him. The names of God are given by God and belong to God, and are to be used with a proper care. (Qur'an 7:180).

Shehadi includes some criticism of Cragg in the course of his examination of Ghazzali. He notes that Cragg indicates an awareness of the philosophical issues involved in the fundamental contrast of God's unknowability and his summons to humanity to meet with him. He quotes *The Call of the Minaret*:

> The problem of meaning in language exists for all religions and is not unique to Islam. It can only be solved within the conviction that the Divine and the human are truly meaningful to each other: only in the confidence that the relationships God has with man are really indicative of His Nature. We only put these convictions more shortly—and sublimely—when we say: 'God is Love.' Islam has never felt able to say that. The pressure of these problems is the measure of its reluctance.[37] [*Call*, p. 49]

Despite an acknowledgement that Cragg is not concerned to write a philosophical treatise, Shehadi objects to his use of terms like 'in the conviction that' and 'in the confidence that': 'the conviction and the confidence that God *does* truly reveal Himself do not answer in the least the philosophical question of *how* this is possible.' [emphasis original] He clearly thinks that the confidence and conviction Cragg calls to be placed in God as love might in logic be equally validly placed elsewhere, for example in the *sunna* of Islam. To cite 'confidence' and 'conviction' does

---

36 Gairdner, *op. cit.*, p. 145.
37 Shehadi, *op. cit.*, p. 79.

not in itself resolve the problem of where they should be employed. He clearly feels that Cragg has substituted assertion for argument.

Shehadi's book, however, raises a final point in this context which goes some way towards justifying Cragg's strictures on Islamic 'reluctance' to identify God as Love, or indeed, anything else. Shehadi asks whether, in view of the unknowability of God insisted on by Ghazzali, it is possible to speak realistically (at least in philosophical terms) of 'God revealing' anything at all, however that revelation might be defined. He concludes that there needs, logically, to be a shift in the 'locus of authority' in Islam from 'the directness of God's authority to that of the prophet ... The Prophet would then have to be trusted in a special way for supplying man with a theistic perspective that directs his religious and ethical life.' The Islamic bridge, in other words, from the properly agnostic character of theology to the practicalities of daily religion is to be Muhammad. Such a shift from Allah the Transcendent to Muhammad as mediator of his ways is of course amply testified in Islamic preaching and informs daily Muslim life.[38]

Some such bridge is surely inevitable if the intelligent mind and the worshipping heart are to find any harmony with one another. Gairdner, like Shehadi, finds Ghazzali unsatisfactory on this point but speaks with much greater force of the 'incorrigible inconsistency' of Ghazzali's position. Ghazzali, he complains, bases his whole treatise of *Mishkat al-Anwar* ('The Niche for Lights') on the analogy of light for God which is given by the Qur'an itself (Surah 24:35). In Ash'arite style Ghazzali seems to deny in the very same work that the analogy really applies to Allah, who is 'transcendent of and separate from every characterization that in the foregoing we have made.' Yet Ghazzali also speaks in the identical passage of an 'Obeyed-One' whose relation to the 'Real Existence is as the relation of the Sun to Essential Light, or of the live coal to the Elemental Fire.'[39] This alarmed some Muslim thinkers. Ibn Rushd/Averroes (d. 1198) alleged that Ghazzali had compromised the divine unity and taught (like Ibn Sina/Avicenna d. 1037 and al-Farabi d. 950) a doctrine of emanations from God, because he spoke of the angelic intelligences of the spheres, and seemed to imply, with his talk of the sun and Light and the coal and Fire that these intelligences somehow shared the nature of God in diluted

38 *Ibid.*, p. 125; cf. Schimmel, Annemarie, *And Muhammad is His Messenger. The Veneration of the Prophet in Islamic Piety*, University of North Carolina, Chapel Hill, 1985.
39 Gairdner, *op. cit.* (1924), s. 29, 55.

form. Gairdner's own lengthy examination of Ibn Rushd's accusation exonerates Ghazzali from such heresy by emphasizing Ghazzali's normal language of the heavenly beings reflecting God's glory, and in no sense themselves a source of it,[40] but the confusion remains.

We have already seen that this difficulty of speaking descriptively of God is not exclusively an Islamic issue. Pseudo-Dionysius, the Neo-Platonist, writes of The One as 'neither soul nor spirit, nor representation, nor opinion, nor thought, nor equality, nor disparity … nor night, nor light, nor living, nor life … ' John of Damascus (d. 749) was the first Christian theologian to write about Islam, and he is positively Ash'arite in speaking of the idiomata or *sifat* (attributes) of God: these are to be applied 'only in so far as He is the cause of these, and in so far as He is immaterial and the Creator of the universe and almighty.'[41] He might almost be using the Islamic expression 'without (asking) how'. Maimonides, the medieval Jewish theologian who wrote in Arabic, rejected both likeness and relationship:

> In view of the fact that the relationship between us and Him, may He be exalted, is considered as non-existent—I mean the relation between Him and that which is other than He—it follows necessarily that likeness between Him and us should also be considered non-existent … The meaning of the qualificative attributions ascribed to Him and the meaning of the attributes known to us have nothing in common in any respect or in any mode; these attributes have in common only the name and nothing else.[42]

Then listen to the Russian theologian Vladimir Lossky (d. 1958), expressing the common understanding of the Orthodox Church:

> God is not determined by any of His attributes; all determinations are inferior to Him, logically posterior to His being in itself, in its essence. When we say that God is Wisdom, Life, Truth, Love—we understand the

---

40 Gairdner, *op. cit.* (1914), pp. 133-145.

41 Wensinck, *op. cit.*, pp. 71-2.

42 Maimonides, Moses, *The Guide of the Perplexed*, 2 vols, Eng. tr., University of Chicago Press, Chicago, 1963, c. 56.

> energies, which are subsequent to the essence and are its natural manifestations, but are *external* to the very being of the Trinity … Like the energies, the divine names are innumerable, so likewise the nature which they reveal remains nameless and *unknowable*—darkness hidden by the abundance of light.[43] [emphasis added]

Here the Orthodox Church is surely in fundamental agreement with Ghazzali about the nature of God against Western Christians like Cragg and Gore, and is even found using the same imagery of concealing light as the *Mishkat al-Anwar*. Nor is such negative theology confined to the Eastern tradition. Though developed by Clement, Origen, Basil and Gregory of Nyssa, it finds scriptural justification in texts like Matthew 11:27—'No one knows the Father but the Son'—and Western followers as significant as St John of the Cross, Meister Eckart and Pascal. Maimonides reckoned that 'We are only able to apprehend the fact that He is and cannot apprehend His quiddity.'[44] Aquinas, though he disagreed with Maimonides on the question of attributes, did agree on this last point: 'Sed quia de Deo scire non possumus quid sit, sed quid non sit, non possumus considerare de Deo quomodo sit, sed potius quomodo non sit.'[45]

At this point it may be well to raise some more general questions in a short digression. The point just discussed raises the question of whether, like many other writers, Cragg is not pursuing some 'hidden agenda' of his own in the guise of an engagement with Islam, without necessarily realising the fact. Is he really conducting an argument with other Christians in order to establish a particular viewpoint of the nature of God for which Islam simply serves as a convenient negative illustration? If however we grant—as without question we must—his genuine concern for Islam, other related issues arise. We need, for example, to be clear at this point that two elements are involved in the general aspect of Cragg's thought under discussion at this stage. Cragg's position is that the *doctrines* of God and humanity are reciprocal—that is to say, that what is thought about God profoundly affects what is thought about humanity (which

43 Lossky, Vladimir, *The Mystical Theology of the Eastern Church*, James Clarke, Cambridge, 1957, p. 80.

44 Maimonides, *op. cit.*, c. 58.

45 'But because we cannot know about God what he is, but what he is not, so we cannot know about God how he is but rather how he is not.' Patterson, R L, *The Conception of God in the Philosophy of Aquinas*, Allen & Unwin, London, 1933, p. 113.

is hardly in question), but equally that what is thought about humanity profoundly affects what is thought about God. As already suggested, this is controversial with Muslims. But the implications of this line of thought go beyond the formulation of doctrines about what God is like and what humanity is like. There is inevitably in its development the claim that God is somehow subject in some degree to the will of humanity, as well as the reverse. If it be claimed that Islam will have none of such a doctrine, Cragg's answer is that the implication is already there, for those who have eyes to see it, in the doctrine of creation and the pages of the Qur'an. This inevitably involves him in the claim that he sees deeper into the meaning and implications of Islam than Muslims do. It is also likely to involve him in the practice of searching out congenial interpreters from Muslim ranks who show signs of reaching his own conclusions, while others (like the classical theologians and moderns such as Mawdudi) are neglected.

This is not necessarily a condemnation of his theological method. It may be that time and further Muslim thought will prove him right. Among contemporary Muslim authors Fazlur Rahman is quite prepared to speak (from painful personal experience) of 'the real picture' of revelation in Islam being 'anathema' to the 'general Muslim mind', and of the Qur'anic 'intentions', e.g. about monogamy being 'thwarted' by Muslims over many centuries.[46] Sayyid Qutb and others have spoken of the principles of Islam having been crippled in Islamic countries for many centuries. [*Call*, p. 339, n. 10] Arguments open to Muslim thinkers must, at least in principle, be open to non-Muslims also. Cragg may indeed see and understand things in the fundamental doctrines of Islam which very few Muslims themselves have yet seen. The possibility must at least be entertained, if a non-Muslim venture of interpreting Islam with some basic sympathy is to be sustained. How otherwise is a non-Muslim interpreter of Islam to proceed? If he has turned away from those Christian views which see Islam only in the negative terms of demonology or apocalypse, and yet is unwilling to throw in the intellectual towel by assuming a valid plurality of (mutually contradictory) religious philosophies, is some such path as Cragg's not inescapable? The issue then turns on the cogency and comprehensiveness of his treatment of Islam according to carefully stated starting-points. Clearly the further he diverges from generally accepted dogmatic markers in Islam, the more cogent his argument will have to be, and the more his refutation or neglect of opposing views will have to be

46 Fazlur Rahman, *op. cit.*, 1979, pp. 14, 38.

examined. Is he engaging only with a selected, minority viewpoint within Islam? Does he wrestle with the question of what is normative Islam (or normative Christianity)? We shall deal later with the awareness which he shows of these wider issues. Here we need to know more about the way he elaborates his doctrine of God and humanity.

It should not be thought that Cragg is crudely anthropocentric in his understanding of God, as though human beings made God in their own image. In the discussion of the Islamic cry 'Allahu akbar' he maintains that 'the criteria of divine greatness cannot well be those of our devising or requiring. It takes God to show us what they are.'[47] But he is insistent that such criteria be consonant with what we know of human nature. 'If God is arbitrarily beyond our nature, we cannot approach him except in the denial of our own.' In fact to concede the omnipotence of God as meaning an utter arbitrariness would be to make our *islam*/submission impossible. 'To say: "Let God be God" makes it impossible to eliminate ourselves from the answer.'[48] In other words we have here a relationship, a mutuality. In a 1984 essay Cragg acknowledges the 'very proper instinct for divine "indescribability"' which is characteristic of negative theology in Jewish and Christian, especially Orthodox, tradition as well as in Islam, as we have seen. But he continues to plead for the same 'confidence' that Shehadi found philosophically problematic:

> Need we, in the negative theology, deny that God, as He transcends all our knowing and telling, also belongs within it? Need the ineffable, the incomprehensible, be also the nugatory, the contradictory? Or can we not rely on a confidence that, although we must always be aware of the poverty of our concepts, we can nevertheless take them in the seriousness of the created order and the prophetic revelation which gives them to us and, giving, does not mock or tantalize?[49]

47 Cragg, Kenneth, art. 'Islam and Incarnation' in John Hick ed., *Truth and Dialogue in World Religions. Conflicting Truth Claims*, Sheldon, London, 1974, p. 136.

48 Cragg, Kenneth, art. 'Legacies and Hopes in Muslim-Christian Theology' in *Islamochristiana* 3 (1977), p. 5.

49 Cragg, Kenneth, art. 'Tadabbur al-Qur'an: reading and meaning' in A H Green ed., *In Quest of an Islamic Humanism. Arabic and Islamic Studies in memory of Mohamed al-Nuwaihi*, American University in Cairo Press, Cairo, 1984, p. 191.

The difficulty of language about God, as Cragg sees it, is that theologians suppose that God is reluctant to be named or described, and the confidence he calls for is in God's willingness to be addressed by the creatures he has made himself responsible for. Can this possibility of communication not bring about 'a certain mutuality between God and man, proper to both?'[50] Reflecting on the Qur'anic description of Abraham as the *khalil* or 'friend' of God (in, e.g., 4:125), he writes

> God, having 'a friend', thereby becomes (or, rather, is) one—a truth which must make the two words *Allah* and *khalil* somehow alike. A relationality in respect of man enters, in some sense, into the being of God. [*Troubled*, p. 62]

In Cragg's view, then, the bridge we spoke of earlier between theology and religion is the possibility of mutual communication between God and humanity which God has implanted in the very character of his creation. Here we see again how Cragg's theology is based on the fundamental possibility of communication and the existential need of it.

There have been voices within Islam which come very close to acknowledging Cragg's viewpoint. In his review of *The Call of the Minaret*, written while he was still a Muslim, Daud Rahbar (b. 1926) blamed the theologians of Islam for so emphasizing divine transcendence that the divine personality revealed in the Qur'an was obscured. 'Thus the concept of God was left completely devoid of the element of intimacy with and challenge to human affairs.'[51] Nuwaihi also said, quoting Cragg, that 'The Qur'an is nothing if it is not "a suffering identity with creation and humanity." '[52]

However, the mainstream of Islamic thought is probably better represented here by Fazlur Rahman. He credits Cragg with 'an extraordinarily sensitive response to Islamic scripture (for) a Christian', and he has no doubt that the God of the Qur'an is not arbitrary, and that it is a Western slur upon Islam to allege that it is. But he has a different understanding of God and humanity which emerges in the way that his use of the word 'nature' differs from that of Cragg. For Fazlur Rahman the

50 *Ibid.*, p. 190.

51 Rahbar, Daud, review article on *The Call of the Minaret* in *The Muslim World* 48: 1 (January 1958).

52 Nuwaihi, *op. cit.*, p. 221; cf. Cragg: art 'Constance E Padwick 1886-1968' in *The Muslim World* 59: 4 (Oct. 1969), p. 38, and 'Tadabbur al-Qur'an', *op. cit.*, p. 191.

qadar or capacity of God to 'measure out' the potentialities of everything created, including of course humanity, 'expresses the most fundamental, unbridgeable difference between the nature of God and the nature of man.'[53] So the 'relatedness' of God to humanity which we observed earlier in Fazlur Rahman's thinking is strictly in these 'measured' terms. If God is a friend of humanity, it is as a 'protector-friend', or so Fazlur Rahman translates the *wali* of Surah 6:14. It is instructive to compare the two authors on the consequences of failing to acknowledge God. For Fazlur Rahman, who discusses the point in the context of *shirk*, the result is the loss of order in nature, 'the entire chain falls to pieces.'[54] For Cragg the consequence is rather that where God is not acknowledged, there can be no real understanding or concept of human nature. In Cragg's terms, it is not a matter of 'a broken command but (of) a disrupted communion.'[55] Cragg quotes Sartre to make the point by its corollary: '"There is no human nature, because there is no God to have a conception of it" Sartre once wrote, in his darkest mood.' [*Privilege*, p. 138]. The question is about humanity as well as about God.

3 The Khalifate of Humanity

For Cragg then, reciprocity means this relational, existential link between God and humanity. [Almost all of Cragg's published work employs the older vocabulary, now regarded as sexist, which refers to 'man' rather than 'humanity', and no attempt will be made to change his usage in the quotations which follow.] It is this link which matters, rather than some philosophical abstraction, and it is celebrated in worship, which takes on in consequence the significance that it ennobles humanity as well as honours God. So we need to see the Qur'an, for example, primarily 'as a mission to retrieve idolaters for a true worship', writes Cragg in introducing it. [*Event*, p. 15] For humanity is constituted by worship, by the relationship which a person has with the one who created and therefore defines him. God must be 'worshippable', both in the sense that he is big enough for human adoration, and in the sense that people are enabled to worship him. We discover our true selves as we worship.

53 Fazlur Rahman, *op. cit.*, 1980, pp. xv, 15, 13.
54 *Ibid.*, pp. 14, 10.
55 Cragg, Kenneth, *op. cit.*, 'Tadabbur al-Qur'an', p. 191.

'Man is king and priest, but neither in isolation. For he only truly rules when he validly praises, only governs as he kneels, only masters in that he prays.' [*Sandals*, p. 117] And if it be thought that such an outlook stems from Christianity and finds no home in Islam Cragg is ready with exegeses of the passages about Adam and Satan in the Qur'an. (2:30-34, 7:11-14, 15:26-35) Iblis, the Devil, refuses to bow before Adam at the command of God.

> His defiance of God takes the form of a denial of man: it is in rejecting the status with which the creature is endowed that *Iblis* repudiates the Creator's authority. There could hardly be, in terms of myth and symbol, a clearer affirmation of the lordship of man as that which may not be spurned without impugning the authority of God ... God is flouted where man is despised. [*Privilege*, p. 28]

All the relevant Qur'anic passages Cragg understands as making it clear that the proper recognition of God involves the recognition of humanity, and vice-versa. 'Non-recognition of man is non-submission to God. Satan's obduracy in rejecting prostration before man in recognition of his responsible dignity is Qur'anically understood as the crowning defiance of God.' [*Sandals*, p. 117] To refuse to see the significance of humanity is to fail in duty to God.

But is this a proper understanding of the Qur'an? Here we have to examine how far Cragg's exegesis is consonant with Muslim understanding of the same passages. This heavenly dispute of Satan with God concerns the risk God proposes to take in creating the human race. According to the Qur'an the angels are anxious about the whole enterprise. 'Wilt Thou, said the angels, place therein one who will do harm therein and will shed blood?' (2:30). Commenting on a parallel passage (38:71), the Mu'tazilite Zamakhshari (d. 1144) identifies the fault of Iblis not in a refusal to recognise the 'responsible dignity of man', as Cragg has it, but in setting his own judgement before the command of God. 'The reason why Iblis detested and scorned bowing down before Adam is that this would be prostration before something created ... He should have known that, by bowing down before a lower being at the command of God, the angels devoted themselves more strongly to the service of God than if they had bowed down before God himself.'[56] Zamakhshari goes on to give examples which make it clear that he regards the status of the angels, and of Iblis, to be superior to that of Adam. Other commentators took a different view of their comparative status, some relying on Surah 7.19f., where Satan says 'Your Lord has only prohibited you from this tree lest you become angels, or lest you become immortals.' Baidawi (d. 1316) is at pains to deny that there is 'evidence here for the absolute superiority of the angels.'[57] Whatever the exact status of angels and of human beings, however, the classical exegetes seem to be agreed that some cosmic drama was being enacted, something more significant than merely the emergence of the human race. Creation was not brought about for humanity but for another purpose altogether. Human nature is too ambivalent to bear the whole weight of God's purpose in creation. 'It may be argued', writes Ayoub, summarizing the classical exegetes,

> that the purpose of the entire drama of creation was for God to manifest His knowledge and power and to expose the pride of Iblis. This is clearly shown in the creation of man. According to Tabari, God sent Gabriel, then Michael, to fetch clay, but the earth said, 'I take refuge in God from you, if you have come to diminish and deform me.' [58]

Human existence, so far from being the crown of the rest of creation, was perceived as a threat to it. We shall see shortly how the classical writers understood the status of Adam as *khalifah*.

Cragg is characteristically modern in not being much impressed by angels, and they find little if any place in his writing. For him the emergence of the human race is overwhelmingly more important than whatever rôle angels may have in the divine economy. But if that is so, does his understanding run entirely counter to conventional Muslim thought when he reads the passages in the Qur'an about the creation of humanity in the way that he does? There are modern Muslims who go as far, if not further than Cragg himself. Al-Mashriqi (Md 'Inayat Allah Khan, b. 1888) for example, has God saying to the human race:

---

56 Gätje, Helmut, *The Qur'an and its Exegesis. Selected Texts with Classical and Modern Muslim Interpretations*, Eng. tr., RKP, London, 1976, p. 167-8.

57 *Ibid.*, pp. 278, 171.

58 Ayoub, Mahmoud M, *The Qur'an and its Interpreters*, Vol. 1, SUNY Press, Albany, 1984, p. 75.

> Be aware that I am God; you should be God's counterpart, and incarnation in little of the divine attributes; hear and see, like I do ('so We have made him hearing, seeing'). My spirit I breathe into you ('and I breathed into him of My spirit'). This is so because I want you to be what I am … powerful and mighty … I am the great Creator; similarly I expect from you great creations and inventions.[59]

This sort of language goes much further even than Nasr and Schuon's theomorphism, and is not of course typical of Muslim writing, but what is the link between the classical exegesis and such human-centred 'modernism'? The answer seems to lie in the esoteric contribution of the Sufis mediated to modern non-Sufi Muslims through the poet-precursor of Pakistan, Muhammad Iqbal (d. 1938).

For Sufi devotees the Prophet is the representative human being, icon of all humanity. In very early times the famous contemporary and nominated poet of Muhammad, Hassan ibn Thabit, is credited with the verse:

> God derived for him, in order to honour him, part of His name;
> Thus the Lord of the Throne is called *mahmud*, and this one *muhammad*.[60]

In this way Muhammad is related directly to one of the names (attributes) of God, and the human race potentially through him, as we saw in the implications of Ghazzali's thought. Later speculation fastened on Muhammad's name in the form *Ahmad*, and the alleged *hadith qudsi* (tradition recording words of Allah) which ran '*ana Ahmad bi-la mim*', that is 'I am Ahmad (= Muhammad) without the letter *m*', or in other words *Ahad*, which means 'the One', God. From this developed the idea of Muhammad as the perfect human being, the *al-insan al-kamil*, made in the image of God and a perfect copy of his Creator.[61]

---

59 Baljon, J M S, *Modern Muslim Koran Interpretation 1880-1960*, Brill, Leiden, 1961, p. 55f.

60 Schimmel 1985, *op. cit.*, p. 105f.

61 Schimmel 1975, *op. cit.*, p. 224f.

As Ibn 'Arabi (d. 1240) saw it, human beings are themselves each a theophany *(tajalli)*, since everything that is real is an emanation from God, God manifesting himself in a infinity of forms. When someone prays it is God praying within him. But divine consciousness reaches its perfect expression in the perfect human, whom Ibn 'Arabi identifies with the spirit (rather than the earthly person) of Muhammad. 'God, wrote Ibn 'Arabi, made him His Vicegerent *(khalifah)* in the guardianship of the universe, and it continues to be guarded whilst this Perfect Man is there.'[62] In reaction the Indian Naqshbandi Sufi Sirhindi (d. 1624) tried to free Sufism from the legacy of Ibn 'Arabi by distinguishing between prophethood *(nubuwwat)* and sainthood *(walayat)*. For him sainthood indeed brought with it 'illuminations and appearances' *(tajalliyat wa zuhurat)* of the divine, but these were inferior, mere shadows of the Real compared to the direct knowledge of Real experienced by the prophets, a subjective and not an objective knowledge.[63]

Is Cragg then relating essentially to Sufi understandings of the Qur'an? Here we need to look closely at the question of the interpretation of Adam as *khalifah*, or vicegerent. Among non-Sufis there seem to have been two principal interpretations, as noted in the great Qur'an commentator Tabari (d. 923). Relying as he frequently did on Ibn 'Abbas, one of the Prophet's Companions, Tabari says that Adam was the *khalifah* (in the sense of substitute and successor) of the *jinn*, who had been the first to inhabit the earth, but who had been defeated by Iblis because they had spread corruption and murder there. This sense is hardly complimentary to Adam, but Tabari offers a second interpretation (in which he is followed by, for example, Qurtubi the Spanish jurist, d. 1273). Now Adam is identified as the vicegerent of God himself, 'who shall represent me in judging among my creatures', because, adds Qurtubi, 'he was the first messenger to earth.' (But note that it is Adam himself as prophet, and not the human race in principle, who is *khalifah*.)[64] We have to be aware, especially in the earliest of the classical writers, of the political implications of any exegesis of the word *khalifah*. Al-Hajjaj, the notorious governor of Baghdad under the Umayyads, used the text at 2:30 to claim that the Caliph was superior even to angels and prophets, while other supporters

62 Landau, Rom, *The Philosophy of Ibn 'Arabi*, Allen & Unwin, London, 1959, p. 56f., 73.

63 Ansari, Md Abdul Haq, *Sufism and Shari'ah. A Study of Shaykh Ahmad Sirhindi's Effort to Reform Sufism*, Leicester, The Islamic Foundation, 1986, p. 212.

64 Ayoub 1984, *op. cit.*, pp. 74, 76.

of the regime understood the title as meaning the 'Deputy of God'. Abu Bakr is said to have rejected that interpretation decisively in favour of the sense 'Deputy (or Successor) of the *Apostle* of God.'[65] [emphasis added]

However, the *mufassir* (Qur'an commentator) Ibn Kathir (d. 1373) is one classical writer who does see the text as evidence of the special favour of humanity as a whole with God, and among the Sufis that theme was developed extensively. Nisaburi (d. 1329) says that 'when man's lamp is so illumined with the fire of the light of God, he becomes God's vicegerent in His earth, manifesting the lights of His attributes in this world through justice, well-doing, compassion, mercy, kindliness, and domination. These attributes,' comments Nisaburi, 'are manifested in neither animal nor angelic beings.'[66] Here we come close to the theomorphic conception of man which we saw in S H Nasr and Frithjof Schuon. Ibn 'Arabi, noting like Nisaburi, that Surah 2:30 does not speak of God 'creating' *(khalaq)* man but of 'placing' *(ja'al)* him on the earth, develops an interpretation in which God says: 'Man is My vicegerent forming his character according to My character, and is known by My characteristics.'[67] A century earlier than Ibn 'Arabi, Ghazzali was capable of similar, though more cautious statements. Quoting Surah 15:29, about God 'fashioning man and breathing into him of my spirit', he says

> For this reason the angels of God made obeisance to Adam. It is understood also from this verse: I have made you my successor in the world. The Prophet Adam would not have been fit for *khilafat* unless he was given the connection *(munasabah)* of spirit. The Prophet said, hinting at this connection: God created Adam according to His image.[68]

This linking of the Sufi exegesis of *khilafat* and the tradition about humanity being made in the image of God appears, however, to induce a certain nervousness in Ghazzali, for at two points in the *Ihya'* he says that the special endowment of humanity must not be spelt out in detail in a book.[69] But his use of the word *munasabah* (Lane: = 'resemblance,

65 Watt, *op. cit.*, p. 84.
66 Ayoub, 1984, *op. cit.*, p. 78.
67 *Ibid.*, p. 79.
68 Al-Ghazzali, *Ihya' Ulum id-Din*, 4 vols., Eng.tr., Sind Sagar Academy, Lahore, 1971, s. IV:310=IV: 6: 675 Egyptian Arabic ed.
69 *Ibid.*, IV:294, 675.

similarity, analogy, correspondence, conformity: in logic the relation of subject to predicate') does seem at this point to justify Cragg's theme of reciprocity between God and man, despite the earlier philosophical issues which we noted, and Ghazzali's evident misgivings at too much publicity for the details of such a view. The *Ihya'* passage quoted above actually continues with a reference to the tradition of God's rebuke to Moses that 'I was sick, and thou visitedst me not', with its close similarity to Matthew 25:31f. [cf. *Alive*, p. 99 and *Common*, p. 53]

Modern Muslim interpreters, however, decline to be drawn into using this dangerous theomorphic language, with its echoes of al-Hallaj, and read Surah 2:30 in terms of human responsibility, not resemblance, to God.[70] Iqbal maintains that

> Three things are perfectly clear from the Quran:
> (i) That man is the chosen of God …
> (ii) That man, with all his faults, is meant to be the representative of God on earth …
> (iii) That man is the trustee of a free personality which he accepted at his peril … [71]

Whatever the views of classical writers about *khilafat* as succession, and the status of Adam himself as *khalifah* and prophet, the moderns follow Iqbal in affirming that the term refers to a human vicegerency from God. The Indian scholar Vahiduddin affirms Cragg's metaphysical exegesis of the relevant passages and reckons that 'the traditional exegesis which understands the Khalifah primarily in its involvement with the political succession to the Prophet has gone a long way in clouding the original Qur'anic intention.'[72] Tabataba'i says: 'Many are the texts which support the fact that the vicegerency is meant to include the descendants of Adam.'[73] Mawdudi uses the same theme to attack Western ideas: 'this knowledge (of his origins) raises the status of man from the helpless and mean creature of evolution to the noblest creation of Allah, His vicegerent on earth, to whom the angels and everything in their charge were made

70 E.g. Parwez in Baljon, *op. cit.*, p. 57.

71 Iqbal, Allama Md, *The Reconstruction of Religious Thought in Islam*, Ashraf, Lahore, 1971, p. 95.

72 Vahiduddin, Syed, review article of *The Privilege of Man* in *Islamic Culture* 44:1 (January 1970), p. 67.

73 Ayoub, 1984, *op. cit.*, p. 89.

to bow.'[74] Leaving Paradise, he asserts, was not a punishment for Adam, but 'a matter of course', because the real purpose of creation was this vicegerency on earth. The Garden was merely a trial and a training. Sayyid Qutb (d. 1966) agrees: 'Thus God's mercy had decreed for this creature that he descend to the place of his vicegerency, having had the experience of this trial which he is to confront always if he is to be ready for the battle, and that it may be for him a lesson and a warning.'[75] Muhammad Asad (convert from Judaism and translator of the Qur'an, d. 1992) supports the interpretation of the human race as *khalifah al-ard* (vicegerent on earth) by citing 6:165, 27:62, and 35:39.[76]

Modern, as compared with classical Muslim exegesis of the Qur'an would then appear to give some support to Cragg's theological programme of promoting the dignity of human status by emphasizing its divine support. He continued to explore the theme of the '*khilafah* of man' in his later writing, especially when considering the issues of secularity and secularisation, often noting the similarity of *khalifah* with the Arabic word for 'created being' *(khaliqah)*. [e.g. *West*, pp. 29, 207]

4 Theodicy and Self-Wronging

Is there, in this modern Muslim shift towards a more human-centred, earth-bound understanding, some faint and inexplicit acknowledgement of the truth of Cragg's contention that 'what is due from man to God belongs with what is due from God to man'? [*Jesus*, p. 45] If the heavenly court, the attendant angels and the *jinn* fade in importance in the modern mind in favour of the earth as the theatre of 'the eternal battle', are not God and humanity drawn closer in what Sayyid Qutb calls 'the covenant of vicegerency', referring perhaps to the *amanah*/trust of 33:72?[77] ['We offered the Trust to the heavens, the earth, and the mountains, yet they refused to undertake it … mankind undertook it.' Cf. 7:172-174] Cragg's abiding conviction is that Islam has not taken the full measure of its own doctrines. He speaks of the classical Muslim theologians' 'reluctance to be fully theist' [*Jesus*, p. 46], and complained earlier (and no doubt more rashly) that:

74 Maududi, S Abul A'la, *The Meaning of the Qur'an*, vol. 1, Islamic Publications, Lahore, 1971, p. 58.
75 Ayoub 1984, *op. cit.*, p. 93.
76 Asad, Muhammad, *The Message of the Qur'an*, al-Andalus, Gibraltar, 1980, on 2.31.
77 Ayoub, 1984, p. 92.

> This Muslim tendency to silence or 'contain' all questionings in the totalitarian fact of God not only compromises the intellectual life and over-simplifies religious surrender: it also closely affects the relation of religion to life. God is not in redemptive relation with man nor is man in redemptive need of God. Just as Islam is intellectually a faith without a theodicy, so it is also a religion without a radical criticism of life.[78]

Such allegations are familiar from Kraemer: 'Islam ... must be called a superficial religion ... that has almost no questions and no answers ... Man has no real place in the relation of God and man ... Man is so evanescent in the hyperbolically theocentric atmosphere of Islam that problems of theodicy, of the cry for a God of *righteousness*, etc., are entirely absent.'[79] [emphasis original]

We must take up later the significance of Cragg's criticism of the political dimension of Islam, but it must be noted here that, given the political character of all theological disputes within Islam, the charge of a non-existent theodicy cannot really stick. What is unexpected for a Western observer is that these disputes were directly related to political issues. The Kharijite refusal, in early Muslim days, to obey a ruler regarded as sinful; the Shi'i criticism of Umayyad worldliness; the Mu'tazilite anxiety to uphold the justice of God; all these are evidence of a practical questioning about the righteousness of God, especially in relation to rulers. It is certainly different in form but no less intense in character than that of Christianity, even if it be finally judged as inadequate to the depth of the issue.

One way of proceeding at this stage is to examine the Qur'anic concept of *zulm* and the other derivatives of the root *Z-L-M*, a term roughly equivalent to 'wrongdoing'. The point is to take serious note of a key Islamic idea and its place in Muslim thought about God and humanity. It is also a term which has interested Cragg, and featured in his writing about Islam. [e.g. *Mind*, p. 99f.] In 1959 he translated, with extensive comment, an article of Kamil Husain entitled 'The Meaning of *zulm* in the Qur'an'.[80] In this Husain notes that words from the root *Z-L-M* are

78 'Islam in the 20th Century', unpublished D.Phil. thesis Oxford University, 1950, pt 1, p. 92.

79 Kraemer, Hendrik, *The Christian Message in a non-Christian World*, Edinburgh House Press, London, 1938, pp. 216, 217, 222.

80 'The Meaning of *zulm* in the Qur'an' (tr. from Md Kamil Husain) in *The Muslim*

recorded 289 times in the concordance of the Qur'an. Cragg agrees that 'Their usage is exceeded only by the most central of all words, like *Allah, Rabb*, and *Rasul*.' [*Mind*, p. 99] Setting aside the primary meaning as noted by Lane, of 'putting a thing in a place not its own' and so 'transgressing the proper limit', Husain concludes that the essential meaning of *zulm* in the Qur'an is injustice or injury, and 'in the majority of cases' self-wronging, or injury to one's own soul, *zulm li'l-nafs*.[81] Surah 65:1 is a characteristic use: 'Anyone who transgresses the limits of God, does verily wrong his own soul.'

From an extensive examination of this word-cluster Husain draws some interesting conclusions. First he sees even so fundamental a term as *shirk*, associating partners with God, as subsumed under *zulm*, which as we have seen is to be thought of as primarily self-injury. The significance of this becomes clear in a second point, that the Muslim 'is unable to conceive of man as being capable of injuring God.' Thirdly (though these points are made more incidentally by Husain than this presentation of them suggests), it is clear to Husain that 'the soul in its essential nature is pure', for if

> the soul was naturally and inherently sinful we would have no ground for regarding acts of evil-doing as a wrong against the self ... Surely an admirable ethical viewpoint this, which characterises every sin you commit and every good you fail to do, as a wrong against your own soul. Those who assess what they do by this criterion will find open before them, clear and sure, the road to the good.[82]

It is interesting to compare this analysis with the conclusions of a Qur'anic (though non-Muslim) scholar like Izutsu, who confirms the sense of *zulm* as injustice (though he finds its antonym in *qist* rather than in *'adl*), but sees a considerable overlap between the roots *Z-L-M* and *K-F-R*, with *kufr* as the key Qur'anic term. He acknowledges the sense of self-injury, but links it not with human incapacity to injure God but with God's innocence of the wrong human beings have brought upon themselves.[83] 'It is not God that hath wronged them, but they wrong

World 49: 3 (July 1959), pp. 196-212.

81 *Ibid.*, p. 200, 201.

82 *Ibid.*, pp. 201, 198, 204.

83 Izutsu, Toshihiko, *The Structure of the Ethical Terms in the Qur'an. A Study in Semantics*, Keio University, Tokyo, 1959, p. 212, 113.159.

themselves.' (Surah 3:117) He finds a close association between *Z-L-M* and *K-DH-B*, meaning 'to lie'. The *zalim* is a liar. For

> Who doth more wrong *('azlamu)* than those who invent a lie *(kadhiban)* against God? They will be turned back to the presence of their Lord, and the witnesses will say, 'These are the ones who lied against their Lord! Behold! the Curse of God is on those who do wrong!—Those who would hinder (men) from the path of God and would seek in it something crooked: these were they who denied the Hereafter! (Surah 11:18, 19; cf. 7:44f.)

In the light of Izutsu's analysis Husain's interpretation begins to seem rather idiosyncratic, but Cragg's interest in it can also be understood more clearly. For his concern is to take up the second two points which we noted from the Husain article, and to argue the inadequacy of Muslim thought as so expressed. On the point of the human incapacity to injure God Cragg responds that this is

> valid enough in the sense that sin and *Shirk*, disobedience and ingratitude, do not affect His being God or His Godness. But the concept is obviously incompatible with any serious faith, with *islam* as such, if it implies that our wrongness is a matter of indifference to Him. Our evils 'harm' Him in the sense, at least, that all law-making authority must be seriously cognisant of law-breaking … God's very demand of *islam* (willed conformity) from man requires that the lack of it (in *Zulm*) matters for Him and, in that sense, 'affects' Him adversely.[84]

On the question of the alleged purity of the human soul as indicated in the concept of self-wronging, Cragg asks 'May there not be a much deeper tragedy—the self-wronging that is conscious and yet persistent?' and he questions the assumption that 'an intellectual recognition of evil is equivalent to salvation from it.' 'Has the realisation we are wronging ourselves any more force or effectiveness, if we are bent on defiance and obstinately ready to take any consequences?' Is not 'the truth about Adamic man' the

84 'The Meaning of *zulm* in the Qur'an', p. 198, n. 3.

Christian concept of original sin 'which seems, though unrecognized, to be latent in Quranic *Zulm al-nafs*'?[85] It is not so much then that Islam is superficial in its understanding of the human situation, as Kraemer claimed (and Cragg appeared to echo in his 1950 thesis). It is rather, as Cragg sees it, that Muslims have not yet fully grasped the implications of the Qur'anic testimony to the human predicament. But this brings us back to the alleged Muslim 'reluctance to be fully theist.' [*Jesus*, p. 46] For the depth of this human predicament, as Cragg sees it, requires an adequate response from God if the purposes of his own creation are to be fulfilled and his laws obeyed, and if authentic worship is to be offered him.

Cragg has argued face to face with Muslims that there is a 'divine responsibility' which God has incurred by the very act of creation. Elsewhere he has talked of the 'divine liability'.[86] To his Muslim partners in the dialogue such divine-human reciprocity was unthinkable. Khurshid Ahmad's view was that 'if men refuse to worship God and to obey Him, God is not affected. It is not God who seeks completion in our worship, but rather we who seek completion through worshipping Him.' But for Cragg: 'You cannot create and be as if you hadn't. You cannot have law and be indifferent to what happens to it. You cannot educate and be indifferent to what is happening in education … God is involved in wrong that *jahiliyyah* does to him.' For Cragg, an 'unobligated deity' meant deism, 'a terribly desolating and finally contradictory concept'.[87]

That 1976 dialogue, Cragg felt later, 'concluded alas, in opacity', because the Muslim participants insisted on understanding the 'responsibility' of God in relation to our misdeeds in terms of the determining of our choice and therefore guilt. God, it seemed to them, was being blamed for wrong-doing which should be laid squarely at the door of human beings. They heard Cragg as advocating a human irresponsibility for wrong. Cragg, however, meant it in the sense of God 'undertaking responsibility for the situation thus ensuing, as a shepherd does the lostness of the sheep.'[88] In Cragg's understanding God's act of creation involves him in the obligation to retrieve the mistakes and fallenness of those created, in a word with 'redemption'. For Islam, it

85 *Ibid.*, pp. 204, n. 8, 209, 211.

86 Contributions passim, *International Review of Mission* LXVI (October 1976), pp. 365-460, and 'Legacies and Hopes in Muslim-Christian Theology' in *Islamochristiana* 3 (1977), p. 5.

87 *International Review of Mission*, *op. cit.*, p. 407.

88 'Legacies and Hopes', *op. cit.*, p. 9.

seems, this compromises the greatness of God, who cannot be under any obligation to humanity. In denying such 'unobligatedness' Cragg is drawn to formulate the most insistent of all his aphorisms concerning the relationship of Christianity and Islam, namely that the question about God's greatness is 'not whether but how'. *How* is God great? And what is the appropriate image of his greatness? Is it that of the King, the Judge, the Teacher or the Shepherd? How can both Christian and Muslim 'let God be God'?—to employ the quotation from Martin Luther which Cragg has almost made his own. [e.g. *Counsels*, p. 193]

On the question of 'obligated deity' it seems clear that Cragg's Muslim opponents, even if they did not take his point, were at least faithful to historic Muslim thought. Early in the *Ihya'* Ghazzali sets out a kind of extended creed, part of which runs:

> (God) recompenses His believing servants for obedience by the command of His generosity and His promise, not for their deserving and because He is obliged to do so, for not a single act is incumbent upon Him and any injustice is inconceivable on His part. No one has any right which imposes an obligation upon Allah.[89]

Later in the same passage Ghazzali denies the Mu'tazilite claim that 'it is incumbent upon God to do whatever is salutary for men.' Human beings, he says, are subject to questions, but there is nobody to question God.[90] In fact in later classical Muslim thought there appears to be a denial that the fact of creation has any special significance in indicating some truth about God, so opposing the very basis of Cragg's argument. The so-called *Fiqh Akbar* of al-Shafi'i declares in its Article 20 that 'Allah was free to create the world as well as not to create it. Allah has not created the world either with a view to what is salutary to humanity, or on any other ground; but He knew from eternity that He would create. Allah is free to make the whole world vanish and to make it return.'[91] Is Cragg then inclining to a modern version of the Mu'tazilite position, rationalising a claim upon God concerning what is 'salutary', i.e. concerning salvation,

89 Sweetman, J W, *Islam and Christian Theology*, 4 vols, Lutterworth, London, 1947-1967, II.2.24 (quoting I.2.2).

90 Ghazzali, *op. cit.*, p. 140.

91 Wensinck, A J, *The Muslim Creed. Its Genesis and Historical Development*, CUP, Cambridge, 1932, p. 266f.

which orthodox Islam cannot allow? In fact historic Mu'tazilite thought took a different turn, based on a concept of God's justice which envisaged him as being obliged to reward faithful servants:

> His actions towards all men are determined by what is most salutary for them from the religious point of view, and by what is best fitted to lead them into the ordered path; nor will He withhold from them anything which He knows they need for the performance of what is ordered and so help them towards the due rewards of obedience.[92]

So on this evidence Cragg's idea of divine responsibility is supported neither by the Mu'tazilites, because where salvation was concerned they conceived divine justice as a necessary response to human deserving, nor by the Ash'arite orthodox who rejected any such necessity of God and refused to consider anything incumbent upon him, declaring that 'He is free to impose suffering on innocent children and animals, without indemnifying them.'[93] Modern Muslim writers too maintain God's total freedom from any obligation. 'Abduh (d.1905) wrote: 'It is not that anything good for the universe is incumbent on Him to take account of because, if He does not do so, He will incur criticism … God is indeed exalted far above all that.' [*Unity*, p. 50]

Cragg's response is that this means that we human beings are 'forbidding things' to God.[94] It seems, however, from the way that Muslim writers frame their objections to an 'obligated deity' that they have in mind principally the supposition of an external necessity operating upon God. 'Abduh makes this quite clear when he says: 'To speak of duty resting upon God suggests obligation and constraint. Or in another phrase it may suggest duress and susceptibility to pressure.' [*Unity*, p. 61] However, it must be noted that 'Abduh also says that 'The intelligent mind … would emphatically never entertain the idea that any of His deeds were essentially necessary to His nature,' so that an inner constraint may be denied as well. [*Ibid.*, p. 57] In the introduction to his translation of 'Abduh's *Risalat al-Tauhid* Cragg acknowledges that in this ''Abduh shows himself in line

92 *Ibid.*, p. 82.
93 *Ibid.*, p. 267.
94 Cragg, Kenneth, art. 'Conversion and Convertibility, with special reference to Muslims' in J R W Stott and R Coote (eds), *Down to Earth: Studies in Christianity and Culture*, Hodder, London, 1981 p. 198.

with a fundamentally Islamic instinct,' [*ibid.*, p. 19] but complains that this lack of 'an imperative within Him' (God), makes it impossible to depend upon a consistency between the Divine knowledge and the Divine will. The Divine nature, Cragg thinks, is 'properly under the "ought" which is its own,' subject to a constraint which is not external but springs out of its inner character. He feels that the acceptance of this understanding of God 'opens the door to a far more secure and authentic practice of prayer and adoration,' as well as revolutionising the understanding of revelation. [*Ibid.*, p. 20] This claim must be taken up in the context of Cragg's understanding of prayer and the Spirit.

5 Christology

It remains at this point to outline the way in which Cragg's doctrine of God relates to his understanding of incarnation, atonement and salvation in Jesus. His complaint about the Muslim understanding of Jesus is that 'whereas, in Christian thought, theology and Christology are mutually necessary and mutually definitive, in Islam theology is largely defined by the exclusion of Christology.' [*Jesus*, p. 45] It is difficult to know precisely what the latter statement means, unless Cragg is asserting that Muslim theology was formulated in conscious opposition to Christianity. In spite of certain Muslim reactions to Christian thought this would be hard to substantiate in general. For the first part of the statement we note simply that there have of course been many who called themselves Christians who would have found it difficult to agree that theology and Christology are mutually definitive. The statement is perhaps best seen as an example of the Christocentric character of Cragg's thought. Not that he gives any impression of being unduly defensive about traditional Christian dogma concerning the person of Jesus. For Cragg

> there is a certain sense in which the issues of the Sonship of Jesus and the Trinitarian understanding of the divine Unity will take care of themselves, if we truly reckon with what it is we mean when we say: 'God is, God reigns, God loves'. For it is out of that conviction, believed to be known in history and experience, that the doctrinal formulations derive.[95]

95 'Legacies and Hopes', *op. cit.*, p. 3.

Is Cragg unduly Christocentric? It is true that his major theological statement about the Christian theology of religion, *The Christian and Other Religion* (1977), is sub-titled *The Measure of Christ*, and that this was in Cragg's view the true title of the book, the other being used only for 'publishing considerations'. But closer examination shows that the phrase refers to Christ as the 'measure' or 'criterion' of God, the Christian's 'point of departure'. [*Other*, p. xiii] It would be rash to propose that Cragg pays inadequate attention to the first person of the Trinity. As we have seen, for Cragg human beings are only truly themselves when they are rightly related to God. The significance of Jesus for him lies precisely at this point. 'The personality of Jesus is the key to the human relatedness of God because it is that relatedness in action.'[96]

This significance of Jesus is first and foremost as the 'Christ of God', the divine answer to the human predicament, expressing the faithfulness of the Creator in his responsibility towards the created order which he, and he alone initiated, and which he, and he alone can redeem. For the doctrine of creation requires a divine involvement with the human race which Cragg sees as in itself a kind of *kenosis*, a freely-willed self-limitation 'implicit in "letting man be" as the creature he is, with an obligation to be *muslim* to God—an obligation which, patently, he is free to refuse.'[97] And when he does refuse it God undertakes a response which culminates in Jesus. If in Jesus we see God it is because 'Jesus, in the flesh, accomplishes the eternal mind,' so that 'what happened in Jesus takes God to explain.' 'What Christology is saying is that the very idea of God involves the relationship to mankind which we can identify in Jesus as the Christ.' [*Jesus*, pp. 292, 291, 198] What is seen in Christ, and what makes him appropriately the 'criterion' of God in a sense very close to what Muslims claim for the Qur'an as the *furqan*, is the power and effectiveness of the love that suffers, that goes to all the lengths necessary to retrieve humanity from their fateful state, and offers to them the new life in fellowship with God originally intended in his creation. What God has done in Christ is therefore more than the sending down of a prophetic warning or the giving of detailed and reliable instructions as to how to live, which is the 'Gospel' of Islam. It is the restoration of relationship with God, which means life itself.

96 *Operation Reach* (pamphlet series), Near East Christian Council Study Program in Islam, Beirut, 1957-1962, 2.4.

97 Cragg, Kenneth, art. 'Being Christian and Being Muslim. A Personal Debate' in *Religion* 10 (Autumn 1980), p. 200f.

This basic conviction about the necessary 'relatedness' of God to humanity and of human beings to one another has profound implications for dialogue and mission, to which we shall come later. It is an 'economic' doctrine of God with which Cragg works rather than an 'essential' one, reflecting a soteriological rather than an ontological concern. All three Semitic faiths, he thinks, operate in the same way. Whether Exodus, Christ or Muhammad, 'the event arouses the recognition of faith and the faith recognises what the event really was.' [*Ibid.*, p. 190] Here he would claim to be in line with the development of Christian doctrine from experience to philosophic reflection, from event to dogma. All true understanding, he implies, takes that path, and cannot circumvent it without becoming trapped in the conserving, defensive habit of mind which Cragg brands as the 'custodial mind'. 'If (doctrinal formulations) are commended and contested as formulae prior to the mediation of the experiential meaning, we not only invite, or incite, contention, but we abandon the apostolic sequence of discovery and conviction.'[98] Again we shall need to examine carefully this alleged priority of experience over dogma, but it is clear that what he intends is a dynamic interpretation of religion which takes the educational sequence of the growth of faith seriously, and is thus enabled to retain a fundamental sympathy with all religious expression while pulling no punches in criticism of the adequacy of particular religious life and language.

Cragg's starting-point with God as above all Creator has profound consequences. It means of course that he can attempt to relate directly to Islam through the Qur'an with its vivid and consistent portrayal of the *rabb al-'alamin*, the 'Lord of the worlds', who constantly sustains us in being. He does not need to keep asking the question whether the God of Islam is the same God as the God of the Bible, since although the two definitions differ in important respects there is clearly enough overlap to be confident that the respective terms refer to the same being. The predicates may differ but their subject is the same, which means that we can (and must, if we are loyal) differ about the nature of God, and how he should properly be described, while at the same time we know that it is the one God we are talking about. If it were not we should have nothing to say to each other. 'We are together *under* Him and *in* Him, even when we are diverging *about* Him.' [*Alive*, p. 18, emphasis original] It also means that he is not constricted by the problems of the ontological relationship of

98 'Legacies and Hopes', *op. cit.*, p. 3.

Christ to God, but, as we have seen, is free to explain how the necessity of the Christ springs out of the nature of God as first and foremost Creator.

The weakness of his approach is a somewhat cavalier attitude towards Muslim sensibilities over the transcendence of God, and their refusal to entertain his notion of God's 'liability', and to engage in his version of the argument about theodicy. Though he acknowledges at several points that the problem of religious language affects all faiths, he does not always indicate that the force of his criticism, if granted, would apply to much Christian theology also. Consequently he does not acknowledge the problem of *which* Christianity is under scrutiny. Moreover, if his idea of divine-human reciprocity be found unconvincing, because of that same issue of transcendence—and we have noted a number of Christian authors who might have problems with it—the question must arise as to whether his theology is basically determined by a certain understanding of the nature of human relationships.

4
PRAYER, FAITH AND ORTHODOXY

1 A God to Worship

> All faiths are the interrogation of life. They are a protest against reality on behalf of reality. Gods are vital hypotheses, horizons towards which people move. As such they deserve reverence. Even though their answers may not be ultimate, their questions may be authentic. The more we think them lacking, the more important this sympathy becomes.[1]

Cragg is writing in this passage for a widely circulated journal read by people of many faiths and varied educational attainment. His language does not show the careful formulation of his more scholarly work, and he should not be held too closely to account for the 'reverence' suggested here for 'faiths' as such. Nevertheless the quotation is significant as indicating an abiding attitude in him. For Cragg does not share the antipathy towards 'religion' of many of his contemporaries, whether we think of agnostics and unbelievers or of some sophisticated theologians for whom Christianity spells the end of 'religion', because 'religion' can only be understood in terms of human attempts to manipulate God. As the quotation shows, Cragg understands religious faith as a long-term endeavour in prayer and ritual and all the activities of religion to discover and live out a right-relatedness to God. It is therefore something deserving of a fundamental sympathy, whatever its imperfections. It should be noted that he is equally appreciative of honest unbelief, believing that authentic protest against inadequate religion is all in the cause of better religion: 'All the articulate reasons for irreligion are essentially religious.'

---

1 Cragg, Kenneth, art. 'The Church and Other Faiths' (contd) in *Interfaith News* (10 February 1986), p. 5.

[*Other*, p. xiii] Again we hear the characteristic note of Cragg's desire to communicate with the other and be engaged in a dialogue with him. And for him dialogue must be more than a courteous exchange of views which leaves the participants unchanged. 'Worthy religious thought lives in the purgatory of external criticism,' he wrote in the introduction to his thesis.[2] Our sternest critics, in other words, are our truest friends—a theme we shall have to return to.

His basic sympathy for the enterprise of religion and the questioning implied in it means an impatience with any easy assumption that humanity has grown out of the need for religion. Of Bonhoeffer's 'religionless Christianity' he has written: 'no careful Christian perspective can ever make a virtue of secularity.' [*Other*, p. 14] It is an illusion to suppose that humanity's alleged autonomy, the 'coming of age' is anything essentially new. Our technological and other capacity is only on a new scale the gift that we have always held, and misused, from God. The human problem has perennially consisted in the exercising of a proper trusteeship, expressed Biblically by the 'dominion' given to Adam over nature, and Qur'anically, at least as modern interpreters understand it, by the 'caliphate' of humanity, our 'standing in the place' of God. For him the secular is simply the reliable, law-abiding 'arena' of our human activities.

> Our being thus volitional requires the secular as its arena. We are back with the reality of our 'caliphate' where 'what we do with what there is' is always at stake as to good or ill, praise or blame, grace or guilt. We humans can only be volitional because all else, from stones to stars, is 'law-abiding' that we might be 'law-acceding'. [*West*, p. 71]

At this point we need to ask how this basic sympathy of Cragg for the activities of religion is undergirded theologically, and whether his insights into religious meaning are sustained by a consistent set of theological principles. It is fine to perceive in another religious tradition the spiritual vitality one covets for one's own, but is such perception the product of genuine insight or of some merely subjective and emotional condition, inwardly engendered? Without a theological framework any modern approbation of Islam is no more soundly based than the

2 'Islam in the 20th Century', unpublished D.Phil. thesis Oxford University 1950, intro., p. 5.

polemical criticism of earlier centuries. We require an examination of Cragg's theological understanding of the nature of religious faith and its varied expressions. Not that faith as such is the fundamental category for Cragg that it is, for example, for Wilfred Cantwell Smith, as expounded in *The Faith of Other Men* (1962), *The Meaning and End of Religion* (1963) and other books. Or perhaps it is that Cragg sees the essential character of faith as the search for a God who is 'worshippable' in the hope that there is such a God to be found. (Cragg credits Daud Rahbar with the coining of the term in *Meet*, p. 201 n. 6.) As he wrote in 1950: 'Christianity holds that a renewal of worship would be both the sign and the means of our salvation. The civilized world can only be saved by worship.'[3] The search may involve false trails and unsatisfactory stopping-places, but it is the animating spirit of the search which matters. Even those who appear not to be involved in the search may contribute to it if they are urgently concerned to point out the wrong turnings. We have seen the positive value Cragg places on theological controversy, and of 'thought that perishes usefully', a quotation from Ruskin.

If the search for a God who is worth worshipping is central to Cragg's thinking, so that humanity and God may relate to one another, then it is the aspect of God which enables us to worship which is the heart of faith. The names of God are not primarily for formulating propositions but for calling upon him. 'The Names are far from being mere attributes to be listed in a theology: they are awesome realities of daily life.' [*Call*, p. 35] Theological issues may not even be felt, as in Muhammad's case, in a mind 'fully possessed with its single mission.' [*Ibid.*, p. 39] The Qur'an says (51:56—Yusuf Ali) 'I have only created jinns and men that they may serve me,' where the Arabic word *'abada* can be translated either 'serve' or (as in Pickthall) 'worship'. It is worship which is central to Cragg's thinking as the heart of faith. So it is best to begin an examination of Cragg's theology of religion with his doctrine of the Spirit as the animator within the human person and community of the response to God in faith.

We saw in the discussion of his doctrine of God that Cragg does not make any extended examination of the question of whether the God worshipped in Islam and the God worshipped in Christianity are identical. 'We worship the same Lord, in worships informed by significantly similar, as well as sharply discordant, theology.' [*Alive*, p. 18] Naturally he acknowledges profound differences in definition, and even in attitudes

3 *Ibid.*, pt 2, p. 99f.

towards the possibility of definition, but on Islamic grounds he resists the use of the term 'Allah' in English translations from Arabic, because 'to do this is to privatize that which Islam, properly understood, must universally affirm. It is precisely the reality of *Allah* in every human speech which the Qur'anic conviction of sovereignty declares.' [*Event*, p. 78] He does not wish to imply that 'there is something about the divine in Islam which only Arabic can say.' What he does want to imply, it seems, is that a true (and truly Christian) understanding of God will include the Islamic while saying significantly more than Islam says.

The question is: what is the source of this universal speech about God? And has Cragg answered *Christian* objections to the use of 'God' to translate *Allah* by referring primarily to *Islamic* principles? He recognises the problem of literary and other associations clinging to a word when he refers to the 'sentimental' associations of the use in English of *Allah*, which 'have more to do with melodrama than theology.' [*Call*, p. 30] But some Muslims have objections of their own. Pickthall wrote in his translation of the Qur'an that he had retained the word *Allah* instead of using the English *God* 'because there is no corresponding word in English.'[4] Nor has it always been so obvious to other Christians that the Islamic usage summarized in *Allah* can be 'included' in the wider term *God*. Would the Dutch-American missionary Zwemer have agreed whole-heartedly with Cragg?

> What is the result of our investigation of the Moslem idea of God? ... In as far as Moslems are monotheists and in as far as Allah has many of the attributes of Jehovah we cannot put Him with the false gods. But neither can there be any doubt that Mohammed's conception of God is inadequate, incomplete, barren and grievously distorted.[5]

We have seen that Cragg would share some at least of Zwemer's criticisms, though he expresses them very differently. But his answer to Zwemer's assertion that 'Islam is anti-Christian'[6] would be in terms of the Holy Spirit, and of hope. 'To let oneself despair that Islam is "deist"

4 Pickthall, M M, *The Meaning of the Glorious Koran. Text and Explanatory Translation*, Taj, Karachi, n.d., Surah 1.

5 Zwemer, S M, *The Moslem Doctrine of God. An Essay on the Character and Attributes of Allah according to the Koran and Orthodox Tradition*, American Tract Society, Boston, 1905, p. 107.

6 *Ibid.*, p. 120.

... would also be to despair of the Holy Spirit, who does not fail until he bring "crisis" through to "truth" (Isaiah 42:3).'[7] Here are several clues to Cragg's theological principles in this area. Here is also another example of that confidence of which Shehadi complained in another context that it expressed conviction that a problem could be solved without suggesting *how* that might be done. What does it mean to appeal to the Holy Spirit in this way? Is Cragg using the Spirit as a kind of theological *deus ex machina*, the solution to all problems? Cragg might take his authority here from the Qur'an, in the words attributed to Jacob: 'Do not despair of the Spirit of God. It is only those who give the lie to him who despair of the Spirit of God.' (12:87) However, Cragg's translation of this verse [*Alive*, p. 142] is supported only by Pickthall. Other translators significantly do not read *ruh* at all but *rauh* and translate 'Soothing Mercy' or 'Comfort' instead of 'Spirit'.[Yusuf Ali, Arberry, Dawood, Asad and Abdel Haleem] But for Cragg the key to the question of the variant Islamic and Christian doctrines of God is to be found in the Holy Spirit, and hence, one presumes, his choice of text here.

His particular emphasis is that the activity of the Holy Spirit is still in process. Cragg urges a dynamic and not simply a static approach to doctrine. It is all very well and necessary to compare the Muslim understanding of God with that emanating from the New Testament experience of Christ, but if the matter is left there a whole and vital dimension of the issue may be missed, namely that that very New Testament experience points to a process which should still be continuing, and which is inherently universal in its scope. To the question of what 'faith we may have in the activity of the Holy Spirit beyond the Scriptures and the Church,' Cragg answers plainly that

> The ways of the Spirit cannot be exclusive of the life and mystery of other faiths unless we are to surrender a Christ for the world. It is precisely the partiality of all human witness that necessitates the universal witness of the Spirit and necessitates, too, the genuine partnership between them ... (Otherwise) the Holy Spirit, far from 'proceeding', is, in brutal language, either redundant or unemployed. So then, the very finality of the Gospel of Christ argues the

7 Cragg, Kenneth, art. 'Temple Gairdner's Legacy' in *International Bulletin of Missionary Research* 5:4 (October 1981), p. 166.

> unceasing and unfailing Spirit of God everywhere at work.' [*Other,* pp. 104, 106]

To suppose otherwise and to despair of mutual understanding between Muslim and Christian on the matter of God, his nature and call, is an 'isolationism of the Spirit' [*Sandals*, p. 20], a refusal to acknowledge the continuing activity of the Spirit except within one's own narrow confessional experience.

Cragg speaks with complete freedom of the activity of the Spirit in other faiths, and in reference to Ghazzali declares that 'there are other masters of the Spirit in the two faiths, who belong in part together, in inward significance if not in outward community.' [*Sandals*, p. 79] In the same vein he refers to the 'dual citizenship of the spirit' achieved by Constance Padwick, the Christian missionary anthologist of Muslim prayer. [*Troubled*, p. 54] Elsewhere, thinking perhaps of Exodus 31:3, he speaks of 'the craftsmen of the Spirit in every people', where the context is clearly broader than a multi-cultural Christianity. [*World*, p. 200] What is implied in Cragg's use of the term 'spirit' here, and has he, as it appears, gone well beyond the rather tentative usage about the Spirit which is characteristic of his theological heritage? For in the context of other faiths the characteristic references to the Spirit of those who share his background are generally limited to the work of the Spirit in bringing about a personal awareness of the significance of Christ, often in terms of the words of Jesus in John 16:14—'He (The Spirit) will glorify me, for everything that he makes known to you he will draw from what is mine.' Anglican Evangelicals would generally prefer to say with Newbigin that 'The work of the Spirit is the confession of Christ'.[8] There is a particular reluctance to credit the structures of a faith with positive spiritual value. Norman Anderson, writing of 'more than one Muslim whose study of the Qur'an made him seek after Christ' feels that 'we must ascribe this to the Spirit of God meeting him in his need, *rather than attribute it to the Qur'an as such*.'[9] [emphasis added] Cragg, one feels, would ask 'But why not attribute it to the Qur'an?', regarding this as an 'isolating' and unwarranted caution about the proceeding of the Spirit even through the Qur'an. His whole thinking about the 'inward significance' which inheres throughout a faith

8 Newbigin, Lesslie, *The Open Secret. Sketches for a Missionary Theology*, SPCK, London, 1978, p. 211.

9 Anderson, Norman, *Christianity and World Religions*, IVP, Leicester, 1984, p. 173.

indicates that he would regard such caution as misplaced. Reflecting on the emergence of Sufism within Islam Cragg has written:

> The historian or observer from without may finally believe himself pondering the ways of the Holy Spirit in the fertility of Islam within itself, its capacity to produce from within its own resources the antidote by which its own characteristic ethos could be queried and even transformed.[10]

Almost all Cragg's books strike some such note, but his *Alive to God. Muslim and Christian Prayer* (1970, revised in 1999 as *Common Prayer. A Muslim-Christian Spiritual Anthology*) is especially important in this respect. To bring together Islamic and Christian texts, both scriptural and other, with the intention that they be prayed in common by members of both faiths, is to affirm one's faith in the Spirit of the One God in very concrete terms. The book frequently illustrates his conviction that God does indeed speak through the institutions of Islam and in the Qur'an in particular. A striking example is his quotation from Surah 90, beginning 'Would that you knew what the steep is! It is the freeing of the slave, Or giving food in the hungry day To an orphan near of kin … ' The next entry in the anthology is one of Cragg's own compositions, and it has clearly been written in response to the previous passage, for it begins: 'In part we know it, Lord, The hard road of compassion, The strenuous demands of mercy, The steep ascent of heaven.' [*Alive*, p. 121] There are similar responses in the anthology to the 'Doubters' of Surah 41:54 and the 'locks upon your hearts' of 47:27. [*Ibid.*, pp. 131,137] (Cragg confirms that unattributed passages are his own composition on p. 52.) Here then Cragg answers the Lord whom he has heard speaking to him out of the Qur'an, and the Qur'an becomes for him a book charged with God's meaning. He speaks without qualification of the 'deep relevance of the Qur'an to contemporary man', [*Event*, p. 16] and suggests more tentatively that it 'has interrogatives that reach beyond the boundaries of institutional Islam and these are lively enough to create a community at least of study, if not of spirit.' [*Mind*, p. 16] In his book *Mosque Sermons. A Listener for the Preacher* (2008) he goes further in presenting imaginary sermons a Christian might preach from the *minbar* of a mosque, if so

10 Cragg, Kenneth, art. 'Sainthood and Spirituality in Islam' in *Studia Missionalia* 35 (1986), 185f.

invited. For, he says 'The New Testament is deeply latent in Qur'an *tafsir* (interpretation).' [*Mosque,* p. xiv]

Anderson justifies his reluctance to attribute any revelation of Christ to the Qur'an itself by quoting with approval the saying of Wilfred Cantwell Smith that 'If there is any truth in the Buddhist tradition, then its truth is not "in Buddhism", it is in the nature of things.'[11] Cragg would accept Cantwell Smith's insistence on using the word 'religion' in the singular and not the plural, as the frequently misquoted title of his *The Christian and Other Religion* confirms. He would surely agree that it is in 'the nature of things' that God can be discovered, since he is responsible for all of them. He quotes Richard Crashaw on religion in the singular with enthusiasm: 'No law controls Our traffic free for heaven.' [*Mind*, p. 16] In any case he reckons that

> It is a dubious and perhaps, in the end, a barren proceeding to enquire how far developments in a religion are from within its own resources and genius or how far they come about by external influence. What is truly original to a faith and what transpires from alien sources do not admit of being identified decisively.[12]

Nevertheless he finds Cantwell Smith's further dictum that 'there are Hindus but no Hinduism' too sharp, 'since one has presumably to identify Hindus by their Hinduism'. He might have said that Muslims are self-described participators in Islam. 'The "-ism" has its claim on our concern.' [*Other*, p. xiif.] The institutional cannot be so lightly dismissed, and Cantwell Smith himself is compelled to reinstate it with his use of the term 'cumulative traditions' to replace the disapproved plural term 'religions'. There is in consequence a 'mission to Islam', as we shall see later, and not merely to Muslims,[13] and such a thing is possible because the Spirit works with the 'inward significance' of a faith and not merely with the individual lives of its practitioners. It is clear that for many Protestants, however, no human institution or cultural form can be credited with such positive value.[14] The inward significance or deeper intention of a faith is opaque to them, perhaps because they pay less attention to the doctrine

11 Anderson, *op. cit.*, p. 173.
12 'Sainthood and Spirituality in Islam', p. 179.
13 'Temple Gairdner's Legacy', p. 165.
14 Cf. Niebuhr, H Richard, *Christ and Culture*, Faber, London, 1952, ch. 2, 'Christ Against Culture'.

of creation, which would affirm all reaching out to God as a response to him, than to the theology of redemption which invariably emphasizes God's one great provision for salvation.

2 The Spirit in Islam

It will be best to return to the wider dimension Cragg gives to the work of the Spirit in the context of his understanding of credal orthodoxy, and to ask meanwhile whether his usage can in any way be paralleled among Muslims. Is it possible, for example, that Cragg has been influenced by Muslim thought at this point? Alternatively, is he using language about Islam which Muslims themselves would find it impossible to acknowledge as Islamically appropriate? We need to know whether the common operation of the Spirit which Cragg assumes is also predicated by Muslims. Such questions are by no means easy to answer, and the discussion which follows is inevitably somewhat technical. Readers unfamiliar with Arabic should note that the convenient distinction in English and other Latin-alphabet languages between 'spirit' and 'Spirit' cannot be made in Arabic, which does not use capital letters. Consequently the lower-case 'spirit' will be used in the following passage, except where a writer is quoted who uses the upper case.

Muslim usage of the term *ruh* (spirit) is complex and varied, and as with Biblical usage ends to shift unpredictably from being part of a discourse about anthropology, the nature of human beings, to being part of talk about God. For example, the Hanbali theologian Ibn Qayyim al-Jawziya (d. 1350, a disciple of Ibn Taimiyya), in extensive discussions of the circumstances of the soul after death seems to employ the term *ruh* interchangeably with *nafs* (meaning 'soul' in the sense of 'person', 'living creature'). Were the two terms equivalent for him? If so they are not equivalent for one modern Muslim scholar who writes that

> the two terms *nafs* and *ruh* are quite different and one cannot be substituted for the other. The word 'yatawaffa' (in S 39:42) which means 'causes to die' is ascribed to *nafs*, not to *ruh*. Ruh, being a glimpse of God's spirit, never dies; it is immortal.[15]

15 Ahmad Subhi in J I Smith and Y Y Haddad, *The Islamic Understanding of Death and Resurrection* Albany, SUNY Press, New York, 1981, p. 202, n. 42.

The Qur'an never uses the plural form *arwah* (spirits), but rather *mala'ika* (angels), or (in a reflexive sense) *anfus*, the plural of *nafs*, and so *ruh* in the Qur'an cannot be understood as meaning the human soul.[16] But what then does it mean?

In a detailed analysis of the word *ruh* as it appears in the Qur'an O'Shaughnessy took particular note of the chronological development in its use. He found that its earliest sense denoted a 'created personal being, either a superior angel or a member of a species above the angels'.[17] Passages of the Qur'an reckoned to have been revealed later seem to indicate a return to the basic meaning of the stem *R-W-H* in the sense of an impersonal breath from Allah, who supplies the breath of life to all living beings.[18] On this reckoning the spirit in Islam is a part of Creation, not another way of speaking about God himself. (Cf. Genesis 2:7, John 20:22)

However, there is also a puzzling set of Qur'anic verses linking *ruh* with the term *amr,* meaning 'command', or 'affair', as in 17:85: 'They ask thee concerning the Spirit (of inspiration). Say: The Spirit (cometh) by command of my Lord: of knowledge it is only a little that is communicated to you (O men!)' The bracketed words in this translation by Yusuf Ali show more clearly than usual his attempt to interpret the Arabic text. O'Shaughnessy renders the same passage: 'They ask thee about the spirit; say: The spirit is from the *amr* of my Lord'.[19] Pickthall's version is: 'the Spirit is by command of my Lord', and Gairdner's: 'The Spirit pertains to my Lord's Word-of-Command'.[20] There are other passages linking the spirit and *amr* in 16:2, 40:15, 42:52. The latest of the Qur'anic verses use the term the 'spirit of holiness' *(bi-ruhi 'l-qudusi)* in association especially with Jesus. (In 2:87, 253; 5:113 and 16:102)

Commentators later identified the spirit who appeared to Mary 'in the form of a human being, shapely' as Gabriel (19:17), and he became associated also with the sending-down of revelation to Muhammad on the basis of 2:97 ('Whoever is an enemy to Gabriel—for he brings down the revelation to thy heart … '—cf. 26:193). S H Nasr refers to 'the archangel Gabriel, whose function in Islam is in many ways like that

---

16 *Ibid.*, pp. 17, 18, 202, n. 43.

17 O'Shaughnessy, Thomas, *The development of the Meaning of Spirit in the Koran*, Pontifical Institute of Oriental Studies, Rome, 1953, p. 23, citing 78:38, 97:4 and 70:4.

18 *Ibid.*, p. 25, citing 15:29, 38:72, 21:91, 32:9, 66:12.

19 *Ibid.*, p. 33.

20 Gairdner, W H T, tr. al-Ghazzali's *Mishkat al-Anwar*, Royal Asiatic Society, London, 1924, s. 22.

of the Holy Ghost in Christianity.'[21] Gairdner rejects this comparison, complaining of the 'arid tameness' of the commentators with their 'stereotyped identification' of the mysterious figure of 81:19-23 with the Angel Gabriel.[22] Nevertheless it is clear that most Muslims understand the spirit in the Qur'an to have a decidedly prophetic function, associated with the expression of God's revelation, although it is difficult to characterise it further.

In the post-Qur'anic period the use of *ruh* developed more variation still, but generally Muslim thought regarded the spirit of God as contingent upon God, and not as deity itself, or in Christian terminology 'consubstantial' with God. Though the distinction cannot be made in Arabic, the spirit in Muslim understanding would be 'it', rather than 'he'. There was, however, a measure of uncertainty as to how to speak of the spirit. The jurist Ibn Hanbal (d. 855) is recorded as saying that 'Whoever says that *al-Ruh* is created *(makhluq)* is a heretic: whoever says that it is eternal *(qadim)* is an infidel.'[23] He was also known to declare the doctrines that the Qur'an was created and that it was uncreated as both equally heretical, presumably by way of saying that such speculation was unwarranted and unprofitable.[24] This could also suggest that he thought of *ruh* as an attribute of God. But Ash'arite orthodoxy does not number it among the seven 'essential' attributes *(sifat)* of knowledge, power, will, life, speech, hearing and seeing, no doubt because its Qur'anic use was very different. Nor is it commonly spoken of as an 'active' attribute of God.

It is exceptionally difficult to find consistency in this area. It is the Qur'anic obscurity—Macdonald calls it a 'suggestive obscurity'[25]—about the doctrine of the spirit that brings about these very varied estimates among Muslim thinkers of its real character. The text 17:85 in particular 'exercised by far the greatest influence' in preventing speculation about it. In Pickthall's translation this *locus classicus* runs:

---

21 Nasr, Seyyid Hossein, *Ideals and Realities of Islam*, 2nd edn, Allen & Unwin, London, 1975, p. 42.

22 Gairdner, *op. cit.*, p. 20.

23 *Ibid.*, p. 40.

24 Fakhry, Majid, *A History of Islamic Philosophy*, 2nd edn, Longman, London, 1983, p. 63.

25 Macdonald, Duncan Black, art. 'The Development of the Idea of Spirit in Islam' in *The Muslim World* 22 (Jan. 1932), p. 30.

> They will ask thee concerning the Spirit. Say: The Spirit is by command of my Lord, and of knowledge ye have been vouchsafed but little.

Ibn Khaldun (d. 1402) used the verse to justify his 'distrust of metaphysical speculation'.[26] Iqbal thought it referred to the soul.[27] At times the Qur'an appears to some readers to place the spirit in a most exalted position, as in the verse which speaks of a special Day in which 'The angels and the Spirit ascend unto Him.' (70:4, cf. 78:38, 97:4) Ghazzali in particular speculated about the spirit on the basis of such verses to the point where Gairdner concluded that in the *Mishkat* the spirit 'figures, virtually, as an Arian Logos', and raises doubts about the author's monotheism.[28] In the Sufi tradition al-Hallaj (d. 922) and others had long since identified God's *amr* or word-of-command with his *ruh*. Ghazzali makes the further identification of *ruh* with *al-muta'*, the One who is to be obeyed. On the basis of 81:19-21 ('Verily this is the word of a most honourable Messenger, endued with Power, with rank before the Lord of the Throne, with authority *(muta'in)* there and faithful to his trust'), Ghazzali, abandoning the usual identification of this Messenger with Gabriel, writes of a Being who is the highest of all possible beings next to Allah, related to Allah as 'the live coal to the Elemental Fire'.[29] One can see how such passages might well bring Ghazzali's monotheism into question.

One whose monotheism is more often queried is Ibn 'Arabi (1165-1240), for whom 'The Spirit … clearly denotes the living reality of God, His living consciousness.' Ibn 'Arabi writes that

> … the Reality is manifest in every created being and in every concept, while He is hidden from all understanding, except for one who holds that the Cosmos is His form and His identity. This is the Name, the Manifest, while He is also unmanifested Spirit, the Unmanifest. In this sense He

26 Ibn Khaldun, *The Muqaddimah. An Introduction to History*, 3 vols, RKP, London, 1958, I:79, cf. III:36.
27 Iqbal, Allama Md, *The Reconstruction of Religious Thought in Islam*, Ashraf, Lahore, 1971, p. 102f.
28 Gairdner, *op. cit.*, p. 23.
29 *Ibid.*, pp. 21, 96.

> is, in relation to the manifested forms of the Cosmos, the Spirit that determines those forms.[30]

On the basis of that passage alone it would seem that for Ibn 'Arabi the 'Spirit' was God, the utterly Transcendent One. 'Attar seems to speak in similar vein of God as the *ruh kulli*, the 'Universal Spirit.'[31] Yet here too consistency eludes us, for it is clear that even in Ibn 'Arabi the spirit is not precisely the Eternal Reality in itself, nor the world of which it is the source but a *tertium quid*, contingent yet joined to the Eternal, and (like the Perfect Human) an intermediate creation, a *barzakh* or isthmus between necessary and contingent existence. In another passage Ibn 'Arabi says that the

> greatest union is that between man and woman, corresponding as it does to the turning of God toward the one He has created in His own image, to make him His vicegerent, so that He might behold Himself in him. Accordingly He shaped him, balanced him, and breathed His spirit into him, which is His Breath, so that his outer aspect is creaturely, while his inner aspect is divine.[32]

The spirit of God conveys to us our divine calling but it does not follow for most Muslim authors that the spirit is itself divine. Since only God is non-corporeal the spirit must be a created being, however imprecisely defined. The Muslim, therefore, cannot say with St John's Gospel that 'God is spirit, and those who worship him must worship in spirit and in truth.' (4:24) God is not spirit. This at least is plain Sunni orthodoxy, as taught, for example by the Hanbali Ibn Qayyim al-Jawziya in his *Kitab al-Ruh*.[33] Sufis may have thought differently, but even the renowned Persian Sufi Hujwiri (d. 1077) reckoned that all Sufi doctrinal error could be traced to faulty thinking about the *ruh*.

> All the errors of these sectaries (the Hululis) are in regard to the spirit *(ruh)* … Belief in the eternity of the spirit is one of the grave errors which prevail among the vulgar.[34]

---

30 Ibn al-Arabi, *The Bezels of Wisdom*, SPCK, London, 1980, pp. 172, 73.
31 Macdonald, *op. cit.*, p. 41.
32 Ibn Arabi, *op. cit.*, p. 275.
33 Smith and Haddad, *op. cit.*, p. 202, n. 43.
34 Al-Hujwiri, Ali, *The Kashf al-Mahjub. The Oldest Persian Treatise on Sufism*, Darul Ishaat,

('Hululi' is from *hulul* or 'incarnation'.) In his understanding, as in that of Ibn Qayyim (d. 1350), the *ruh* was corporeal but subtle *(jism latif)*, originated *(muhdath)* and not eternal *(qadim)*. Al-Baghdadi (d. about 1037) says plainly that 'The life of Allah is without *ruh* and nourishment and all the *arwah* are created, in opposition to the Christian doctrine of the eternity of the Father, Son and Spirit.'[35] The reference to Christian doctrine marks Muslim recognition of the sharpness of the difference. Hujwiri comments that it is the heretics

> who assert that the spirit is eternal *(qadim)*, and worship it, and regard it as the sole agent and governor of things, and call it the uncreated spirit of God, and aver that it passes from one body to another. No popular error has obtained such wide acceptance as this doctrine, which is held by the Christians, although they express it in terms that appear to conflict with it.[36]

Ibn Mas'ud, a Companion of the Prophet, records that the text 17:85, saying that only a little knowledge of the spirit has been given mankind, was revealed on the occasion of some Jews asking Muhammad about it. Ibn 'Abbas, Muhammad's cousin, reported that it was the Quraish who asked the Jews for a question to tax Muhammad with, and were told to ask about the spirit.[37] In a discussion of Islamic art S H Nasr boldly makes a virtue of this particular Muslim agnosticism by saying:

> In contrast to Christianity, where the manifestation of the Spirit is identified always with an affirmation and a positive form, Islamic art makes use of the 'negative' and the 'void' itself in a spiritual and positive sense in the same way that metaphysically the first part of the *shahada* begins with a negation to affirm the vacuity of things vis-à-vis Allah.[38]

Karachi, 1990, pp. 261, 266.

35 Calverley, Edwin, art. 'nafs' in *Encyclopaedia of Islam*, 1st edn, Brill, Leiden, 1913-1934.

36 Al-Hujwiri, *op. cit.*, p. 262f.

37 Von Denffer, A, *'Ulum al-Qur'an. An Introduction to the Sciences of the Qur'an*, Islamic Foundation, Leicester, 1985, p. 101f.; cf. also Hujwiri, *op. cit.*, p. 261.

38 Nasr, Sayyed Hossein, *Islam and the Plight of Modern Man*, Longman, London, 1975, p. 143.

The consequences of all this are momentous between Christianity and Islam. It is not only that Muslim thinkers have been aware of the very different place of the spirit in Christian thought. By its uncertainty over the place of the spirit Islam is prevented from expressing the immanence of God in terms of *ruh*, with its association with the universal breath of life, and confines its rôle to the inspiration granted to the prophets, where the spirit generally becomes hypostasised in the works of the commentators as Gabriel. Alternatively the spirit tends to become a kind of Gnostic demiurge (literally 'craftsman') or inferior creator deity, whose function, one might say, is to protect the utter transcendence of God, who must be beyond such concern with material affairs. We saw with the concept of *khalifah* an early tendency to confine its significance to the prophets or to Islamic rulers, rather than apply it to the human race in general. Similarly there seemed a common reluctance to credit the human race as a whole with being made in the image of God, and a preference to employ that tradition in the development of the idea of Muhammad as *al-insan al-kamil*, the Perfect Human Being, called by some 'Muhammad ... God's kindness *(latif)*. The mystery of the Adamic Creation, Light of Lights, Mystery of Mysteries, Spirit of Spirits.'[39]

So too with the spirit, we observe no sense of a common possession of it among Muslim believers, such as John and Paul identify among Christian believers. In this absence of an indwelling divine helper, prompting love and wisdom in the community, Islam has had two recourses, once the days of prophetic inspiration were past. One is the provisions of the *Shari'ah* and the accumulated wisdom of the way to live, modelled on the example of the Prophet. The other consists of the narrower channels of mystical union. The mainstream of Islamic piety, particularly since Ghazzali, has always tried to hold the two together. In the mystical path with its more precarious hold on orthodoxy the choice has seemed to lie between the mysterious 'Arian Logos' figure of Ghazzali, and the abyss of pantheism. Moreover, the mystical tradition depends upon an esoteric discipline and gnosis unavailable to the ordinary Muslim, and access to the truly spiritual world tends to recede up the gradations of mystical prowess. The spirit was often equated in the Sufi schools with *'aql*, or Intellect, or First Principle, and related to Qur'anic vocabulary through the Pen *(qalam)*. Macdonald

39 Padwick, Constance, *Muslim Devotions. A Study of Prayer-Manuals in Common Use*, SPCK, London, 1961, p. 256.

quotes the tradition: 'The first thing God created was *al-'aql*.'[40] This was the language of ontology, but it carried the corollary that the mark of the spiritual person is *'aql* or 'intellect'. Now although *'aql* may be closer to the Greek *nous* with its implication of religious sensitivity than to the English word 'intellect', its use inevitably introduces a note of elitism. Massignon attributes this to Qarmatian (early Isma'ili and theosophist) influence, and says 'une psychologie ultra-intellectualiste dépersonalise l'âme, reduit *rouh* à *'aql* chez Tirmidhi et Tawhidi.'[41] This elitism is traceable also in Ibn 'Arabi. Among moderns S H Nasr refers to 'the sword of the Intellect and the Spirit'.[42] Plainly intellect, however defined, is not equally distributed, whereas love, a primary mark of the Christian concept of the Holy Spirit, is in principle available to all.

In view of all this is it possible that Cragg's language about the Spirit's (Cragg's upper case) activity within Islam is congruent with Muslim thought, or are we back again with the implication that his understanding of Islam is not one that Muslims themselves could own? Although the orthodox denial of God as spirit seems very discouraging, there is that 'suggestive obscurity' about the spirit in Islam which is exploited by the Sufis, and which might lend itself to Cragg's notion of the Spirit 'proceeding', if that be thought of in terms of a progressive laying bare of the inner meaning, the 'intention' of Islam. This relates closely to the question of his understanding of the nature of religious language, to which we shall come in the next section. But it does seem as though Muslims uninfluenced by Sufi thought would be puzzled by Cragg's theology of the Spirit. On the one hand they associate the spirit with the revelatory activity of God, particularly by means of Gabriel, of which none but a prophet can claim any direct knowledge. Muhammad, as we have seen, is no ordinary man in Muslim understanding. On the other hand the world of the *arwah*/spirits (though the Qur'an does not use this plural form), the unseen *(ghaib)* world, is a matter of intense interest to many Muslims.

Yet Cragg is not much concerned, as we noted before, with angels, nor with *jinn*, or *shaytan* whether one or many. The significance of dreams (cf. 39:42), the prevalence of the evil eye, the world of the spirits in their

40 Macdonald, Duncan Black, *The Religious Attitude and Life in Islam*, University of Chicago Press, Chicago, 1909, p. 230.

41 Massignon, Louis, *Le Lexique Technique de la Mystique Musulmane*, Guenther, Paris, 1922, p. 60.

42 Nasr, *op. cit.*, p. 132.

unmistakably plural form appears not to interest him, as they interested predecessors like Macdonald and Zwemer. Cragg, as we have seen, is primarily interested in Islamic modernism, or rather in Muslim attempts to come to terms with that which has faced Western Christians since the Enlightenment. That movement of thought notoriously dismisses all such talk of spirits, whether evil or good, as so much superstition. The consequence in the Western mind has been a general emptying of the Unseen World of all but God himself, and even his position has been eroded in many minds. Cragg, it seems, shares the assumptions of this thought-world, but refuses the agnosticism in which it typically results. For him the Spirit of God pervades the world, so that he can respond to the 'signs' in it of the divine glory, and rejoice in the abundant recognition in the Qur'an of 'the sacramental earth'. [*Mind* ch. 9]

3 The Theology of Religion

It is time to return to Cragg's understanding of the theology of religion, and to deal with this under two main headings: his understanding of the character of theological affirmations, and his conception of the relationship between Christianity and other faiths. There are scattered through his writings innumerable references to the proper task of theological affirmation, almost all of them emphasizing the insecure, risky and adventurous character of theological statement. Many of these are aphoristic asides in the context of urging the establishment of relationships and making efforts at communication:

> There is a real sense in which we find truer loyalty by taking larger risks. Unrisking minds mean cautious trusts and so, in turn, diminished meanings. The claims of communication ought always to be paramount, since ensuring the truth is properly a function of having it received, and this is the guiding loyalty in having ourselves 'received it.' [*World*, p. 74]

Characteristically the language is highly compressed, and internally structured with great care ('having it received', 'having ourselves received it'), and this does not serve to promote ease in the communication which Cragg continually commends. But if his style is occasionally tortuous it is not so because of a restricted technical vocabulary and thought-forms. For often this urging that people should communicate what they believe to others outside the immediate community of faith is coupled with admonitions not to worry unduly about precise orthodox statement of their faith. 'It is more urgent to be alive to God than orthodox about Him.' [*Alive*, p. 8] Searching for an appropriate exemplar Cragg lights on Dag Hammarskjöld, whose *Markings* achieved some distinction as a spiritual journal to the surprise of those who had not known him articulate as a Christian:

> It is better that such implicit discipleship should ripen into explicit faith in God through Christ than that articulate conviction should wither into barren orthodoxy or conforming unconcern. [*Other*, p. 117]

Cragg searches for words denoting movement and process rather than words with associations of stability and fixity.

> While 'the cistern contains', as William Blake observed, 'the fountain overflows', and 'to overflow' is very much the sense of the verb in John 15:26. Theology has so often, to its loss, preferred the cistern. [*Ibid.*, p. 105]

In one of his latest books Cragg even regrets that Christians did not adopt the Islamic formula *bi-la kaif* (without asking how), comparing Muslim arguments about the attributes of Allah with Christian debates about the nature of Christ. 'In both cases, the issues had to be contained, rather than explained, in the readiness to trust a feasible compatibility between the divine and the human.' [*Lord*, p. 157]

The reference to the Johannine passage about the Spirit in 15.26 is typical, for it is the Spirit in Cragg's theology who is the active agent of truth.

> The Holy Spirit is never a sleeping partner of sleeping partners, but always an active spur, enthusing, employing, never excluding, the mind and will of men, not purveying ready-made answers but enabling responsible decision. [*Ibid.*, p. 80]

This work of the Spirit is contrasted with what people so often settle for, the defensive posture of the 'custodian-mind'. [*World*, p. 74] For

> there are no automatic guarantees in the Holy Spirit, no established creeds, codes, churches, symbols, which avail and achieve just by dint of being there, of being right in form, of holding fast and keeping going. [*Other*, p. 108]

In contrast religious vocabulary has to be flexible enough to do the job demanded of it: 'We only rightly possess our terminology in the capacity to do without it.'[43] The style of writing is again characteristic, and the paradox neatly turned, but it prompts the question of how one may adequately 'do without' the normal means of doctrinal expression. How will one recognise this 'right possession' of our terminology? For Cragg the answer seems to lie in the search in Christianity as well as in Islam for the inner intention, the proper meaning of the doctrine to be commended:

> What then do we mean when we say that God is 'the Father of our Lord Jesus Christ', and that 'Jesus is the Son of God'? What will be our adequately Christian and intelligibly Muslim paraphrase?[44]

And how, it might be asked, will we know when we have it right? And who is to be the judge of that?

It is hardly surprising that Cragg's method involves looking for the operational ('economic' or dispensational) categories rather than the ontological, absolute ones. Cragg sees Gairdner as pointing the way here, by his willingness to replace conventional but misunderstood Christian vocabulary by terms expressing

> divine action on behalf of the sinful world ... It is in line with our present urgency to break free of 'substance' metaphors that set Christology/theology in the realm of abstract

---

43 Cragg, Kenneth, 'Islam and Incarnation' in John Hick ed., *Truth and Dialogue. The Relationship between World Religions*, Sheldon, London, 1974, p. 136f.
44 *Ibid.*, p. 137.

> metaphysics, and bring it firmly into the concrete 'operation' of divine energy to save, fulfilled within the human.[45]

It is with this in mind that Cragg develops his argument about the divine obligation towards his creation, and moves, especially in *Jesus and the Muslim* into a sophisticated form of apologetics. But his dislike of ontological discussion and arguments about status—the status of Jesus as Son of God, the status of the Qur'an as the Word of God—has a special significance when it comes to considering the status of other faiths in Christian understanding. For at this point it seems very much as though he is refusing to answer the question. Here is a critical issue about evasiveness, and whether Cragg is right in regarding much Christian theological formulation on the subject as at best premature. That others do not regard it as premature may be seen from a spate of books on the subject, with British authors prominent among them. [e.g. Race 1983, Anderson 1984, Neill 1984, Cracknell 1986, D'Costa 1986, Ward 1987, Barnes 1989, Newbigin 1989, Smart and Konstantine 1991] An anthology of such writings, published in 1980, significantly excludes any contribution from Cragg.[46]

Cragg has in fact three books which deal explicitly and at length, rather than implicitly and in passing, with the Christian theology of religion. The earlier is *The Christian and Other Religion* (1977), subtitled *The Measure of Christ.* The unexpected singular 'Religion' in the title points to the major thrust of the book, and to his unremitting insistence throughout his writing that he intends to speak not about the Christian religion and other religions, but about the Christian *person* and religion wherever it may be found. So the book takes as its theme the necessity for relationship with other faithful people rather than the dogmatic intention of setting out a conceptual model of relationship between Christian faith and other faiths. In the chapter where he deals with this latter topic by reviewing the work of Christian thinkers from Kraemer to Hick he seems content to question each of the views expressed without in any obvious way setting out his own. Some reviewers found this unsatisfactory, calling chapter five 'somewhat skimpy'.[47] But Cragg in 1977 was clear that 'the

45 'Temple Gairdner's Legacy', *op. cit.*, p. 166.

46 Hick, John and Hebblethwaite, B L eds, *Christianity and Other Religions. Selected Readings*, Collins, Glasgow, 1980.

47 Whaling, Frank, review of *The Christian and Other Religion* in *The Scottish Journal of Theology* 31:5 (1978), p. 499.

task has still a long way to go … if concluded it can ever properly be … we must live with some bewilderment and maybe some aberrations.' [*Other*, p. 81] Theologians do not normally advertise their uncertainties and inconsistencies, but Cragg is unrepentant, for

> what finally matters is the relationships achieved in the actual, in the personal and the social, *in the Spirit.* For, whatever theory may finally satisfy the theology, the fulfilment can only be in the life. [emphasis added]

This is not a simple case of intellectual humility or self-restraint, or an attempt at a profound statement about the limitations of words. In Cragg it is rather a deep conviction about the social dimension of truth, and therefore about the Christian Gospel. 'To be is to meet' [*ibid.*, p. 11], and therefore

> 'meaning *of* … ' can never be divorced from 'meaning *for* … ' Since meaning is a transaction with others, and not a commodity, as it were, in stock, relationship is inseparable from faith, and faith from relationship. [*Ibid.*, p. 24, emphasis original]

Again the reader is struck by the determination to think in a dynamic rather than a static mode, as befits Cragg's emphasis on the Spirit who 'proceeds', and his conviction that it is religious experience which is prior and gives rise to dogma, and not the other way round. Yet there is a definite 'given' in his thought that will make his reader pause. Is there, in this 'relational' and 'transactional' language, sufficient weight given to the claims for objective truth, to what the American Lutheran theologian George Lindbeck calls the status of 'unsurpassability'?[48] Is Cragg saying that whatever language, or conviction, forwards the relationship is 'true' to the demands of the situation? Cragg acknowledges the force of that interpretation while declining to accept it. Referring to John Hick's thought he writes:

> … the Incarnation is true in the truth of the attitude it evokes in the believer. Hick understands it as having no

48 Lindbeck, George, *The Nature of Doctrine. Religion and Theology in a Post-Liberal Age*, SPCK, London, 1984, pp. 47-52.

> other truth. If, to use his verb, we try to 'unpack' the doctrine of the Incarnation we find it takes us only to our experience of Jesus as, for us, 'the way, the truth and the life.' Here are taxing problems. [*Other*, p. 75]

Cragg's answer to them is principally couched in historical terms, where he challenges Hick's assertion that faith-communities lived in mutual ignorance of one another until recent times. He points to the facts of Hindu/Buddhist, Jewish/Christian, and Christian/Muslim geographical proximity and with them antagonism, from earliest times. But 'most important of all', he claims, is the fact that Christians depend for their living faith on the logical priority of Jesus' life as historic actuality. Only on that premiss can the Christian proceed to live out his image of God. But Cragg's thought is tantalisingly compressed here. If the premiss is the mere fact of Jesus having lived, that is important but hardly ground enough for becoming the basis of modern faithful existence. It is the significance attached to the character of Jesus' life that matters, and here Hick would claim that the doctrine of the Incarnation is a much later interpretation of Jesus' life which is not warranted by the claims which we have reason to be sure he made about himself.[49] Cragg has given us his own understanding of the development of early Christian doctrine about Christ in his *What Decided Christianity. Event and Experience in the New Testament* [1989], where it is clear that he is confident that 'in the New Testament literature the apostles were writing their autobiography … interleaved with the story of their Master.' [*Decided*, p. 46, cf. p. 165ff] Some have thought that his attitude to Biblical criticism was to ignore its alleged results while defending its legitimacy as method.[50]

On the other hand he is certainly no fundamentalist, as we shall see more clearly later. He does not insist on people taking the Christian scriptures as their starting-point but recommends a view of 'man as the existential subject of all religious meaning', because 'the earth is our common space ship and … the single territory of our humanness.' [*Other*, p. xiii] His preferred image for religion is the hunger experienced by an audience in front of an empty stage, waiting for the play to begin and longing that it may meet their hope and yearning for meaning. For

49 Hick, John, *God Has Many Names. Britain's New Religious Pluralism*, Macmillan, London, 1980, p. 66f.

50 Edmonds, P, review of *Paul and Peter* in *The Heythrop Journal* 23 (1982), p. 188.

him the action which does so is the history of Israel, culminating in the coming of Israel's Messiah. In that total story is a 'theatre for the world'. [*Ibid.*, p. 63] The artistic metaphor is apt for the historical drama at the heart of Christianity, and also as an expression of the need for internal consistency within each faith.

> What matters is that the point of departure fulfils itself in where it leads. To end authentically is to vindicate one's beginning, and this is what the Christian claims of his Old Testament indebtedness. [*Ibid.*, p. 51]

But the corollary is that 'the play's the thing', and one cannot ask, or answer, the question 'why this play rather than another?' 'A particular beginning', as Cragg rightly says, 'is inescapable in any religion, as in any philosophy. One cannot start presuppositionless.' At the same time there is no way in which one can justify starting-points, or they would of course cease to be starting-points. One has to know one's starting-point, and begin from there, for 'there is no prophecy, honoured or otherwise, without a country of the mind.' [*Event*, p. 19] What is more there is no possibility of offering a hospitality of heart and mind to those of other faiths if one has no home of faith from which to offer it. [*World*, p. 76]

It is this firm loyalty to the 'home' of Christian faith which is most evident in the later books Cragg has published about the Christian theology of religion, *The Christ and the Faiths. Theology in Cross-Reference* (1986), and *To Meet and to Greet. Faith with Faith* (1992). These books carry many of the familiar accents of the previous work about the priority of forming relationships over formulating concepts. 'Pluralism does not primarily require of our theology hypotheses about its being so. It awaits a Christian fidelity of mind and will in the relationships it entails and offers.' [*Christ*, p. 10] But there is a new emphasis on the proper Christian 'custody' of the faith which is all the more significant when set against the much more negative associations of that custodial metaphor in previous writing.

> The Christ-faith has shaped for its credential to all others a custodial community, a house and home from which to pursue the hospitality of God in the homelessness of the world. [*Ibid.*, p. 343]

Cragg is clear that Christians cannot contribute anything to dialogue, or properly encounter other faiths if they have forgotten, or neglected, the upkeep of their own spiritual home. The final chapter of *To Meet and to Greet* is titled 'Where is Home?' and continues the book's theme of hospitality.

> It is surely into homes, however, that genuine encounter must repair. The deepest exchanges cannot well remain where we cannot accede to be guests or offer to be hosts. Meeting is akin to hospitality. [*Meet,* p. 168]

It is from here that loyalty and identity take their meaning and so encounter with others who are different becomes possible. 'There is neither point nor loyalty in encounter with pluralism if "the salt has lost its savour". The summons is not met if we forfeit what is heeding it.' [*Christ*, p. 20] This goes side by side with a plain acknowledgement that the ultimate assumptions by which religious communities operate are not open for negotiation. [*Ibid.*, p. 318] They are 'given' and carry their own authority, which cannot then be subsumed under some other heading. In any case there is no agreed frame of reference. [*Ibid.*, p. 338]

Cragg does not refer to the 'theocentrism', espoused by John Hick and some others, whereby it is recommended that the focus of faith should shift in the Christian case from the person of Christ to the centrality of the God whom Christ confessed.[51] But it is evident that his whole emphasis on the ultimate non-negotiable 'givens' of faith operates against the 'theocentric' proposal. It is certainly *theo*logy which is important to him.

> The gospel through and through is about God. But it is about God in dimensions and *via* indices which are nowhere else reached or read as they are in Jesus as the Christ and the Christ as crucified for love of man. [*Christ*, p. 323]

Though Cragg rejects the term 'unique' for Christ as hostile in tone, and wants to cherish 'overlaps' with other faiths, there is still a 'nowhere else' about God in Christ. Moreover, theism cannot serve as an overarching category, for Buddhism, no less than humanism, fails to embrace it. [*Ibid.*, p. 253f.]

---

51 Hick, *op. cit.*, and *God and the Universe of Faiths*, Macmillan, London, 1973.

What Cragg seems to be saying is that there is no theological umbrella which can be opened to shelter all the faiths of the world under one scheme of thought. We have to learn to live with religious pluralism in faithfulness to the ultimates we have inherited, without relativizing them, and in faithfulness to one another, without ignoring or excluding each other. 'Hospitality' is the key metaphor, and the Spirit the theological door. This stance seems unambiguous, but it carries its problems with it, as Cragg recognises. What is the quality and what are the conditions of such 'hospitality', which Cragg describes in one place as 'surely the closest of all analogies to the meaning of the Gospel'? [*World*, p. 71] We come later to a detailed answer in terms of Cragg's approach to Islam, but in this more general inquiry we note his continual stress on loyalty to Christ and openness to others. We are not to possess exclusively, but we are to affirm loyally. [*Ibid.*, p. 76] When pressed for an answer to the 'mystery and burden of the plurality of religions' Cragg has, it seems, only two kinds of response—one in terms of the attitude of the Christian believer, and one in terms of the work of the Holy Spirit. Theologies, in the sense of conceptual models of relationship, are not so much redundant as premature:

> Perhaps in the end our situation calls for a capacity to hold together the finality of loyalty to Christ and the will to 'concede' the other faiths, without asking for an answer how ... We may seem to be concluding that the right theology of pluralism is the lack of one. Hardly so. What we are saying is that we shall only find it in 'proceeding'—the very word theology uses of the Holy Spirit. [*Ibid.*, pp. 83, 84; cf. *Other*, p. 105]

> In the mystery and the burden of the plurality of religions there lies, surely, the supreme test of the meaning we intend when we say, 'I believe in the Holy Spirit'. [*World*, p. 71]

The insistent question is of course how one may recognise this proceeding of the Spirit, or whether it is simply a catchall term for what, for undeclared or even unexamined reasons, elicits one's approval. Cragg's answer emphasises in equal measure the activity and the suffering humility of the Spirit. God is a God who acts unceasingly as the Creator God, and the Spirit accordingly

> is never a sleeping partner of sleeping partners, but always an active spur, enthusing, employing, never excluding, the mind and will of men, not purveying ready-made answers but enabling responsible decision. [*Other*, p. 80]

This is expressed particularly in the 'creative trusteeship' which men are meant to hold of the Christian scriptures [*World*, p. 56], and Cragg spends considerable effort in demonstrating how that same principle was at work in the creation of the New Testament itself. [*Ibid.*, ch. 2—New Testament Universality: Precedents and Open Questions] Christian faith holds indeed to a 'divine "indicative" warranting us to say that God is love' [*Jesus*, p. 192], but this is not intended to mean that we can simply state it like a theorem. [*Other*, p. 84] Christian language, as Lindbeck says, is 'part and parcel of a wider conformity of the self to God', and in consequence is 'performative', and states, or denies, itself in action. 'Creeds are for living currency, not for deposit in a bank of static security.' [*Meet*, p. 178] For Lindbeck, religious utterance 'acquires' propositional truth through the performance which gives it credibility. This saves it from being merely 'intrasystematically' true, i.e. true only within a given context, true in the sense that Hamlet is Prince of Denmark, but not in any sense which could be called absolute or ontological.[52]

Cragg, however, does not lead us into these philosophical realms, but prefers to remind us that in the Christian understanding divine self-emptying is the continual activity of God 'from the foundation of the world'. [*Other*, p. 119; cf. *Sandals*, p. 87] It is the 'kenosis of the Spirit', in his favourite phrase from Wheeler-Robinson, which calls upon us to recreate in our own time and in our own idiom the meaning of the Incarnation, and to encourage others to find their own way through the deeper implications of their inherited faiths to the same understanding. This way of understanding the activity of the Holy Spirit both ensures a full and eager participation of Christians *with others* in the business of exploring religious faith, and also guards Christians against any temptation to arrogance at being in possession of truth others have not grasped. For the Christian story is one which is 'only safe in the custody of those for whom every antagonism is an opportunity. For that, precisely, is the heart of the story itself.' [*Call*, p. 164] 'No one can be in true trusteeship of the good news of Bethlehem and serve his trust with arrogance.' [*Sandals*, p. 86] Yet the contrary is so

52 Lindbeck, *op. cit.*, p. 65f.

often in evidence, and 'it is not seldom that faith erects a dogma where it would better hold a confidence', and religious belief becomes fossilized instead of vibrant and creative. [*Event*, p. 21] Alternatively, as with Judaism, or so Cragg alleges, there comes to be a 'kind of imperialism of the Spirit' which insists on the joining of the right party before access to truth can be guaranteed. [*World*, p. 33, cf. *Sandals*, p. 142]

We take up this theme again in another context, that of Cragg's understanding of the respective natures of truth and power. For the moment the question remains as to whether this talk of holding confidence rather than erecting dogma is, on reflection, theologically satisfactory, or whether the agnosticism about precisely how other faiths may be conceded within a fundamental loyalty to Christ does not give too much leeway for error and too little guidance in the Spirit. Granted that the Spirit proceeds, is he not also a Spirit of order? (1 Corinthians 14:33) However, this question has large dimensions and cannot be answered simply by the presence or absence of codified guidelines. Positively, the whole manner and style of Cragg's treatment of Islamic themes has to form part of the evidence here. Negatively, we have to observe also what he finds unacceptable in Islamic belief and practice and why he finds it so.

5
TRUTH AND POWER

1 The Theme of Custody

We have seen the emphasis that Cragg places upon 'creative trusteeship', as the legacy which the Christian Church receives from the New Testament itself. [*World*, p. 56] The scriptures are not simply there, to be assented to, and stored in the mind. They are to serve as a 'field of precedents' [*ibid.*, p. 55f.; cf. *Other*, p. 80], not only authority but also paradigm for the believer in the task of working out how he is to live and communicate his faith. The Spirit 'proceeds' in establishing the relevance of the Christ-event in all the minds which are open to him, and in developing all the deeper implications of a particular religious tradition, what Cragg in one place calls the 'pro-Christian emphases'.[1] But Cragg, like other thinkers, also finds it effective to state his point negatively, and the opposite of the dynamic, relational pattern of Christian obedience which he commends is that which sees the fulfilment of its responsibilities in terms of guarding the deposit of faith, in terms of custody. The term is meant to imply a rigid, unmoving and unimaginative loyalty which intends the refusal of compromise, but also thereby refuses adventure and the hopeful, open attitude. Consequently it is backward-looking, static, and potentially stagnant, preferring the cistern to the fountain, the still to the running water. [*Other*, p. 105]

It is in the context of a discussion of the term 'non-Christian' that Cragg introduces the concept of the 'custodian-mind', marked by 'habits of exclusion and assertion.' [*World*, p. 74] For most of Cragg's writing 'custody' and its variants is a term with strong negative connotations, and it is only in his later work that it is used in a more positive sense. [*Christ*, p. 343] Noting that negative terms like 'non-Christian' fail to reveal anything

1 Cragg, Kenneth, art. 'Temple Gairdner's Legacy' in *International Bulletin of Missionary Research* 5:4 (October 1981), p. 166.

about the inner content of the cultures and faiths so labelled (what about calling Christians 'non-Buddhists'?), Cragg dubs such usage as confusing and even treacherous because it 'implies the negation of kinship, the exclusion of hope, and perhaps even of the acknowledgement of human neighbourhood.' [*World*, p. 74] Yet he sees that such defensiveness, such denial of relationship, appears to those who practise it as loyal necessity, a negation in the best of causes, a vigorous and uncompromising defence of what must at all costs be defended. He notes the paradox that religions which exist for surrender, for yielding to the ultimate cause, for the sake of the God who is ultimate, are fiercely protective and unyielding of the doctrine they enshrine. This paradox may be understood as a tension between the necessity of creed and the necessity of worship.

> Seen from the standpoint of beliefs, faiths appear, substantially, as ends in themselves: seen from the perspective of worship they are themselves for ends beyond them. [*Ibid.*, p. 75]

We have observed the centrality of worship in Cragg's thought, and his determination to search out, so that it may be actively encouraged, every sign of human turning God-wards, however it may be expressed. When he considers the characteristic temper of the mind which sets itself to consolidate and to protect the Godward turning already established, he finds that the tension between creed and worship is particularly acute in Christianity.

> Their conjuncture is nowhere more pressing than for Christianity where the self-preservation, *to which creeds tend*, is the very principle which Christ crucified refuses and abjures. So we have, for example, a long doctrinal contention for the status of the Incarnate Son; yet that very status in itself consists, not in prestige reserved, but glory self-expending. This is not to say that controversialists had a wrong concept to defend, but that their defence had, nevertheless, to do with a freely defenceless Christ. [*Ibid.*—emphasis added]

Tillich seems to be saying something very similar in his *Christianity and the Encounter of the World Religions* (1963): 'What is particular in him

(Christ) is that he crucified the particular in himself for the sake of the universal.'[2] In Tillich's view this results in a tension between 'Christianity as a religion and Christianity as the negation of religion'. Cragg would not accept Tillich's use of the term 'religion' as contrasted with a secular realm, but he would be happy with Tillich's statement that 'the principle of love in him (Christ) embraces the cosmos,' and that 'with this image ... the criteria are given under which Christianity must judge itself and, by judging itself, judge also the other religions.'

The whole of Cragg's passage is very revealing of his theological presuppositions. First we note that there is a universal pattern in religious life—a paradox or tension between creed and worship—which is found in its sharpest form in Christianity. The events of Christ's coming, and the life and thought they give rise to, are archetypal versions of experiences to be found in less focussed form everywhere. By looking at Christ you can make sense of the world. Rejecting the dialectical theology which saw metaphysics as irrelevant to faith, Cragg engages in theology as a single debate, where Christians have to take in all possible data. This is not to be thought of as something threatening, for 'Christian theology, like the arch, grows stronger through the weight it bears.'[3] (The arch is a metaphor that has lived with Cragg all through his writing career.) [Cf. *Christ*, p. 325]

Secondly, and more explicitly, the crucifixion willingly suffered by Christ makes plain a universal truth, that in the presence of God there is no immunity which can be claimed, no status which can be preserved and no prestige which can be clung to. *Islam*, or surrender, is always required of us. We do not mean of course, that this is the only meaning of the Cross, or that that is what Cragg supposes. He is careful not to say that Christ contended for a 'principle' of any sort. Cragg merely says, negatively, that Christ refused the principle of self-preservation.

Thirdly, that obedient refusal in Christ is the mark of divine glory. 'Jesus, in the flesh, accomplishes the eternal mind, just as the poem translates into accessibility the mind of the poet.' [*Jesus*, p. 292] That understanding has somehow to be contended for, in a manner which is appropriate to the message itself, which 'performs' the word to be offered,[4]

---

2 Hick, John and Hebblethwaite, B L eds, *Christianity and Other Religions. Selected Readings*, Collins, Glasgow, 1980, p. 111.

3 Cragg, Kenneth, 'Islam in the 20th Century', unpublished D.Phil. thesis Oxford University, 1950, pt 2, p. 55.

4 Cf, Lindbeck, George, *The Nature of Doctrine. Religion and Theology in a Post-Liberal Age*, SPCK, London, 1984, p. 65.

and does not betray it. The manner of holding one's faith, therefore, matters intensely, as we shall see when we come to examine Cragg's dictum 'not whether but how'.

The fourth implication of the passage is that Cragg has succeeded in turning the tables on those who argue from positions of entrenched conservatism that their opponents are betraying the faith. For Cragg there may be more betrayal in the way that some go about defending 'the true faith' than there is in the apparent failure by others to hold fast to it. In the saying attributed to Father Kelly, 'the opposite of faith is not doubt but certainty,' and religious certainty can lead people into committing grave injustice in its name. We have seen that Cragg also accuses such conservatives of confusion of thought, again returning their own accusation.

Cragg is clearly challenged by Toynbee's thought that Christianity itself needs to die in order to live [*Other*, p. 79], and says, in relation to the tension between the guardianship of the faith and the self-surrender the faith prescribes, that 'It is urgent not to surrender either side of this paradox.' [*World*, p. 75] Nevertheless it is clear that his own emphasis is consistently to remind us that theology is produced to enable authentic worship (as opposed to idolatry), and worship is enacted to serve God. Conversely, it is God who has acted to save human beings in Jesus, and they are entrusted with the task of making sense of what has happened. The event is prior to the doctrine, but the doctrine is necessary to keep hold of the event, and make it accessible to others. 'Damascus visions can be turned into preaching only as they accept to be commended in the form of convictions that have a structure of doctrine and community.' [*Paul*, p. 11] Consequently there should be, as Cragg sees it, a freedom for theological formulation, a sense of adventure. We shall see how for Cragg soteriology takes precedence over ontology. 'The divine energy to save' is a more important focus than 'substance metaphors that set Christology/ theology in the realm of abstract metaphysics.'[5]

Many Muslims would agree with the central thrust of Cragg's thought here (though not of course with his emphasis on soteriology), finding in the defensive habit of mind he criticises what Islam has known as *taqlid. Taqlid* means literally 'the wearing of a necklace', and is associated also with the ancient Arab practice of hanging certain objects around the necks of animals due to be sacrificed at Mecca. It came to mean 'clothing

5 'Temple Gairdner's Legacy', *op. cit.*, p. 166.

with authority', and so complete dependence on the ancient authorities of the faith. In this sense it was the opposite of *ijtihad*, the exercise of independent judgement on matters of law or belief. It might be supposed that attacks on such dependence were more characteristic of modern, or 'modernist' thinkers, than of classical Islam, but in fact there is a long tradition of interpreting certain Qur'anic passages in just this sense. This suspicion of *taqlid* stems from the opposition Muhammad faced in Mecca from those who alleged that he was contravening the customs of their forefathers, and wanted him to adopt their own unquestioning obedience to those ancient authorities. [See Qur'an 2:170, 5:107, 21:53, 43:22f.] To the objection 'Nay, we shall follow the ways of our fathers', the Qur'anic reply (almost a refrain) is 'What! Even though their fathers were void of wisdom and guidance?' [2:170]

Baidawi (d. 1282) is only one of the classical commentators who makes a vigorous attack on such *taqlid.* He comments trenchantly on those who criticised the change of *qiblah* from Jerusalem to Mecca, ('The Fools among the people will say … '—2:142f.), calling them

> those people who exhibit only little capacity for insight and who depreciate even this through their blind acceptance *(taqlid)* of other views and neglect any examination of such views on their own. Referred to are those among the hypocrites *(munafiqun)*, Jews, and pagans, who want to know nothing of the change of the direction of prayer.[6]

The un-Islamic, pagan character of *taqlid* is further emphasized in another comment of Baidawi, this time on 2:170, but he goes on to make a point about religious obedience which somewhat qualifies his sharper language about *taqlid*:

> This verse was sent down concerning the pagans, who were ordered to follow the Qur'an … but who had held instead to the blind acceptance *(taqlid)* of traditional beliefs and practices … This passage shows that blind acceptance of what is capable of individual insight and independent research is to be rejected. If one follows freely in the religion of another

6 Gätje, Helmut, *The Qur'an and its Exegesis. Selected Texts with Classical and Modern Muslim Interpretations*, RKP, London, 1976, p. 131.

> and thus has assurance through some kind of proof that he is correct, as is the case with the prophets and those who investigate the statements of revelation independently, then it is not in fact a matter of blind acceptance, but on the contrary one then follows what God has sent down ...[7] [In quoting Gätje I have omitted the brackets he uses to indicate where his translation becomes paraphrase]

Baidawi here reflects an abiding puzzle in Islam as in all religion. Believers are called seriously to investigate what they believe, and not simply to accept things 'on trust'. Yet few have the facilities or perhaps the aptitude to spend the necessary time in study and critical reflection, and are thus compelled to rely on other people's judgements. Islam recognises this fact in the doctrine of the *ijma'* or consensus of the believers, and all independent judgement has to be exercised within that established consensus. Since about the end of the third Islamic century it has been widely reckoned that the 'gate of *ijtihad*' was closed, and that henceforth there was minimal room for further decision-making, at least on points of law. Religious obedience now consisted of following the decisions of one of the recognised *madhahib* (schools of law), and it was an issue much debated as to whether one could change one's allegiance from one *madhab* to another, much less pick and choose among them the judgements which one approved. As Schacht says, 'combining elements of the doctrine of several schools was practically unheard of, because it was the allegiance to the teaching of a common master that held the schools together.'[8] So a form of *taqlid* was in practice approved, and even prescribed, and the checks to be made on the authority accepted became, even with Baidawi, extremely vague—'... assurance through some kind of proof.' [See above]

Mention of the *madhahib*, however, recalls one critical peculiarity of Islam as compared with Christianity, which is the prior significance of law over theology. This is a matter of some complexity since neither term has a precise equivalent in Arabic and Islamic usage, but all that is said above about *taqlid* really applies only to the religious law, the *Shari'ah*, the extensive code of behaviour for private and public life which was based on the Qur'an and the traditions of the Prophet and elaborated by the

7 *Ibid.*, p. 140.

8 Schacht, Joseph, art. 'Theology and Law in Islam' in G von Grunebaum ed., *Theology and Law in Islam*, Harrassowitz, Wiesbaden, 1971, p. 14.

jurists. As Schacht points out, 'there were no recognised masters (in the field of theology), comparable with Abu Hanifa, Malik and Shafi'i until Ash'ari and Maturidi well into the third Islamic century, the time of the closing of the "gate of *ijtihad*".'[9] *Taqlid*, writes a modern Pakistani scholar, 'conserved the legal heritage of the first three centuries,'[10] but the same judgement is not self-evidently true of theological statement in Islam. In theology it seems that not only was there wide variety and a profusion of doctrinal viewpoints, falling only into the most general patterns or schools of thought, but also that theological speculation was likely to pass unremarked and uncontrolled by any authority unless it carried obvious political implications. Frequently, however, it did just this. Goldziher and Schacht are broadly agreed in tracing the origins of theological dispute in Islam to politics, piety and Christian polemics.[11] Governments could be content to allow the various schools of religious law to grow in peace until they had reached the maturity implied in the general adoption of *taqlid*, as noted above. But Islamic theological dispute both arose from and was stimulated by such questions as the standing of 'Ali among the first four Caliphs, the issue of whether a grave sinner should be obeyed as ruler, and the extent to which human action (and inaction) was predetermined by God. Neither Umayyad nor 'Abbasid rulers could remain indifferent to the debate about such questions, and the consequence, at least from time to time, was 'massive government interference'.[12]

In such circumstances the mere recommendation to follow in the ways of the Prophet and his companions, the prescription of *taqlid*, seemed inadequate, for the issues were new in their sharpness and urgency. Consequently theologians, whatever they thought of Mu'tazilite theology, in practice followed the Mu'tazilite conviction that '*nazar*, the speculative cognition of God, was every person's duty.' *Taqlid* as the unthinking acquiescence in received opinion was to be condemned, for

> it was not enough for a Muslim to say that he believed in Allah as the only God and in the prophethood of Muhammad, merely on the authority of his teacher, and

9 *Ibid.*

10 Hasan Ahmad, *The Doctrine of Ijma' in Islam. A Study of the Juridical Principle of Consensus*, Islamic Research Institute, Islamabad, 1978, p. 7.

11 Goldziher, Ignaz, *Introduction to Islamic Theology and Law*, Princeton University Press, Princeton, 1910, pp. 68f., 81, and Schacht, *op. cit.*, p. 18.

12 Schacht, *op. cit.*, p. 20.

> finally on the authority of the founder of his school of theology, but that he must know, that is to say, be personally convinced of it himself, even if he does not know all the scholastic proofs and distinctions.[13]

These considerations have to be borne carefully in mind when trying to compare Cragg's attitude to religious conservatism, coloured by his original Christian environment, with Islamic notions of *taqlid*. Religious law in its Muslim or Jewish form plays virtually no part at all in Christian life or thought, and therefore it is very easy to misread the whole Islamic debate on the subject of *taqlid*, since Christians have so little familiarity with the kind of circumstances in which it became approved. Moreover, since the New Testament is claimed to be, among other things, a radical critique of Jewish law it is not to be expected that Christians will find an easy understanding of the Muslim version of codified religious guidance. Catholic canon law provides only a very partial parallel. So there is likely to be an equivalent Christian misreading of Muslim theology, for what has been called the 'Queen of the Sciences' in Christian circles has often been viewed with deep suspicion by Muslims considering its Islamic version. This is not only because of the political context noted above, but also because one force in the formulation of scholastic theology, or *kalam*, seems to have been the inheritance of Greek philosophy mediated through Iraqi and Persian non-Muslims who challenged Islamic beliefs on philosophic grounds. Muslim thinkers learnt to reply to their interrogators in the same idiom, but also came to use such rationalist arguments in debate with other Muslims. Consequently *kalam* was attacked as a form of *zandaqa* (dualism), particularly by the followers of the jurist Ibn Hanbal.[14] It is this character of theology in Islam which leads Schacht to describe it as 'essentially defensive apologetics', though a similar judgement could easily be made about Christian theology.[15]

It has become a truism to say that the genius of Islam is law rather than theology. Gibb said: 'The master science of the Muslim world was law.'[16] Zaehner said: 'Theology has never plagued Islam to the extent it has

13 Goldziher, *op. cit.*, p. 106; Schacht, *op. cit.*, p. 21.

14 Watt, W Montgomery, *The Formative Period of Islamic Thought*, Edinburgh University Press, Edinburgh, 1973, pp. 243, 186.

15 Schacht, *op. cit.*, pp. 21, 4.

16 Gibb, H A R, *Islam. A Historical Survey*, 2nd edn, Oxford University Press, London, 1953, p. 7. Compare Cragg, Kenneth, 'Tadabbur al-Qur'an: Reading and Meaning'

Christianity.'[17] Watt has written: 'Jurisprudence was the central intellectual discipline in the Islamic world.'[18] Certainly the intellectual formation even of the Mu'tazilite theologians and men like Ghazzali was in the studies of *Shari'ah* and tradition. If one looks for a complementary focus in the Muslim mind to law, it would be *tasawwuf* rather than *kalam*. The *taqlid* of the law might be challenged more cogently by the Sufi than the *mutakallim* (scholastic theologian). So the Persian poet 'Attar of Nishapur (d. 1221) represents famous mystics of Islam grouped around the gibbet of the dying al-Hallaj, and one of them, Shibli, asking him whether his saying *ana-l haqq*/I am the Reality' conformed to the law. 'Attar has al-Hallaj answering 'You are in *taqlid*, I in *tawhid*/Unity.'[19]

How does Cragg's understanding of religious language and study fit with these Islamic realities? We have to note first of all that the whole of his doctoral thesis was devoted to the examination of modern Muslim apologetics contrasted with their Christian equivalents, and that he frequently speaks in that context of the inadequacy and timidity of Muslim theological thought. He reckons that the *Azhar Journal* reflects 'a dichotomy of mind in which the final problems of theology remain in permanent abeyance,' and writes of Muhammad Ali of India that his work was 'not so much apology, as the lack of it made virtuous.'[20] Later, speaking of the maxim that the genius of Islam lies in law rather than in theology, he writes that 'it would be truer to say that its strength lies in theology as law … Law, we may say, is religion, and religion is law.' [*House*, p. 44] Nevertheless he writes very little about Islamic law, and much about the 'renewers' of Islam—men in the vein of Muhammad 'Abduh, whom, despite some reservations, he exempts from his general strictures on Muslim thinkers. 'Abduh, he thought, showed 'no trace of the impatience of theology which sometimes inspires modernism elsewhere,' though even he could be guilty of a 'spirit of intellectual docility'.[21]

A lawyer like Schacht will see the significant current development of Islam in terms of 'legal modernism', the attempt by modern Muslim

---

in A H Green, *In Quest of an Islamic Humanism. Arabic and Islamic Studies in memory of Mohamed al-Nowaihi*, American University in Cairo Press, Cairo, 1984, p. 186.

17 Zaehner, R C, 'Why not Islam?' in *Religious Studies* 11:2 (June 1975), p. 169.

18 Watt, *op. cit.*, p. 182.

19 Massignon, Louis, *The Passion of al-Hallaj, Mystic and Martyr of Islam*, 4 vols, Princeton University Press, Princeton, 1982, II, p. 384.

20 Cragg, 'Islam in the 20th Century', pp. 296, 398.

21 *Ibid.*, pt 1, pp. 145, 151.

nation-states to modify classical Islamic law to suit modern conditions. Cragg, looking at the same events, advocates the shifting of the criminal codes of Muslim countries to a civil basis: 'What is obvious is that the whole current of modern life, and its tempo, are running against both the spirit and the feasibility of the religious legalism of Islam.'[22] Schacht dismisses 'Abduh as unimportant:

> By contrast, there has been nothing similar in the field of theology; there has been only the well-meaning, but anodyne and tame effort of Muhammad 'Abduh (himself a progressive thinker in the field of Islamic law), who tried to eliminate from traditional Islamic theology those features that seemed to him most incompatible with modern thought.[23]

We should note, however, that Iqbal is less easy to ignore as a theological influence because of his tremendous reputation in Pakistan. [Cf. *Muhammad*, p. 74f]

Is Cragg's interest in men like 'Abduh and Iqbal then misplaced? Or perhaps we should ask what it is that interests Cragg, and other Western scholars, in them? Is his, and their, focus on Islam misdirected? Cragg quotes Juvenal's tag *quis custodiet ipsos custodes?* in his thesis, in the context of Christian 'interior self-consistency', which is judged to be 'more delicate in the realm of theology than in the realm of law or society.'[24] Nevertheless it may have been 'Abduh who fixed in Cragg's mind the metaphor of custody to describe the entrenched and unthinking conservatism both men attack. 'Abduh employs the image in two key passages of his *Risalat al-Tauhid* (translated by Cragg as *The Theology of Unity*):

> There were in every people custodians of religion concerned with its protection and propagation, of which the first prerequisite is expression. They had, however, little recourse to rational judgement in their custody of belief ... Indeed there is an almost total contrast between the intellectual cut and thrust of science and the forms of religious persuasion and assurance of heart. Oftentimes religion on the authority

22 *Ibid.*, pt 1, p. 97.
23 Schacht, *op. cit.*, p. 22.
24 Cragg, 'Islam in the 20th Century', pt 2, p. 106.

> of its own leaders was the avowed enemy of reason, and all its works. [*Unity*, p. 30]

The Qur'an, in contrast, 'spoke to the rational mind and alerted the intelligence.' In the second passage 'Abduh couples his custodian-image with a repudiation of *taqlid*, which is identified as essentially pagan:

> Islam will have no truck with traditionalism, against which it campaigns relentlessly, to break its power over men's minds and eradicate its deep-seated influence. The underlying bases of *taqlid* in the beliefs of the nations have been shattered by Islam.
>
> In the same cause, it has alerted and aroused the powers of reason, out of long sleep. For whenever the rays of truth had penetrated, the temple custodians intervened with their jealous forebodings. 'Sleep on, the night is pitch dark, the way is rough and the goal distant, and rest is scant and there's poor provision for the road.' [*Ibid.*, p. 126]

The metaphor still served Cragg nineteen years later, when he commended Hasan Askari for developing his theological insights from within the discipline of sociology, and therefore as one who did not belong to 'the professional dogmatists, with their stock in trade of *Tafsir, Kalam*, and—it may be—*Taqlid*. These tend to obscure the deeper issues or obfuscate the mind. Custodians habitually confine their study to secure authority and safe precedent.' [*Pen*, p. 110]

Why is it that Cragg declines to engage with the legal themes in Islam pursued by Schacht and other Western scholars as the acknowledged focus of Islamic thought, and avoids also any extended study of the mystics of Islam, even Ghazzali? Commenting on Gibb's dictum about the most highly developed expression of Islam being, because of its practical bent, in law rather than theology, Cragg argues that 'The pre-eminence of the *Shari'ah*, however, is not primarily "the practical bent" of a community but the pattern of the divine relationship, both given and received.'[25] However, we have seen that many Muslims find this way of thought alien. Another reason for Cragg's avoidance of the study of *Shari'ah* may lie in his preoccupation with contemporary history, and the relationship

25 Cragg, 'Tadabbur al-Qur'an', p. 186.

of religious faith and political power. 'Are there,' he asks, 'limits to the competence of power in the care of truth?' [*Event*, p. 24]

2 Truth in the Custody of Power

> ... the most fundamental question of all religion, namely the relation and the relevance of power to truth. [*Event*, p. 134]

One of the refrains of Cragg's writing about Islam is the criticism that Islam too easily assumes that spiritual truth can survive uncorrupted in the custody of human beings exercising political power, or more decidedly, that spiritual truth actually needs political patronage. The 1950 thesis already bears much evidence of this, from the commendation of 'Ali 'Abd-ar-Raziq to the criticism of Indian Islam. 'Ali 'Abd-ar-Raziq (d. 1966), in the course of arguing that the Caliphate was unnecessary to Islam, had claimed that Muhammad's mission was essentially spiritual and not political. Muhammad was never the head of a state. Cragg is equally glad of Hasan Askari's statement that 'The Prophet of Islam did *not* create a state.' [*Pen*, p. 118—emphasis original] Cragg's comment on 'Ali 'Abd-ar-Raziq was: 'Though Muslim opinion is slowly and inevitably coming round to the views expressed by 'Ali 'Abd-ar-Raziq, they were rank heresy when first set down.'[26] That 'inevitable coming round' has been slow to happen, however, and raises questions about Cragg's interpretation of Islam, especially as similar observations continued to be expressed later. [E.g. *Valley*, p. 10, n. 8] In 1950 he felt that 'Muslim political pre-occupations are no solution of Islam's modern secular problem', for

> In the conditions of the modern world, it is difficult to see how any religious force within the State can truly fulfil itself, if it is so closely identified with the State, as Islam is, and *if it is so much bounden for its very life upon the cause of the State* ... Only if its being is independent of political props, if its power lies finally in its theological self-respect, can it rightly or safely fulfil its undoubted obligations to the State.[27] [emphasis original]

---

26 Cragg 'Islam in the 20th Century', pt 1, p. 221.
27 *Ibid.*, pp. 199, 200.

At that time he felt that the Islam of the Indian sub-continent was characterised by 'an unfortunate political quality to adventures of thought, which required a more spiritual detachment.' Pakistan, he thought, had diverted Indian Muslim attention from more fundamental problems, and he was able to quote Cantwell Smith as saying that the movement for Pakistan, as the 'rise of a separate Muslim nationalism has postponed the religious crisis.' Pakistan is seen as 'perhaps the crowning evidence of the absence of what this Thesis is seeking for in Islam', namely a lively sense of self-criticism issuing in a realistic theological apologetic to the modern world. Fundamentally Cragg agrees with Arnold Toynbee that 'all religions finally suffer when they accept political patronage', and declares that whereas Muhammad founded Islam as a religious force with a political form, 'too often today Islam presents at least the appearance of a political force with a religious form,—an inversion which the Prophet himself would hardly have tolerated.'[28]

It seems to me that we run into serious problems of definition here, and that it is by no means clear what Cragg is really saying. It is plainly possible simply to apply the criticism nearer home and declare that many circumstances of Christian history, even to the present day, could equally well be described as religious in form but political in substance. But what does this really mean? Is there not too easy an assumption here of the distinction between religion and politics—an assumption characteristic of Western Protestants, especially in the Lutheran tradition, but puzzling to Muslims as well as to many other Christians? We shall want to examine later some rare remarks of Cragg about liberation theology in the case of the Mexican Miranda. [*Muhammad*, pp. 157,158] In his advocacy of 'a religious ministry to the world of politics' Cragg is ready to admit that 'Christianity has to confess with pain both the difficulty of, and failure in, this urgent task and that, despite the fact that the Church, by definition and temper, has been so much more independent of the political.'[29] But he does not seem ready to reconsider his categories at this point. There is an uneasy juxtaposition of sociological observation and theological judgement continually made in much of this early writing which makes the reader ask by what criteria Cragg is interpreting the contemporary Muslim world. Some may recall the classic remarks on the difficulty of such interpretation by the anthropologist Clifford Geertz:

---

28 *Ibid.*, pt 1, pp. 326, 476, 478: pt 2, pp. 80 n. 1, 201.
29 *Ibid.*, pt 2, p. 201.

> The comparative study of religion has always been plagued by this peculiar embarrassment: the elusiveness of its subject matter. The problem is not one of constructing definitions of religion. We have had quite enough of those; their very number is a symptom of our malaise. It is a matter of discovering just what sorts of beliefs and practices support what sorts of faith under what sorts of conditions. Our problem, and it grows worse by the day, is not to define religion but to find it.[30]

The predictable response of some Muslim reviewers of Cragg's books has been to complain that he had not accurately 'found' Islam as they understood it, particularly on the issue of the political patronage of religion. (The Muslim response to Cragg's writings will concern us later on.) Many Muslims of course want to carry the war into the enemy's camp. Reviewing *The Call of the Minaret* the Pakistani scholar Hamidullah wrote that

> the author's defence of the separation of church and state raises questions not of dogmas but of facts. Christianity wishes to leave unto Caesar what is Caesar's. In the absence of Christian guidance, a Christian ruler will follow not Christ but Machiavelli, whereas Islamic guidance to a ruler is as imperative as it is to one who prays and fasts.[31]

The problem is that the issue of the engagement of religion and politics inescapably involves questions of historical interpretation, and historians cannot easily deal in broad abstractions like 'Islam' or 'Christianity', except insofar as they are living realities in the minds of Muslims, Christians and others. For most contemporary historians it is Muslims and Christians whose acts make history, and not Islam and Christianity. Cragg might demur at this, to point out that Muslims and Christians are after all defined by their Islam and their Christianity [*Other*, p. xiif. and *Christ*, p. 316 n. 2], and to that extent it is these great

30 Geertz, Clifford, *Islam Observed. Religious Development in Morocco and Indonesia*, 2nd edn, University of Chicago Press, Chicago, 1971, p. 1.

31 Hamidullah, M, review of *The Call of the Minaret* in *The Islamic Quarterly* 3:3 and 4 (October 1956 and January 1957), p. 247.

movements of faith which bring about the events we call history. One of his frequent complaints about modern Muslim apologetic in the thesis is the exoneration of Islam. Muslim writers continually plead

> … the perfection of Islam and the defection of Muslims. If anything is to be criticised it is the faithful and never the faith. The true Islam is incorruptible … We have pointed out how suspicious this argument often looks, the more so when no attempt is made to enquire how the faith could be served by, if not in fact produce such 'believing' delinquency over long periods of its history … It is much easier to admire Islam and to blame Muslims than to suspect Islam and reform Muslims.[32]

There is real cogency in this argument, and especially in the parallel drawn with the doctrine that 'the King can do no wrong; it is always his ministers who are at fault.' (One could cite a modern version in which the policies of a particular political party are always correct: it is their presentation to the electorate which needs to be amended.) But is Cragg entirely innocent of similar assertions about Christianity? He is entirely ready to admit that in the case of Christianity too

> we must recognize what failure implies for the religion so failing and not seek evasive exoneration in reprobating its confessors. For what the confessors are, or are not, is part of the record of the religion and some clue to its nature. [*Call*, p. 294]

But as his argument proceeds it becomes clear that 'Christendom' is not a Christian concept *[ibid.]*, and that 'Christianity belongs to and inheres in people who believe. It is never coterminous as such with any given society.' [*Ibid.*, p. 295] Consequently Christianity can in fact be exonerated from all the ills which its confessors may perpetrate, and remain innocent in any judgements delivered by history.

But is there not a deeper problem about observation (whether historical or contemporary) and evaluation, as Geertz has hinted? Bijlefeld raised in 1959, partly in reference to Cragg's work, the need to distinguish

32 Cragg, 'Islam in the 20th Century', pt 1, p. 550f.

between understanding religion with the tools of phenomenological science, and evaluating it theologically from a Christian (or other) perspective. One should not therefore, in his view, talk of 'Christian understanding' or 'theological interpretation' before Islam has been thoroughly understood in its own terms. Bijlefeld thought that this task was still largely to be accomplished, and that it was too soon to make judgements about Islam being either 'Satanic' or 'pro-' or 'semi-Christian'. Nor should one draw up lists of 'common elements' between the two faiths, as though it was firmly established that the two religions were talking about the same things. Though he commended Cragg's Operation Reach as 'the best planned attempt in the whole history of Muslim evangelism to equip and prepare Christians', he rejected Cragg's argument that the God of Christianity and of Islam was the same God, though differing in definition—the subject the same but the predicate different. We do not yet know.[33] Though some were critical of Bijlefeld's distinction between observation and evaluation, it does seem a useful working distinction, even if, as in thc natural sciences, it is sometimes next to impossible to decide where observation ends and evaluation begins.

Such a distinction may well make one more critical of typical and oft-repeated Craggian references to 'the uninhibited political character and assurance of Islam'.[34] These references are evident, as we have seen, in his earliest writing—'the Prophetic office and the claim to power were inseparable'[35]—and become more sharply phrased in the later, where there is a significant tendency to make the *Hijrah* the hinge of Islamic development. [*Event*, p. 66 and *Christ*, p. 44] Speaking of Sufism as the product of 'suffering, privation, tragedy and the fragility of all things mortal', Cragg continues

> These were precisely the features absent from post-*hijrah* Islam where they were displaced by triumph, success, victory and achievement in martial terms. *Al-Fauz al-mubin*, 'manifest victory' is the frequent cry of the Medinan Qur'an and ... its reading of the divine will and way is in terms of the battles of Badr and Uhud, or the capitulation of Mecca

33 Carman, John B, review of W Bijlefeld's *De Islam als Na-Christelijke Religie* in *Bulletin of the Henry Martyn Institute*, 1960.

34 Cragg, Kenneth, 'Sainthood and Spirituality in Islam' in *Studia Missionalia* 35 (1986), p. 181.

35 Cragg, 'Islam in the 20th Century', pt 2, p. 273.

> and the success of Hunain ... The Islamic faith, never in the catacombs, was its own empire.[36]

Muhammad, in other words, was his own Constantine. [*Call*, 1956 edn, p. 256] The contrast with the way of Jesus is of course commonplace in Christian thinking about Islam, but it has never been more powerfully stated than by Cragg. Writing of the third temptation of Jesus, which he calls 'the option for power' Cragg says

> Satan has Jesus visualize political empire with its compelling short cuts to the goal and, because of these, its inevitable compromise with evil, with brutality and force. The supremely Islamic principle with which Jesus refuses this temptation—'You shall worship the Lord your God and Him only shall you serve'—excludes the option of a *Hijrah*, a shift, a diversion into force and, therefore, away from the quiet strength of truth and the sure fidelities of love. There *are* 'the kingdoms of this world'—to be sure—but Messiahship is *in* them not *of* them. Those kingdoms are nationalist, competitive, exclusivist, political and coercive. As such they leave areas of life, reaches of humanity and depths of need outside both their range and their capacity, and even their achievements generate their contradiction. At the very centre of Jesus' reading of his destiny, in the sort of world the reception of his ministry disclosed, was the perception that the Messianic task and the political arm were not compatible. [*Jesus*, p. 154—emphasis original]

It might be said that Cragg comes close to accusing Muhammad of *shirk* in this passage. How does he actually understand the career of Muhammad at this point of its 'hinge' in the *Hijrah*? This was the 'supreme decision of all religious truth: How does one, how should one, react, in the name of truth, to untruth, to denial of that to which we are pledged witnesses?'[37] Cragg expressly dissociates himself from those who have seen 'a fatal break' at this juncture, leading to a decline in integrity and

---

36 Cragg, 'Sainthood and Spirituality', p. 180f.

37 Cragg, Kenneth, *Operation Reach* (pamphlet series), Near East Christian Council Study Program in Islam 1957-1962, Beirut, 1.27.

even morality in the personality of Muhammad. Goldziher, following Caetani, wrote that 'the change was detrimental to his character.'[38] 'It is truer', wrote Cragg,

> to see the whole pre- and post-Hijrah story as a single unity of commitment to a mission, received as from God, the means to which developed from word to action, from preaching to power, by an inner logic that the 'divine' must necessarily 'succeed'. [*Muhammad*, p. 50]

This leads him finally to the conclusion that Muhammad was a prophet, and that 'Christian response to the main theme of his prophethood has surely to be a positive acknowledgement of its significance.' At the same time more than prophecy is required if the full measure of the world's evil is to be taken, and our salvation achieved. [*Ibid.*, pp. 140, 145] It may seem that Cragg is taking away with one hand what he gives with the other, but he insists that the two judgements belong together. Muhammad can only be called to account for the decision of *hijrah* because his original call was genuine and permanent in its significance. [*Ibid.*, p. 142f.]

Perhaps the central difference between Cragg and other Christian interpreters of Islam at this point is that Cragg attempts to recruit Islam itself to this critique of Muslim confidence in 'the option for power', with the allegation that it is a transgression of the 'supremely Islamic principle' of the worship of God alone—in the final analysis a form of *shirk*. His later writing often states the primacy of the preaching of the message in Mecca over the politics to empower it in Medina. Reflecting on Usamah bin Laden and 'the war on terror' he writes:

> There is no misreading the fact that here is a crisis within and about Islam, only to be addressed, if never resolved, by returning to the equation first made by the Hijrah between the truth of witness and the necessity of power. Mecca was seen to require Medina, but Medina's whole meaning was for Mecca's sake. [*Iron*, p. 77f.]

Elsewhere he sees dis-empowered Muslim migrants living in the West as 'sharing the honour' of the pre-*Hijrah* circumstances of Mecca,

38 Goldziher, *op. cit.*, p. 23.

'where ... the whole genius of Islam began'. [*Lord*, p. 209] It is Cragg's profound conviction that there is within the resources of Islam the capacity to reach a Christian understanding of creation and history. So Sufism, which as he sees it has flourished among Muslims in spite of this power-assurance, can be seen as a kind of corrective to it, a response to the

> non-*islam* of institutional Islam ... Islam had the genius within its own resources of Scripture to respond to the exigencies that history presented when the institutions about which it had been so sanguine failed to actualise a true vocation under God.[39]

Nevertheless the clear implication of Cragg's view is that the *Hijrah* itself, and all that it represents in terms of the search for a 'manifest victory' plainly visible to doubting human minds, was an aberration from the true vocation of Islam and of Muhammad. In his book about suicide bombing, *Faith at Suicide* (2005), Cragg comes close to representing the suicide bombers of 2001 and their imitators as heirs of the *Hijrah*. He says plainly that 'Islam has one origin but a second version', and needs to return to 'the first edition of Islam', acknowledging 'the absolute priority of the Meccan'. [*Suicide*, pp. 92, 101, 102] Though Cragg may appeal to *islam* against Islam, he has to carry the burden of that judgement in the face both of the scholar of Islam who finds it untrue to historical Islam, and of the Muslim scholar who finds it offensively contrary to revelation. For there is no doubt that in Muslim minds the *Hijrah* carries a deep spiritual importance as 'migration in the way of God.' Quoting Surah 4:97, Elkholy sets the duty of migration in the context of a chapter on the concept of community in Islam:

> When the Muslim is politically oppressed and is unable to change the prevailing system, he is religiously required to migrate to any other place, where he has greater freedom. 'When those who had done themselves injustice die, the angels will ask them: in what were you engaged? They will say: we were oppressed in the land. The angels will admonish them saying: Wasn't God's globe spacious enough that you

39 Cragg, 'Sainthood and Spirituality in Islam', *op. cit.*, p. 187.

> could have migrated therein? For this, their resort will be Hell, the worst habitation.[40]

Has Cragg's theological evaluation of Islam begun to interfere with his observation and understanding of one of its major features at this point? Muslims will certainly reckon that it has. Khurram Murad, reviewing four introductory books on Islam (including Cragg's *The House of Islam*) entitles his piece '*hira* and *madina*: the West's Dilemma'. (*Hira'* is the name of the cave in which Muhammad first received the revelation of the Qur'an, and *Madina* here represents the stage of his career after the *Hijrah*.) He argues that Westerners, including westernised Muslims like Fazlur Rahman whose *Islam* is one of the four books he is reviewing, are incapable of understanding Islam because they do not grasp the true significance of prophethood in Islam, and therefore adequately acknowledge the prophethood of Muhammad. (Fazlur Rahman is included as one who accepts only its moral and not its legal dimension, which seems a very questionable judgement).[41] Murad writes:

> Islam cannot be understood unless *hira* and *madina* are understood and accorded the place they have in Islam ... On *hira* depends the truth and nature of Muhammad's experience of revelation and his claim to prophethood; while *madina*, often represented as a deviation, even a 'flight' from prophethood into politics, defines the nature of his mission and the destiny of his people in history. *Hira* by itself is troublesome enough, but *madina* seems to make Islam more complex, even impossible for a Christian-Western mind to comprehend.[42]

Murad finds it puzzling that those who have seen the development of Christianity from Galilee to Constantine through to the great basilica of St Peter's and beyond should find it impossible to portray correctly a similar development in Islam from *Hira'* to *Hijrah*, with the legal dimensions of

40 Elkholy, Abdo, art. 'The Concept of Community in Islam' in K Ahmad and Z I Ansari eds, *Islamic Perspectives. Studies in Honour of Mawlana Sayyid Abul 'Ala Mawdudi*, Islamic Foundation, Leicester, 1979, p. 174.

41 Fazlur Rahman, *Islam*, 2nd edn, University of Chicago Press, Chicago, 1979, p. 19.

42 Murad, Khurram, review of *The House of Islam* in 'Hira and Madina: the West's Dilemma', *Muslim World Book Review* 1:3 (Spring 1981), p. 4.

religion in *madina* following the preaching mode in *makka*. Murad does not actually single out Cragg for particular criticism on this point, but clearly regards him with the others as representative of a general Western failure to come to grips with the full significance of the Qur'anic revelation. (His judgement on Cragg is in fact mainly favourable: 'in large measure Cragg succeeds in the task he has set himself.') Murad has focussed attention on the Muslim response to this common non-Muslim interpretation of Islam, and raised the question of whether it is soundly based. Not only Christians have made it. The great Orientalist Goldziher, a Jew who moved from Orthodoxy to Reform Judaism, also shared this view.[43]

Other Muslim opinion defends Islam either by attacking the Christian record for failing to provide the proper guidance to rulers [see Hamidullah above], or by alleging an inherent failure in Christianity to represent a complete revelation. Ibn Khaldun (d. 1406) criticised Christians for not admitting the duty of *jihad*, while Ibn Taimiyya (d. 1328) reckoned that 'the right religion must have in it the guiding Book with the helping sword.' [*Jesus*, p. 300 n. 10—cf. *Muhammad*, p. 33] The Iranian revolutionary 'Ali Shari'ati (d. 1977) seems to belong to the first group in writing that 'ideal man holds the sword of Caesar in his hand and he has the heart of Jesus in his breast.' [quoted in *Jesus*, p. 52]

These characteristic Muslim responses give us something of the measure of the problem of the political dimension of Islam as a context for Cragg's treatment of it. There are Christian scholars who would in general support his strictures on the Muslim confidence about the use of power. A K S Lambton, in a study of the Persian theory of government, notes that 'theoretically the problem of *quis custodiet custodes* did not arise in Islam. Muslim thinkers in early and medieval times, with rare exceptions, disregard the question of power.'[44] It may perhaps be argued that they raised it in other ways. Other Christian thinkers who follow Cragg much of the way have complained that he has allowed the political issue to get out of proportion. Redmond Fitzmaurice has noted that the 'activist' Hebrew leaders, men like Moses and David, accounted 'prophets' in Islam, had small compunction in resorting to the sword for the defence of God's cause, and that many Christian leaders have followed their example.[45] The

43 Goldziher, *op. cit.*, p. 24.

44 Lambton, A K S, 'Quis Custodiet custodes: Some Reflections on the Persian Theory of Government' in *Studia Islamica* 5 (1956), p. 125.

45 Fitzmaurice, Redmond, review of *Muhammad and the Christian* in *Newsletter* of the Centre for the Study of Islam, Selly Oak Colleges, Birmingham, no.11 (May

point raises questions about Cragg's understanding of the relation of the New Testament to the Old which we shall need to return to in chapter 7, but also makes one ask how Cragg's position differs from pacifism. 'God and coercion', he says, 'do not belong together.' [*Christ*, p. 90] There is also the question of whether he confuses the issue by identifying the political expression of faith almost exclusively with violence and forcible coercion. Does political commitment necessarily involve coercion? To answer more fully the question of his portrayal of the issue of power we need to examine his understanding of the way that power is seen to corrupt true religion.

3 Morality and the Collective

Hendrik Kraemer expressed perhaps the most trenchant criticism of Islam in the twentieth century when he called it 'a thoroughly secularized theocracy', by which he seemed to mean 'religious imperialism'. 'Its real "god" is group solidarity', he thought. While Cragg, as we have seen, has moved some way beyond Kraemer's judgement that Islam is only 'to a certain degree' a prophetic religion,[46] it is legitimate to ask whether his criticism of the 'power-assurance' of Islam does not simply represent Kraemer's view about Islamic idolatry of the *umma* in a more sophisticated form. Certainly Cragg complains that some contemporary Muslims are correctly interpreted as meaning *Islamu akbar* (Islam is great) when they say *Allahu akbar* (God is great). Yet the second can never rightly come to mean the first. [*Jesus*, p. 297 and *Muhammad*, p. 133] He refers to another corruption of religion in the name of Islam when he says that 'There can be few attitudes more blasphemous than crying *Allahu akbar* with a clenched fist. For then we clearly mean: Down with our enemies. Religious faith, even piety in practice, may be a sadly inverted assertion of ourselves.'[47] But this is far from a blanket condemnation, and both the Shi'ite and the Sufi forms of Islam are recruited by Cragg for evidence that Islam is by no means monolithic even in the consequences of its

---

1984), p. 46.

46 Kraemer, Hendrik, *The Christian Message in a Non-Christian World*, Edinburgh House Press, London, 1938, pp. 223, 353, 142.

47 Cragg, Kenneth, art. '"Greater is God", Contemporary takbir: Muslim and Christian' in *The Muslim World* 71:1 (January 1981), p. 35; cf. Cragg, *Muhammad and the Christian*, p. 131f.

assumption of political power. Despite the vigour of its protest the Party of 'Ali has had to cope with tragedy and failure throughout Muslim history.

The last quotation indicates that Cragg's fundamental concern is not to denigrate Islam, but rather to explore the intrinsic problem of all religion, what he once called 'the pride and perjury of all religion, its inherent vocation to possess and serve the absolute, and its inevitable temptation to forget that the absolute is not itself.' [*Event*, p. 37] 'Precisely because faiths have to do with ultimacy they falsely locate it in themselves.' [*Christ*, p. 86] That forgetting, or confusion of priorities, is a consistent theme throughout his writing, and is often associated with a particular quotation from T S Eliot's *Murder in the Cathedral*:

> Servant of God has chance of greater sin …
> For those who serve the greater cause may make the cause
> serve them,
> Still doing right: and striving with political men
> May make that cause political.[48]
> [*Sandals*, p. 100, *Other*, p. 110, *Suicide*, p. 59]

It is not, as might be supposed from the argument of the preceding section, that Cragg espouses a political quietism and regards the world of public affairs as necessarily contaminating. Some Sufi and other mystics may have adopted such a line of thought, but Cragg is not of them, and indeed writes little about them. The focus of his thought is rather—as we have noted before—the authenticity of worship, and therefore the perils that attend it, and the imminence of idolatry at all times. This is not a Kraemerian theme. True worship Cragg finds most threatened not by the refusal to worship but by false worship, by 'the treachery of the pseudo-faithful. *Corruptio optimi pessima*.' [*Other*, p. 110] As he continues writing it seems that he finds the focus of that treachery increasingly in the attempt to ensure valid worship in the community through the use of political power, with all the sanctions of violence and the need for compromise that goes with it. Above all it is this question of the morality of the collective which continually recurs in his later writing, and he shows a keen perception of Qur'anic passages concerning it and a particular fondness for writers who themselves reflect an awareness of it—men like Fazlur Rahman, Hasan Askari, Kamil Husain and Najib Mahfuz in Islam

48 *Ibid.*, p. 33.

(all of them subjects of *The Pen and the Faith*, itself a book on Qur'anic exposition), and others like Martin Buber and Abraham Heschel among Jewish writers. The Qur'an itself indicates its concern with the problem in the struggle against the hypocrites *(munafiqun)* and the desert Arabs who, as the Qur'an says, submitted to Islam but did not believe. [49:14, cf. *Event*, p. 155]

Kamil Husain provided Cragg's great discovery of a Muslim writer who did not deviate from Islamic orthodoxy, and yet was able to delve imaginatively not only into the events of Good Friday, but thereby also into the complexities and moral evasions characteristic of political power acting in custody of truth and innocence. As Cragg understands Husain's *Qaryah Zalimah*, which he translated into English as *City of Wrong*:

> It is in the circumstances of the Friday when the world, epitomised in Jerusalem under Caiaphas and Pilate, was in the throes of its moral encounter with truth and right, embodied in Jesus of Nazareth, that the writer finds the heart occasion and the essential core of his theme.

Quoting Buber's *Between Man and Man* he describes the latter as expressing 'the same disquiet about the collective as man's all too frequent plea to justify wrong.' [*City*, p. xiv]

There is no doubt that this theme is powerfully expressed in Husain's book. The Mufti of Jerusalem is made to sound Cragg's own warning against *Islamu akbar*:

> I shall give no more fatwas from now on. They have misconstrued the ones I gave and seek by them to murder a man whose death my conscience cannot approve ... I do not wish to be a deceiver of the people or be on their behalf a guarantor of particular ideas ... When men of religion adopt the attitudes of politicians it is because they have set politics above religion, or rather the politics of religion above religion itself. And that is manifest error. [*Ibid.*, pp. 33, 34]

The final phrase, as Cragg points out in a footnote, is very familiar from the Qur'an (*fi dalalin mubinin*—found in 3:164, 6:74, 7:60 and some thirty other passages), and refers to 'the state of unbelief and idolatry preceding Islam', but is here extended 'to cover the vagaries and obtuseness of men of the true faith and even of the very custodians of orthodoxy'. [*Ibid.*, p. 214]

Elsewhere Husain indicates that his own interest in the story as he understands it is also, even equally, the uncertainty and vacillation of Jesus' disciples on the question of whether to attempt to rescue him from the hands of his captors—an attempt which he himself has forbidden them to make. In an appendix Husain outlines his theory, suggested by Freud's *Moses and Monotheism*, that religious groups are powerfully influenced by some formative event in the life of their community, as the Jews were by the event of the Exodus, and the Muslims by the battle of Badr.[49] For Christians he identifies the key event in the failure of the disciples to rescue Jesus despite Jesus' prohibition. In a long debate on the matter between the disciples the two themes of the book come together. One disciple is opposed to the use of force in any rescue attempt, and argues that religion has to do with limits and prohibitions which must be observed. Another answers:

> —'This notion of yours is weak to the point of near treachery. It is open to such vacillation that it is almost stupid. Would not a successful outcome for us be also the victory of religion? What then is the point of your impeding a religious victory in the name of religion?'
> —'I have no desire to perpetrate a crime for the sake of making religion secure. Religion has a Lord Who is well able to secure it, and has no need to require a transgression on my part in the worthy cause. Such fantasies are the product of the feeble in faith who are half-baked in their religiosity.'
> —'God makes us factors in the execution of His will. It is up to us to guard jealously the security of religion ... Of course it is permissible to depart from religious principles for the sake of defending religion itself. There is, for example, no alternative but to destroy false belief by death, if such false belief is seditious. Sedition is a worse evil than killing.' [*City*, pp. 108, 109]

49 Kenneth Cragg, 'The Exodus: an Egyptian View' (tr. with an intro. from Md Kamil Husain in *The Muslim World* 49:1 [January 1959]).

The last sentence is a direct quotation from surah 2:191 *(wa'l-fitnah ashaddu min al-qatl)*, and can be answered by the other disciple only in terms of the uncertainty of proving heresy compared with the certainty that 'murder is a definite transgression of religion which no exegesis can sustain.' Cragg confessed himself puzzled by the emphasis Husain puts on the inability or failure of the disciples to rescue Jesus, and the way he links it with the alleged 'besetting mood of Christianity (as) one of self-reproach and an excessive pre-occupation with the sense of sin.' [*Ibid.*, p. xixf.] Husain himself says that 'The best Christian in his most sublime moments is a sad man.' [*Ibid.*, p. 224] The case against defending religion with force is powerfully put, but Husain seems to retain a certain ambivalence on the point, and in an extensive comment on the nature of conscience remarks that 'the main power of conscience being inhibitive and prohibitive it is mainly a guide to us in avoiding wrong. When it acts excessively it can have a paralysing effect.' [*Ibid.*, p. 222] It appears therefore that, despite a real sympathy with the argument against the disciples rescuing Jesus he concludes that an over-active conscience left them with a paralysis of the will which has marked subsequent Christian character also.

The same ambivalence continues into Husain's later work. In *Qaryah Zalimah* Cragg finds in Husain the recognition that *shirk* can take many forms, and that 'it is possible even for Islam in certain manifestations to displace in men's loyalty the very God to whom it witnesses, if it becomes thereby an end in and unto itself.' [*Ibid.*, p. xviii] In *Al-Wadi Al-Muqaddas*, translated by Cragg as *The Hallowed Valley*, Husain identifies this issue, in more philosophic vein, with the problems of large-scale collectives:

> The greater the numbers of a community the weaker its sense of guidance and the more likely its becoming perverse. The larger a collective the more prone it is to approximate to sheer animal instincts. The laws that govern mass societies are close indeed to those of the jungle. Saints and good men do not differ much from politicians and business men when they act corporately.
>
> It is no easy matter to define one's relationship to the community to which one belongs. In its misguidedness it may impose obligations that are altogether wrong. Being subject to such an order may bring out hidden virtues within a man, such as courage or sincerity or sacrifice. But

> the dictates of the collective may be sound and in that event one's energy in doing what is due may be quite inadequate and one could be parading as sensitivity of conscience a withholding of oneself which is in fact either cowardice or self-interest. People do deceive themselves in ways like these and their judgements become disorganised in a confusion of right and wrong, of truth and error. [*Valley*, pp. 55, 57, 61]

In *Sandals at the Mosque* Cragg had written that 'Plural selves are more prone than private ones to miss the duty of losing themselves in what their selfhood serves.' [*Sandals*, p. 101] He was clearly dissatisfied with Husain's analysis of the obligations of religion and society. As early as 1932 in the West, Reinhold Niebuhr was among the first of those Christian thinkers who questioned the prevalent middle class liberal idealism and advocated a shift to the right in theology and the left in politics.[50] Cragg never shows much sign of adopting a socialist outlook, but his experience of the Palestinian conflict would hardly have encouraged him to emulate Husain's retreat from political engagement, as his books on Israel/Palestine witness. One reviewer regarded *The Hallowed Valley* as 'a work which, at times, seems both to have intrigued and irritated' its translator.[51]

'Maybe,' wrote Cragg of Husain, 'we should understand *The Hallowed Valley*, with his other writings, as a call to quietude.' [*Valley*, p. 7] In spite of twenty years of friendship, there seems in the later book to be a certain distancing on Cragg's part from his previous enthusiasm for the author, an emphasis that 'Dr Husain is hardly to be taken as representative' and that his is 'a unique perspective on a personal Islam'. [*Ibid.*, p. 2] It is true that Husain's 'quietude' extends to an apparent unconcern for the claims to truth of credal statements: 'Creeds are good so long as they correspond to your patterns of thought ... Beliefs may conflict and contradict each other and yet constitute evidence of deep faith.' [*Ibid.*, p. 38] In a criticism that, ironically, some conservative Christians have made of Cragg himself Cragg refers to Husain's

> posture (as) almost unique to himself in what we might perhaps call his nonchalance, his mild 'unassuming

50 Niebuhr, Reinhold, *Moral Man and Immoral Society. A Study in Ethics and Politics*, 1st edn 1932, SCM, London, 1963.

51 Fitzgerald, Michael, review of *The Hallowed Valley* in *Islamochristiana* 5 1979, p. 261.

> assumption' of the case, that does not gird itself for any controversy, in hope to obviate it by intelligent neglect. This irenic temper may be a wise strategy in context, but it can hardly be seen as the end of the road or the limit of the liability. [*Ibid.*, p. 7]

To serve that liability, Cragg felt, it will be necessary to 'deepen the categories; to explore the ultimate sources of evil in the masses and the collectives ... and to strive without dismay for at least a measure of social justice and a proximate compassion in societies as such.' [*Ibid.*, p. 9]

In response, then, to Husain's familiar Islamic characterisation of Christians as unduly preoccupied with evil, Cragg like Kraemer calls for a deeper grappling with the issue.[52] But, unlike Kraemer and many others, he does not charge Islam itself with superficiality— 'This, religiously speaking, rather shallow and superficial religion'[53]—for there is sufficient depth implicit in the call to *islam* and the avoidance of *shirk* if only Muslims can be encouraged to explore it. Husain was on the right lines, but, perhaps to Cragg's eventual disappointment, did not go far enough. Indeed the promise, in Christian terms, of *City of Wrong* in its treatment of the events of Good Friday seems to be plainly nullified by one passage in the later book. Speaking about theological differences between members of different faiths and the dispute between Christians and Muslims over the crucifixion of Jesus, (and somewhat contradicting his earlier remarks about creeds—[cf. *Valley*, p. 38]) Husain writes:

> If it were merely a contention about a historical happening the situation would be easy. People can differ about events without being sharply divided among themselves. The real issue that divides lies in the fact that Christians believe in atonement and redemption ... With us: 'No burden bearer can bear any other's burden.' Thus we cannot find purifying through what we do not believe. And that is what is deeply at stake for us when we deny the crucifixion. [*Ibid.*, p. 76]

But if Husain eventually declined to pursue the issue of Jesus' crucifixion there have been a handful of other Muslims who were prepared

52 Kraemer, *op. cit.*, p. 218.
53 *Ibid.*, p. 219.

to take the question further. Among them was a personal friend of Cragg, Mohamed al-Nuwaihi of Cairo. In an address to a mixed audience of Muslims and Christians in Cairo Cathedral in 1974, Nuwaihi, partly in response to some words of Cragg's own, spoke about 'the sheer beauty and nobility of the idea of redemption, not, indeed, as a literal fact ... but as ... a magnificent and uplifting symbol' of human willingness for self-sacrifice, and went on to speak about the use of the symbol of the Cross in the recent work of Arab poets.[54] Later in the same address, but without linking the two, he went on to interpret surah 36:30—'Ah! Alas for My servants!' *(ya hasratan 'ala 'l-'ibad!)* as expressing God's sorrow and regret over the reception which met all his messengers. Cragg, while questioning Nuwaihi's exegesis, welcomed the alertness to the inner Qur'anic meaning that it demonstrated.[55] Kamil Husain, he must have felt, was not after all destined to be unique among Muslims.

4 God's Omnipotence: The Sacred and the Secular

The questions that remain about Cragg's understanding of Truth and Power in Islam concern the nature of God's omnipotence and what this means for the human handling of the divine demands on human society. In a rare personal confession Cragg, after detailing much common ground with Islam, admits that 'Broadly my discomfort about the Qur'an is its view of divine omnipotence.'[56] Much of his argument turns on the divine involvement with humanity to which God has committed himself by the very logic of creation, the *kenosis* (or freely-willed divine self-limitation) implicit in it by the decision to let human beings be free either to offer their *islam* to God or to withhold it. We have already seen how this theme is developed in his writing. The implications of this understanding, however, are crucial for his attitude to Islam. Rejecting the dictum of Dorothee Soelle that 'There is no way to combine omnipotence with love,' Cragg asks if there is not to be found 'a more resourceful divine response' to the problems of human recalcitrance and evil than the threats and warnings of judgement to come. He sees, of course, such a response as involving

54 Al-Nowaihi, Md, 'The Religion of Islam. A Presentation to Christians' in *The International Review of Mission* 65:258 (April 1976), pp. 218, 221.

55 Cragg, 'Tadabbur al-Qur'an', p. 191f.

56 Cragg, art. 'Being Christian and Being Muslim: a Personal Debate' in *Religion* 10 (Autumn 1980), pp. 202, 200, 204ff.

the participation of the human in Jesus, and indeed, if Muslims would see it properly, in a different way in Muhammad also. For Muslims this would be limiting God, but 'The Christian Gospel sees almightiness precisely where Islam excludes it.'[57]

Asking then if the whole question may be said to 'matter', since Kamil Husain, for one, would reckon that the significance of creeds lies in the purified lives of those who hold them, Cragg answers with what appears to be his final judgement on Islam.

> If we have an ultimately repressive theism, we shall have repressive society. It matters what is transcendently enthroned ... And Islam has been the most power-assured of all faiths, the most frank and uninhibited in its confidence that state and law and rule can effectuate genuine religion. Its calendar dates, significantly, not from a founder's birth, nor from a Book's being mediated into time, but from a state's inauguration.[58]

It is worth noting at this point that Cragg is supported by a historian of Islam. A K S Lambton, in an article already referred to on the theory of Persian government, claims that

> (Islamic) medieval theory ... because of the absence of a dualism between 'Church' and State, and because of its assumption of perfection and perfectibility in the ruler, led inescapably to despotism ... This in effect meant that the State belonged to the latest despot who usurped it.[59]

In similar manner Cragg roundly rejects the 'perverse pleading' for an absolute 'Islamic' God whose acts need no inquiry and no justification made by R C Zaehner at the end of his life.[60]

---

57 *Ibid.*, p. 205.
58 *Ibid.*, p. 206.
59 Lambton, *op. cit.*, 6 (1956), p. 146.
60 Zaehner, *op. cit.*; cf. Cragg, Kenneth, art. 'How not Islam?' in *Religious Studies* 13:4 (1977), pp. 387-94.

Cragg refuses to commend the inscrutable, as he hears Zaehner doing, or to enthrone repression, which he identifies as the danger of Islam, as of other religious establishments. The question that remains, however, is how Cragg perceives the corporate dimension of human obedience to God's summons within society. In rejecting the 'repressive theism' of Islam has he taken the measure either of the failure of Christian grappling with the same issues, or of the possibility that his understanding of Islam is to some degree 'contaminated' by his Western vantage-point and its economic and political vested interests? Cragg briefly rehearses the latter thesis as developed in the writings of Edward Said, but concludes, with some justice, that vested interests can be found on all sides. [*Call*, p. 196f] On the former issue he is ready to admit the folly of views prevalent in the Christian West in the 1960s, and their 'criminally sanguine' notion of a secular future, views he attempted to rebut at the time in *Christianity in World Perspective.* [*Christ*, p. 85 and n. 17] But since he does not deal with *Shari'ah* in his writings, his response to this issue is mainly theoretical, and centres on the issue of human freedom.

> God and coercion do not belong together … Take the issue of 'sacred' and 'secular'. The 'sacred' has to concede the distinction, and with it the autonomy of human life, or else there is nothing to be 'sanctified'. This autonomy which, distorted, means the 'secular' unhallowed, can only be so hallowed, not by domination but by consent … The more any truth or right is coercive the less it is religious. [*Christ*, p. 90]

But 'there is no separation of realms', for the whole man, personal and political, is made in God's image and responsible to him. So the problem is transcended in the divine patience, or included in the human tragedy. We have yet to see whether this constitutes a proper reckoning with the significance of Islam.

6
CHRISTIAN MISSION TO ISLAM

1 Cragg's Missionary Inheritance

Where does Cragg stand in terms of his missionary inheritance? And how does he understand himself in the flow of that history? Two biographical articles breathe a warm affection for Temple Gairdner (1873-1928) and Constance Padwick (1886-1968), CMS missionaries in Egypt and the Middle East, and the second the biographer of the first.[1] Of Temple Gairdner Cragg's attitude is almost of homage:

> For the present writer it is a work of piety to reflect on a personality whose biography, as almost lyrically written by Constance Padwick, played a large part in his own beginnings and continuing from Oxford to Cairo.

Padwick he knew personally, and corresponded with, having access also to letters she exchanged with Louis Massignon (1883-1962).[2] Her biography of Gairdner was of key importance in providing the 'emotional fire' to Cragg's life as an undergraduate, and her article on the ancient glories of the North African Church he read at a critical moment after his arrival in Beirut.[3]

It was the combination in both these personalities of a long and costly personal engagement with Muslims and their world, and a resolute intention to understand Islam at depth that moved Cragg to admire and

---

1 Cragg, Kenneth, art. 'Temple Gairdner's Legacy' in *International Bulletin of Missionary Research* 5:4 (October 1981), pp. 164-7; art. 'Constance E Padwick 1886-1968' in *The Muslim World* 59:4 (October 1969), pp. 29-39.

2 Cragg, 'Constance E Padwick', pp. 33f., 37.

3 Padwick, Constance, *Temple Gairdner of Cairo*, SPCK, London, 1929; art. 'North African Reverie' in *The International Review of Missions* 27:107 (July 1938), pp. 341-54.

to emulate them. Both spent the major part of their adult lives in the Middle East, attaining formidable competence in Arabic, and both were deeply rooted in the life of the Church. Both had made a significant contribution to Islamic studies, Gairdner in his translation of Ghazzali's *Mishkat al-Anwar*, and Padwick with her *Muslim Devotions. A Study of Prayer-Manuals in Common Use.*[4] It was the Islamic scholar and mentor of Christian missionaries Duncan Black Macdonald (1863-1943) who had urged Gairdner into serious Islamic study. It was Constance Padwick's study of Muslim prayer which seems to have impressed Cragg as 'a gesture of imagination inspired by one faith towards the inner genius of another.'[5] The personal links were crucial in each case, and resulted in a revelation of the inner heart of so much Muslim worship. Here could be seen the instincts of that heart which called for a Christian initiative in response.

We have noted the importance for Cragg of the theological theme and the daily reality of relationships, between God and humanity, and between Christian and Muslim. We have seen too the centrality of worship for him. What Gairdner and particularly Padwick seem to have left with him was the further logical step of Christian 'hospitality' to the worshipping Muslim world, not merely in terms of meeting with people, and so accepting Muslim hospitality, but in the demanding hospitality of the Christian mind to the true intentions, the inner heart of Islam itself. Padwick in particular held together 'the Christian conviction and the Islamic hospitality.'[6] By making the theme of hospitality a key element in his approach to Islam Cragg makes it plain that he is not prepared to follow the dual method of observation while suspending judgement, followed by evaluation according to carefully stated Christian criteria. That would be too much like making God an academic topic, 'a blasphemous, and indeed also a ludicrous impossibility.' [*Sandals*, p. 68]

> It is supposed in some quarters that no faith can be sympathetically studied except in a neutrality, or abeyance, of belief. (Padwick) is a signal disproof of this assumption. All that she wrote, she wrote out of a profound, and missionary,

---

4 Gairdner, W H T tr., *al-Ghazzali's Mishkat al-Anwar*, Royal Asiatic Society, London, 1924; Padwick, Constance, *Muslim Devotions. A Study of Prayer-Manuals in Common Use*, SPCK, London, 1961.

5 Cragg, 'Constance E Padwick', p. 35.

6 *Ibid.*, p. 36; cf. Padwick, Constance, *Call to Istanbul*, Longmans Green, London and New York, 1958.

> commitment to Christ as Christianity receives Him. Yet she attained a patient kinship with Muslim norms and themes and made their world her own.[7]

There is an affective, emotional content to this kind of language which presumes that conviction can relate directly to conviction, without the intermediate *epoche*, the temporary setting aside of personal beliefs so as to enable an allegedly more reliable, because objective and dispassionate, assessment. 'Hospitality' assumes a face-to-face relationship in which both the participants are themselves, sharing a home with others. This is clearly not the language of assessment and evaluation. In fact any cool and distant assessment is forgotten in the encounter, or rather is itself absorbed in an appeal to the other to share the deepest things of heart and mind together. The result is that writing in this vein always becomes a kind of preaching. This may account for the widely divergent estimates of Cragg's books given by different Muslim readers. It is not easy to remain indifferent when the sermon reaches its climax. The hearer is sure to be drawn into either approval or hostility. Nor is the preacher, caught up in his message, primarily concerned to evaluate the precise spiritual condition of his hearers, except as is necessary more effectively to move them in heart and mind to a new realisation of God. And in the execution of that task many possible but needless judgements may safely be left aside. Cragg is not inclined to apologize for this manner of approach, with its uncompromising Christian discipleship:

> It may be that Christian commitment, with its concern for the significance of God and humankind, is a surer context for the study of Islam than the academicism that knows only how to analyze and not how to worship. [*Call*, p. vii]

Consequently Cragg can feel confident that he is not touched by the accusation of an incomplete or inauthentic relationship with Muslims, in which friendships would be based upon the avoidance of controversial topics or corrupted by the attempt to win the other to his Christian cause. If the metaphor of preaching leaves that impression it needs to be balanced again with the theme of hospitality. It is not accidental that in his tribute to her Cragg links Constance Padwick with Louis Massignon,

7 *Ibid.*, p. 35.

for the great French Islamicist claimed to have been converted to an adult Christian faith through the rescuing hospitality of Muslims and the strange influence of the long-dead Sufi martyr al-Hallaj (d. 922). Massignon told Padwick that his first prayer was in Muslim Arabic.[8] Here was a man who used as a daily personal discipline the three prayers of Abraham; for Isaac, representing the Jews, for Ishmael, representing the Muslims, and for Sodom and Gomorrah, whose sin he identified as a failure in hospitality (Genesis 19), representing the Christians.[9] There is no doubt that Massignon felt keenly the historic failure of Christians to offer any kind of hospitality to Muslims, and that both Padwick and Cragg came to share that view. They did not, however, share his very Catholic concept of *badaliyya*, or substitution, whereby Christians offered prayer and received the Mass on behalf of Muslims, so making up in the self-offering of the Church what was lacking in Islam.

Cragg's approach was different, though no less theological in its implications. Hospitality he describes as 'surely the closest of all analogies to the meaning of the Gospel'. [*World*, p. 71] Christian existence he thinks of as a 'divine hospitality within the world'.[10] The language of hospitality is always in his mind: 'Are we not ourselves the guests of God in Christ?'[11] But his reflections take a more inward, and psychological turn. Cragg clearly thought much about the inner dynamic of the emotional life of the Christian representative among other faiths. We saw that theologically he is inclined to trust in the 'proceeding' of the Spirit without attempting to define at all closely how that may be recognised. Ethically, or pastorally, he is inclined to rely in a similar way on 'the reasons of the heart', without waiting for more explicit arguments. Constance Padwick's great collection of Muslim prayer-manuals entailed special qualities of mind and personality to obtain them, because the piety of booksellers sometimes made them unwilling to sell such works to a non-Muslim. Writing of these qualities, Cragg says

> There is the yearning to 'belong' with the other party in genuine openness of soul and reverence of heart, even

8 *Ibid.*, p. 37.

9 Massignon, Louis, *Les Trois Prières d'Abraham*, Guenther, Paris, 1935.

10 Cragg, Kenneth, art. 'Christianity as a World Religion in *N.E.S.T. Theological Review* III:2 (1980), p. 17.

11 Cragg, Kenneth, art. 'The Hinge and the Lock *(an 'ala qulubin aqfaluha)*' Editorial in *The Muslim World* 47:4 (1957), p. 269.

> before the dogmatic prohibitions or communal restraints have been fully handled. The heart has its instincts which may not wait for sanctions it has somehow left behind. Yet within the transaction there is also an abiding loyalty, refined perhaps, but no less secure, because it has ventured beyond its traditional moorings and moved without specific leave from its institutions of authority.[12]

It should not be thought that Cragg, who was after all an Anglican bishop, was careless of authority, or happy for the whim of religion to be indulged wherever it might lead. *Alive to God*, his anthology of Muslim and Christian prayer, has a 55-page introduction in justification of the exercise and of the common worship it anticipates and hopes to serve. If the themes of preaching and hospitality both suggest the unguardedness and emotion of enthusiasm rather than a carefully disciplined approach, there must be added from Cragg's stock vocabulary the metaphor of embassy. To be a 'resident alien' (a phrase which, like 'the kenosis of the Spirit', he attributes to Wheeler-Robinson),[13] is one description of the missionary, and suggests the extensive adjustment of mind and manner required to be at home in a faith not one's own. There is a 'country of the mind' to be explored and inhabited. [*Event*, p. 19] But further, the Christian in that country is in a representative capacity, and must learn to speak the local language so as to be understood. Protesting against the 'strongly domestic accent', the dogmatic Western character of contemporary Christianity, Cragg pleads for

> a much more total, and willing, acceptance of a world perspective ... of continuing cultural pluralism ... and so, in turn, of genuine theological and spiritual 'embassy', representing Christ but in full residential capacity, with credentials that, for all their authority, are subject to local presentation. [*World*, p. 198]

We shall see how the necessity of 'local presentation' can affect ecclesiastical policy, for example towards the administration of baptism to Muslim converts. [*Call*, p. 315f.]

12 Cragg, 'Constance E Padwick', *op. cit.*, p. 36.
13 *Ibid.*, p. 34.

Cragg has gone much further than Paul's original use of the theme of embassy in 2 Corinthians 5:20, though the message of reconciliation remains at the heart of his use of it. For much of his thinking and writing focuses on the resources within the faith and culture where the Christian ambassador is resident. It is these by which the Christian message may be cogently expressed in terms comprehensible to the 'local' people. So an Islamic 'language' becomes available to the Christian missionary whereby he may speak of Christ. Described in this way there is really nothing very new or startling in Cragg's programme, though Christians of the Orthodox Churches would have strong reservations about his ideas about a human, as distinct from a divine *kenosis*. The missionary vocation and method are, of course, instantly recognisable. Cragg himself would argue further that its precedents go back to the New Testament itself, and were practised, if not elucidated, by Paul. One of his chapters in *Christianity in World Perspective* is entitled: 'New Testament Universality: Precedents and Open Questions'. Though there can be no compromise on essentials [*Call*, p. 219], the theme of reconciliation, and the Pauline spirit, are everywhere apparent in Cragg's writing. Writing of the 'harsh world' of Islam, he says

> Yet the harshness has to be transcended, for much of it is well intentioned. And in any event the story to be told is only safe in the custody of those for whom every antagonism is an opportunity. For that, precisely, is the heart of the story itself. [*Ibid.*, p. 164]

It would not be right to suggest that all the influence and learning that Cragg anticipates as a result of this Christian spiritual embassy is to be one way, that only Muslims will change. The introduction to his classic book, *The Call of the Minaret*, makes clear that the book is intended to be a call for Christians, not merely to talk about one for Muslims:

> Its title tells what it would constitute, as well as what it would describe. And the one because of the other. Can we so become aware of Islam as to enter into all its implications for the Christian? [*Ibid.*, p. x]

It is difficult, however, to summarize the full extent of these implications as Cragg sees them. Apart from the necessity for a world perspective which we have already noted, and a willingness to perceive the Spirit 'proceeding' into all kinds of unexpected places beyond the cultural world of the Mediterranean basin, the chief implication for the Christian seems to be a willingness to loosen the rigidity of his doctrinal vocabulary, because the encounter with Islam has led him to a greater depth in the grasp of his own faith, and so to discover a greater inventiveness and flexibility in expressing it. Speaking of the common Muslim belief that Jesus has been improperly 'Hellenised' in the westward expansion of the Church, Cragg asks whether Islam may not 'now be seen as presenting to us in characteristically simple form the perennial question about Jesus?' [*Jesus*, p. 14] Islam presents a radical challenge in its 'alternative Jesus' to conventional Christian categories. But apart from the opportunity for new sympathies, and strenuous thought, does the Christian take anything from Islam for himself, as new? Cragg would probably answer No, if by 'new' is meant anything in contrast, or addition, to the Good News of God in Christ. But we have not thereby gone beyond the reach of the Gospel, for properly understood, all the central themes of Islam, *islam* itself, *shirk* and the rest, are involved in the inner intention of all Godward faiths. [*Christ*, p. 12]

It is clear by now that in directing his approach to Islam under the metaphor of embassy, Cragg intends a mission not merely to Muslims but to Islam, to that country of the mind where he has found such fascination. Here is something new in the missionary inheritance, though Cragg would never claim sole credit for it:

> If there is legitimate point in the distinction between Christian mission to Muslims intending their conversion, and a Christian mission to Islam intending a relevance to its mind and society, it was a distinction hardly operative in Christian awareness in Gairdner's generation.[14]

The distinction, however, was very early in Cragg's mind. He wrote in his thesis of the debt of witness owed by the Christian Church to Islam, a debt which 'may perhaps best be discharged in an attempt to help Islam to a more critical awareness of itself—an objective, which, in turn, may require serious modifications in the evangelistic approach.'[15] As previously

14 Cragg, 'Temple Gairdner's Legacy', *op. cit.*, p. 165.

15 Cragg, 'Islam in the 20th Century.' Unpublished D.Phil. thesis, Oxford University

noted, his aim was to examine contemporary Muslim apologetic writing as Muslims struggled to come to terms with the modern world, and to set it side by side with the equivalent efforts of Christian thinkers over a much longer period of parallel engagement.

> Our study has shown that Muslim reaction to the intellectual summons of the time is still largely in the defensive stage. It must one day pass … into a stage more concerned to unlearn and less to justify, more ready to seek and less to suspect. Such a development is to be anticipated by all that we can deduce from modern religious history in general. As and when that stage arrives, Christianity, already doctrinally and historically qualified, should equip and discipline itself to be also spiritually qualified, as the handmaid of Muslim intellectual activity.[16]

This in sum is what Cragg means by 'the mission to Islam'. It is built on the parallel confidence that 'if Christianity be as it is claimed the tests that time and change impose on any faith will pre-dispose it (Islam) Christwards.'[17] The Church must strive to mediate to Muslims the relevance of its own theological experience in the modern world, in the hope that the necessary realism of apology will achieve from within Islam what controversy conducted by Christians from without had failed to produce, namely, the 'Muslim discovery of Christ'. For 'Islam in Christian minds must always be the object of a policy of hope.'[18]

The hopes of 1950 were refined but not abandoned. Thirty years later Cragg was writing of 'the Islamic reasons for being Christian', and calling for a Christian study of the Qur'an in which we 'maximize legitimately all its deeply pro-Christian emphases.'[19] We should note that in 1950 he reckoned that another fifty years would be required before the 'problems under review' could be assessed in an adequate perspective.[20] Over fifty years later his main concern was that Islam should return to its 'first edition', focusing on the *balagh*/preaching of the pre-*Hijrah* time,

---

1950, pt 1, p. 22.

16 *Ibid.*, pt 2, p. 279.

17 *Ibid.*, pt 1, p. 23.

18 *Ibid.*, pt 1, pp. 562f., 32.

19 Cragg, 'Temple Gairdner's Legacy', p. 166.

20 Cragg, 'Islam in the 20th Century', pt 1, p. 33.

acknowledging the 'absolute priority of the Meccan' period. [*Suicide*, p. 102] In the interim Cragg continued his study of those Muslims who have attempted an apologetic stance to the modern world in such books as *City of Wrong, Counsels in Contemporary Islam, The Theology of Unity, A Passage to France, The Hallowed Valley*, *The Pen and the Faith*, and *Troubled by Truth*. He has made some of their work available to the English-speaking world, including of course English-speaking Muslims, through translation. He has also made a particular study of Muslim prayer and devotional writing, and of the Qur'an, in *Alive to God, The Event of the Qur'an, The Mind of the Qur'an, The Wisdom of the Sufis*, *Readings in the Qur'an, Muhammad in the Qur'an, Am I not your Lord?* and *The Qur'an and the West.* We shall see in greater detail how he has handled this material. Here we need to note the way in which he enables the 'maximizing' of the 'pro-Christian emphases' of the Qur'an and other literature of Islam by avoiding the traditional controversies. In fact it does amount to a form of abeyance, or *epoche*, but without the religious 'neutrality' he finds objectionable in those terms:

> The *I'jaz* of the Qur'an ... is then the form by which Muslim conviction possesses its relevance. The outsider then can take it pragmatically in this way without holding it credally. In doing so he will differ from, and with, orthodoxy, but only about the form in which orthodoxy receives the significance he aims to share and, indeed, to revere. [*Event*, p. 21]

The alert Muslim may want to ask how this differs from the contrasting ways in which Muslims and Christians receive the significance of Christ, and indeed revere *him*. But Cragg's theological aim is not to do away with controversy, but to refine it so that it focuses on the points he believes are ultimately at issue. The old battlegrounds of the status of the Qur'an and of Christ can happily be abandoned for a more fundamental debate about the nature of God and his liability for our salvation. Here he believes himself to be entirely at one with Gairdner, who believed that 'Christian mission had decisive "quarrel" with Islam, which irenic sensitivity must refine but could in no way loyally evade.'[21] The old controversy has then become a 'loyal controversy', loyal to the deepest meaning of Islam itself, loyal to the Gospel, and loyal to the human relationships, including

21 Cragg, 'Temple Gairdner's Legacy', p. 165f.

the Muslim/Christian relationships, which the Gospel entails.[22] For the proper abandonment of the polemics of the past should not mean that we refuse to recognise our solidarity in a much older and more basic dispute still—the controversy that God has with his world. In one place Cragg describes the initial prophetic experience of Muhammad as a realisation that he himself was being commissioned to be an 'agent of the eternal contention of God with the city and its world.' [*Event*, p. 32]

But Cragg generally prefers the more conciliatory language of 'clarification', and especially of 'retrieval'. Writing as editor of *The Muslim World* about Muslim understanding of the death of Christ Cragg maintained that

> the service of this journal is patiently devoted to the tasks and stimulus of such essays in clarification. There is still too much in Islamic disqualification of Christianity which has mistaken both the Christian thing and its own Quranic document.[23]

The theme of 'retrieval' requires a section to itself.

2 The Concept of Retrieval

> The positive implications for the faith of the Christian within Islamic theology are significant and must, at all costs be imaginatively and loyally retrieved.[24]

In the highly revealing article about the 'legacy' of Temple Gairdner, Cragg embodies much of his missionary theology in two seminal sentences. Referring to the 'enmities and asperities' of the nineteenth-century Christian response to Islam, he continues

22 Cragg, Kenneth, art. 'The Christian Church and Islam Today' in *The Muslim World* 42:4 (October 1952), p. 280, 281; cf. '" Greater is God" Contemporary takbir; Muslim and Christian' in *The Muslim World* 71:1 (January 1981), p. 20.

23 Cragg, Kenneth, 'The Days of our Lord *(yawma wulidtu wa yawma amutu wa yawma bu'athu hayyan)*', editorial in *The Muslim World* 50:2 (1960), p. 82.

24 Cragg, Kenneth, art. 'Conversion and Convertibility, with special reference to Muslims' in J R W Stott and R Coote eds, *Down to Earth. Studies in Christianity and Culture*, Hodder, London, 1981, p. 195.

> May it not be a still more authentic relation to Islam of a suffering Christian theology to refuse to concede that Islam is impervious *on its own terms* to the theological relevance of the cross? Have we sufficiently rescued the implications in the firm Quranic doctrine of creation?[25] [emphasis original]

There are at least three concepts of real novelty here, expressed in the phrases 'suffering Christian theology'; 'sufficiently rescued the implications'; and '*on its own terms*'.

The conjunction of 'suffering' and 'theology' is hardly new in Christian thought, but it normally takes some such form as 'a theology *of* suffering'. I think, however, that we can be confident that Cragg is being characteristically deliberate with his words, and means more than this here; that he intended something other, though not less, than a straight objective genitive. Can theology itself be said to suffer—not merely in the conventional sense that some missing element or some incoherence renders it defective (as in 'his theology suffers from … '), but in the sense that it experiences pain and adversity? Cragg, as so often, is extending the boundaries of the English language at this point, and the formulation may appeal or not. It gives an invaluable clue, however, to the character of his intellectual mission to Islam, his pursuit of the relevance of Christian theology to its mind and heart. Not only must Christian theology not be 'secluded' [*Sandals*, p. 21], it must take the full weight of the Islamic understanding of God and the world and its critique of Christianity, and conceding all its force, reach a deeper logic and a profounder analysis of the human situation and God's answer to it. It must 'suffer', as Bushnell taught that God through his Holy Spirit continues to suffer as he indwells us.[26]

Cragg's method can be illustrated by a simple comparison. Many Christians have wanted to argue with what they regard as the severe limitation placed on the significance of Jesus by his Islamic status as a prophet, and books with such titles as *Jesus. A Prophet of Islam* have been answered by others such as *Jesus. More than a Prophet.*[27] Such Christian books are generally silent about the status of Muhammad, to the added resentment of Muslims. Cragg in contrast is prepared to concede the

25 Cragg, 'Temple Gairdner's Legacy', p. 166.

26 Cragg, Kenneth, *Operation Reach* pamphlet series Near East Christian Council Study Program in Islam, Beirut, 1957, no. 1, p. 20.

27 ur-Rahim, Md 'Ata, *Jesus. A Prophet of Islam*, 2nd ed, MWH, London, 1979; Wootton, R W F, *Jesus. More than a Prophet*, IVP, Leicester, 1982.

status of prophet to Muhammad, while asking if prophethood, either on the Christian or the Muslim model, is adequate to achieve what needs to be achieved in relation to 'man's inward remaking'.[*Sandals*, p. 77]

> Take, for example, Jesus' reported phrase about John the Baptist: 'Yea, I say unto you, and more than a prophet.' On Quranic grounds one cannot speak of anything 'more' than prophets in divine dealing with the human world. In the divine education of humanity prophets are all we have and their guidance all we need ... On such an understanding, Jesus' words have a strange ring. For they hint at other dimensions entailed by prophethood itself ... depths of travail and tragedy where behaviour might speak with a deeper eloquence than words. [*Jesus*, p. 27, cf. *Muhammad*, p. 125f.]

In this passage Cragg follows the New Testament correctly in making the phrase 'more than a prophet' refer to John the Baptist, rather than Jesus, but more importantly questions the whole Islamic concept of prophethood, inviting Muslims to a 'radical readiness for new frontiers of thought' about God's provision for the world. It may be argued that Islam does in practice know God as offering more than merely a 'divine *education* of humanity' which is the real target of Cragg's criticism here. Do not millions of Muslims look to Muhammad and the saints for intercession? We must take up Cragg's lacunae in interpreting Islam later. Here we note simply the attempt by Cragg to face the full force of Islam. In so doing he aims to make his theology consonant with the story of travail and tragedy that shapes it, and to arrive at a 'suffering Christian theology', enacting the self-surrender that the faith prescribes even in the arena of its thought about other, rival, interpretations of God and the world. There are close analogies here with a colourful passage in Gairdner's early book *The Reproach of Islam* (1909), quoted by Padwick in her influential biography:

> Why must we for ever renounce all the favourable conditions, giving, like the Scottish King at Flodden, *all* the advantages to the opponent? Why must we strive always up the hill, the wind and the rain for ever driving in our faces; ever, ever conceding, never, never receiving the handicap

> and the odds! ... If Islam's forces are indeed nature, the world and the flesh, then Islam has left us one weapon in taking away all the others—it has abandoned to us the Sword of *the Spirit—The Spirit of Jesus is the only asset of the Church.*[28] [emphasis original]

Cragg undoubtedly believes that by handling themes common to Christianity and Islam in this way he is 'rescuing their implications'. Prophecy, for example, being the forthtelling of the divine word, 'exists to bring and bring home the divine imperative ... ', to instruct and subdue the human mastery over the created order to conform to the pattern God intended. The question, for Cragg, then arises:

> Should there, on prophecy's own showing, be something more than prophecy? Does law, by prohibition and injunction, make good its own intention? Or must there be dimensions to divine sovereignty greater than those of 'education' and 'command'? [*Muhammad*, pp. 125, 126]

This is Cragg's method of retrieval, or the rescue of an ancient and fruitless controversy by initiating, and so requiring a more theological handling of its terms. It may be said that he has merely shifted the ground of the controversy, and that to argue that there should be something more than prophecy 'on prophecy's own showing', is merely tendentious. We must examine the validity of the method shortly, but further examples will serve to clarify the issues involved.

A similar intervention to that on the question of prophethood has produced some movement in the deadlocked argument about the death of Jesus. Berating the 'rather supine' assumption[29] that the Qur'an totally negates the Christian account of the crucifixion, Cragg sets about explaining that, on either New Testament or Qur'anic reckoning, the Jews *intended* to execute Christ and thought that they were doing so. (He does not reckon here with the contemporary claims of some Jewish and Christian scholars that it was the Romans rather than the Jews who were primarily responsible for the death of Jesus.) In both Scriptures, therefore, the human response

28 Padwick, Constance, *Temple Gairdner of Cairo*, p. 184f.; cf. Gairdner, W H T, *The Reproach of Islam*, CMS, London, 1909, pp. 325, 326.

29 Cragg, 'The Days of our Lord', p. 81.

to the Sermon on the Mount and the rest of Jesus' teaching is the intention to crucify the preacher. [*City*, p. xiiif., *Jesus*, p. 167f., and several other places] Moreover, claims Cragg, the very rescue of Jesus from the Cross which the Qur'an is understood to teach, argues his unwillingness to rescue himself by compromise or abandonment of his task, and so his willingness to go through with the suffering it entailed. [*Jesus*, p. 168] Considered then as human will, and as the will of Jesus, the Cross was an actuality.

The question that remains is the will of God, and what historically happened. Some Muslims are prepared to say that this cannot be known. 'Christ,' says the Indian Muslim philosopher Vahiduddin, 'is a mystery which unfolds itself at different levels, and the termination of his earthly career on a fateful Friday in Jerusalem is equally wrapped in mystery.'[30] All these Muslims do, however, firmly reject the Christian doctrine of redemption built upon the event alleged. But this procedure enables Cragg to shift the whole focus of the debate about the Cross away from the logjam of disagreement about what actually happened to the question of what we may expect from God in his active mercy to the world. The discussion about redemption can itself be redeemed from futility by focussing on the reception given to God's message in the person of his messenger, and asking what God may be expected to do about it. Cragg has given away nothing of Christian truth in this procedure. Nor has he pretended there is agreement where there is none. But his concentration on genuine areas of agreement throws into sharper focus the real area of disagreement, and so the 'quarrel' is refined.

These two illustrations give some indication of what is meant by Cragg to be involved in his term 'The Call to Retrieval', which is the title of a critical chapter in his seminal book *The Call of the Minaret.* The rise of Islam was due in part to the failure of the Church in the past:[31]

> a failure in love, in purity, and in fervour, a failure of the spirit … It is for these reasons that the call of the minaret must always seem to Christians a call to retrieval. They yearn to undo the alienation and to make amends for the past by as full a restitution as they can achieve of the Christ

30 Vahiduddin, Syed, *The Islamic Experience in Contemporary Thought*, vol. 3 of C W Troll ed., *Islam in India. Studies and Commentaries*, Chanakya Publications, Delhi, 1986, p. 182; cf. Yusuf 'Ali tr., *The Holy Qur'an*, 1975, commentary on 4:157, 158; Kamil Husain in *City*, p. 222.

31 Cf Gairdner, W H T, *The Reproach of Islam*, p. 53 and *passim*.

> to whom Islam is a stranger … All that the minaret both says and fails to say is included in this call to retrieval as the listening Christian hears it. [*Call*, pp. 219, 220]

The chapter continues with detailed references to what Cragg describes as the Muslim *jahiliyya*/darkness or ignorance about Christ and Christianity, running through such representative Muslim writers as Sayyid Qutb, Muhammad Ali and Muhammad Husain Haykal, as well as outlining the views of the Ahmadiyya, despite their rather unrepresentative character. [*Ibid.*, 221-227] Some would dispute Cragg's use of the word *jahiliyya* at this point, arguing that the gulf between the Jesus of the New Testament and the Jesus of the Qur'an has been much overestimated. So Raïsänen argues, focussing on Luke's account and attacking Cragg's assumption of the inadequacy of the portrait of Jesus in the Qur'an.[32] Again we note Cragg's conservatism in Biblical studies compared to New Testament scholars like Raïsänen. As Cragg sees it, the need for 'retrieval' is made most evident by the Qur'anic picture of Jesus, 'sadly attenuated' and 'emasculated' as he finds it. [*Call*, p. 235] But 'the loss of Christ necessarily argues a delinquent Christianity' [*ibid.*, 236], and there is no problem in finding such a thing, from seventh-century ecclesiastical disputes and poisoned theological controversies, through the Crusades to the corrupting influence of the 'Christian' West on Muslim lands today.

In *The Call of the Minaret* the discussion of Christian and Muslim theology then continues under the heading of 'The Call to Interpretation' (Ch. 10), but that chapter itself begins with the quotation 'Rescue a word … discover a universe', and it seems appropriate to discuss the whole thrust of Cragg's missionary theology under this concept of 'retrieval', complemented with such words as 'rescue' and 'restitution', with which it obviously belongs. For

> let it be clear that the retrieval is not territorial. Christianity is not a territorial expression. The retrieval is spiritual. It aims not to have the map more Christian but Christ more widely known.' [*Ibid.*, 230]

32 Raïsänen, Heikki, art. 'The Portrait of Jesus in the Qur'an: Reflections of a Biblical Scholar' in *The Muslim World* 70:2 (April 1980), p. 122.

> 'There can be no ultimate territorial expression of the Gospel. Rather it creates its own interpenetrating community ... whose badge is the new heart and suffering.' [*Sandals*, p. 37]

The spiritual character of this retrieval is not limited to the correction of the Muslim understanding of Christ, as though what was required was merely a flow of more accurate information in the Muslim world about the true nature of Christianity, and the establishment of better personal and communal relationships between Christians and Muslims, important though that is. Properly understood, retrieval is the task of God himself in relation to the creation which has gone awry. His creation has to be made good, and the work begun in it completed. As Cragg sees it, Islam in its origins was part of that task of restoration, and not an interruption or a subversion of it. So he is able to set aside even the limitations of the Qur'an about Christ, and the 'antagonisms' thus incurred, and plead that the Qur'an should be

> primarily seen as a mission to retrieve idolaters for a true worship ... The living context is Arabian paganism, where prophetic duty must be done, in order that the undivided Lordship may prevail and so *islam* come to pass. [*Event*, pp. 15, 16]

Idolaters must be retrieved, or rescued, and their God-given energies turned to creative use through the right human and divine mastery over them, through *islam*. The problem with historical Islam is that this retrieval has not happened because those energies, become evil, have been fought with their own weapons. Writing about the expectation of Islam for manifest success, Cragg says that

> the evil must be mastered, but mastered in terms other than its own. For these have a way of perpetuating the deeper antipathies and even confirming them. Then there is a toughening, rather than a retrieving, of the inner wrongness. Or the success hypothesis leaves its full task unaccomplished, and perhaps also unknown. [*Ibid.,* p. 174]

This understanding of God's task of retrieval suggests a Christian attempt to retrieve the Qur'an in particular, to 'rescue all its implications', from Christian ignorance and inattention as much as from Muslim misunderstanding. And not merely the Qur'an. We need to pursue, says Cragg, the Qur'anic 'potential towards a New Testament situation.' As we do so, we find that the message of the Qur'an is bound up with the faithfulness of the messenger in proclaiming it. He is 'veritably prophet. To that degree the message becomes the messenger.' [*Christ*, p. 64] Here Cragg has gone way beyond Gairdner, and developed the thinking of Padwick in a Christian recognition of the central figure of Islam, a retrieval of Muhammad for Christian understanding, and, in a measure, admiration. For it was Padwick who wrote: 'No one can estimate the power of Islam as a religion who does not take into account the love at the heart of it for this figure (Muhammad).'[33]

We are now in a better position to understand what Cragg means by saying that we must 'refuse to concede that Islam is impervious *on its own terms* to the theological relevance of the cross'.[34] For Cragg has attempted to take Islam with full seriousness and complete acknowledgement of its primary theological thrust as part of God's retrieval of the world. For Cragg Islam is not essentially a social and political question, or a religious and humanitarian one. Nor is it a problem in the growth of the Church. It is above all a theological issue, at the heart of the *missio Dei*. Being so, its imperviousness in principle cannot be allowed. But to search out its implications and its potential is the task of those called to be partners in God's redemptive activity. Their work may involve concentrating on minority voices within Islam, and those who speak, for example about the Qur'an, 'in other terms than those of traditional belief'. [*Christ*, p. 61] Such voices are vital for the mediation of Christian understanding to Muslim consciousness. Moreover their existence argues what Cragg would describe as a self-correcting mechanism within Islam. Sufism is a case in point. The emergence and endurance of Sufism in spite of all the 'power-assurance' of Islam that militated against it, meant, says Cragg, that it had to 'abandon the formula whereby *Jihad* is externally directed ... That it did so bespeaks the resources of religion to generate their own

33 Padwick, *Muslim Devotions*, p. 145.
34 Cragg, 'Temple Gairdner's Legacy', p. 166.

corrective even from the most unlikely setting.'[35] In a manner reminiscent of Massignon Cragg refers boldly to

> the ways of the Holy Spirit in the fertility of Islam within itself, its capacity to produce from within its own resources the antidote by which its own characteristic ethos could be queried and even transformed.

So early Sufism in particular was 'a conscious response to what we may well call the non-*islam* of institutional Islam.'[36]

It will be questioned whether Cragg is right in his assessment that Sufism was a corrective and not an aberration from institutional Islam, as many, both Christian and Muslim have claimed. Furthermore it may be objected that many Sufis, e.g. the Sanusiyya against the Italian invaders of North Africa, did not at all reject the 'external direction of *jihad*', but carried their mysticism into battle. The larger question of the exploitation of minority and numerically unrepresentative viewpoints from within Islam must occupy us when we consider his criteria of interpretation. Here it may be said simply that his principle of retrieval in a sense bypasses the issue of what is representative or characteristic of Islam in finding a means of Christian affirmation of its theological authenticity.

3 The Mission to Islam in Action

> It is 'the flesh' in St John's sense, that becomes the point of Divine-human translation. Continually then the bearers of the Word must bring their treasure and the ken of men together. Their task is to carry God's meaning into men's minds and hearts, that it may win their wills to obedience. All the resources of the Holy Spirit, working in us humility and fidelity, imagination and zeal, wait upon this task. [*Sandals*, p. 95]

35 Cragg, art. 'Sainthood and Spirituality in Islam' in *Studia Missionalia* 35 (1986), p. 181.

36 Cragg, *ibid.*, pp. 186, 187.

If the mission to Islam is to be conceived in terms of residence, hospitality, embassy and retrieval, what is its final goal? And what are the detailed conditions under which the missioner works, and the intermediate decisions he needs to make along the way? And has Cragg, as some have said, demanded too much of him?

There can be no doubt that Cragg regards the goal of mission to Islam to be a recognition by Muslims of Jesus as the Christ of God, as Christians understand that term. His opening words as editor of *The Muslim World* make the issue quite clear:

> Too long the news of God in Christ has been greeted with incredulity. It is news of God to which, in God's name, minds have been closed. How shall those truths find entrance into hearts where their exclusion has been regarded as a first duty toward the God whom they concern?[37]

The language, it should be noted, is the language of persuasion, almost of courtship, not the military vocabulary so often used in Christian missionary circles. Cragg knows he is dealing with profound theological issues, which can only be taken in their own seriousness. Consequently the ultimacy of Islamic conviction has to be met with a like appeal to what finally matters. Cragg is quite willing to be provocative in order to make the point, by using what for some involved in inter-faith dialogue is the offensive term 'conversionist'. He does not think, as many do, that good relationships between people of different faiths preclude the possibility of and desire for conversion to faith in Christ. 'The Christian gospel is conversionist through and through. The singular Christ (Cragg's context here is Hinduism) requires the soul-seeking Church.' [*Christ*, p. 17] 'The Gospel of Jesus and the Christian faith with it are inherently conversionist. "Except you be converted … " were his words even to those of high religious esteem.' [*Jesus*, p. 10] It is evident that the hospitality which we have already expounded from Cragg's early writings, is 'an ardent hospitality' [*Christ*, p. 17] which, like all love, looks for response, above all in baptism and membership of the family of the Church.

We saw, however, that in his thesis Cragg foresaw 'serious modifications in the evangelistic approach', which would be required

37 Cragg, Kenneth, 'The All-Great … the All-Loving', editorial in *The Muslim World* 43:1 (1953), p. 1f.

because of the Christian attempt 'to help Islam to a more critical awareness of itself.'[38] Perhaps the most far-reaching proposal of this kind is the suggestion at the end of *The Call of the Minaret* that in Muslim society the individual is not necessarily 'the appropriate unit of baptism'. [*Call*, p. 317] While denying neither the costliness of true Christian discipleship nor the right of every new Christian believer to claim baptism, Cragg insists that

> it would be wrong to administer baptism as a seal of individual confession, without regard to how the form was understood in the community we are also calling into discipleship. The baptism of the one cannot be in disconnection with the evangelizing of the many. [*Ibid.*, p. 316]

The point here is that the baptism of Muslims is commonly understood in the Muslim world as a kind of treason, because of the strong national and communal ties associated with Islam. 'Faith,' says Khurshid Ahmad, 'is not just like an overcoat which one may put on and put off as one likes. It is also the foundation of the state. Change of loyalty in faith has implications for loyalty to the state.'[39] Somehow it must be conveyed to the Muslim community that the baptism of one of its members does not rob it of a servant, a friend and a fellow-citizen. What Cragg seems to be advocating here is not secret belief but some kind of catechumenate, or unbaptised probationary status, in which Muslim believers in Christ can share with one another in the new meaning they have found, and fill their continued practice of prayer and fasting with the vitality of that new understanding. This sort of group may become a living answer to the question: 'How can we demonstrate that to become a Christian is to remain responsible in some sense for "Muslim" citizenship?' [*Call*, p. 318]

There is no thought here that less responsibility will devolve upon the Church than in the normal case of converts baptised singly. Cragg rather envisages a closer sharing of the cost. He refers to Paul's discussion about the eating of meat in pagan contexts to suggest that if a liberty of that sort may be properly foregone for the sake of 'the weaker brethren' whose consciences may be scandalised, cannot the same principle apply

38 Cragg, 'Islam in the 20th Century', pt 1, p. 22.

39 Ahmad, Khurshid, contributions passim, *The International Review of Mission* LXV:260 (Oct. 1976), p. 448.

to refraining from urging baptism on new believers so that their brethren in Islam may not be scandalised.

There are a number of complex issues involved here which Cragg does not take up either in the original edition of *The Call of the Minaret* or in the second, revised one. In a footnote he quotes a contrary opinion from Bishop Stephen Neill, writing in 1955 before the publication of his own book, but denies that his proposal is affected by Neill's objections to the encouragement of secret belief. [*Call*, p. 340 n. 8] (Neill had maintained that the record of history showed that secret belief led inevitably to compromise and the still-birth of any Christian movement.[40]) But Cragg does not spell out precisely how he envisages such 'catachumens' remaining within the Muslim community, since their new faith would be in no way concealed. Nor does the enigmatic reference to 'forms of prayer and fasting that will be invaded by new liberty and new meaning' [*Call*, p. 318] make clear whether these are the prescribed forms of Islam continued by the new believers with a different understanding, or whether they will devise new forms for themselves and practise them without Muslims, or perhaps baptised Christians, participating. It seems from later work that he does not envisage them joining in *salat*. 'Christians will not share the ritual … ' He discusses the whole issue briefly in this one later publication, but the only new element is a suggestion of the danger that the demand of baptism might become equivalent to the 'Judaizing' circumcision for Gentiles criticised by Paul in Galatians.[41] Cragg's whole proposal here is tentative, and he seems to be reserving his own final position with phrases like, 'it is argued that … ', 'its advocates insist … ', though we are never told who these people are.

It is curious that Cragg has not developed the discussion which he started in *The Call of the Minaret.* Phil Parshall, an American missionary with long experience in Bangladesh, has taken up many of the issues rehearsed above, and others too, in a book entitled *New Paths in Muslim Evangelism. Evangelical Approaches to Contextualization.* In a chapter called 'Problematic Christian Practices' and under the heading 'Delayed Baptism' Parshall quotes at length from this passage of *The Call of the Minaret,* but he cannot quote any further contributions from Cragg to the debate.[42] Yet Parshall himself refers to many other writings which indicate that this has been a

40 Neill, Stephen, *Christian faith Today*, Penguin, London, 1955, p. 179f.

41 Cragg, 'Conversion and Convertibility', pp. 202, 205f.

42 Parshall, Phil, *New Paths in Muslim Evangelism. Evangelical Approaches to Contextualization*, Baker, Grand Rapids, 1980, p. 192.

most lively and controversial discussion among missionaries, which has raised questions about the use of the term 'Christian', the appropriate day of worship (whether Sunday or Friday in Muslim lands), the need for ordained and salaried ministry, and the nature of the church building, among many other issues.[43]

Some conclusions can, however, be drawn from the brief pages in which Cragg debates the issue. Clearly he rejects the 'baptism at all costs' school of missionary thought, in which converts to Christian faith are regarded as brands plucked from the fire of destruction. What must be done 'at all costs' is rather the retrieval of the Christian implications of Islamic theology.[44] There is something further at stake merely than the salvation of the individual believer. The corollary to this is of course that Islam cannot be viewed as a 'fire of destruction'. Rather, Muslims are also those *'for whom Christ died'* [*Call*, p. 319—emphasis original], though they have not yet recognised the fact. The atonement is universal in its reach, and it is therefore appropriate to consider the effect of baptism upon those who do not receive it. The mission is to the whole community of Islam and not merely to individual Muslims within that community. Human relationships must not be unnecessarily jeopardised for the sake of dogma, when a willingness to remain visibly part of the community could convey the true meaning of that dogma to those in the community inherently suspicious of it. For theology in the end is all about relationships, human beings with one another as well as with God. If asked to substantiate this proposal from the New Testament Cragg would reply that the Pauline passages about eating meat already referred to (1 Corinthians 8, Romans 14) indicated just such a message. Paul also said 'Christ sent me, not to baptize, but to preach'. (1 Corinthians 1:17) [*Ibid.*, p. 316] Another remarkable citation is from Hebrews 11:40:

> Nor must we have too Western an idea of what response to Christ is going to mean for those who hear us. If we have the right to say of the patriarchs, 'They without us shall not be made perfect', surely Easterners have the right to say it to us. [*Call*, p. 320]

---

43 *Ibid.*, pp. 157-97; cf. Parshall, Phil, *The Fortress and the Fire. Jesus Christ and the Challenge of Islam*, Gospel Literature Service, Bombay, 1975, and McCurry, Don ed., *The Gospel and Islam. A 1978 Compendium*, Monrovia, MARC, California, 1979.

44 Cragg, 'Conversion and Convertibility', p. 195.

The connection between Patriarchs and 'Easterners', by whom Cragg must mean Muslims, is unexpected and problematic, though it is obviously suggested by the idea of Islam, like the Old Testament, being a *praeparatio evangelica.* It is not of course an exact parallel unless it is accepted that Christianity is the fulfilment of Islam. However, the plain implication must be that God who has 'provided some better thing for us' is active in the lives of Muslims as he was in the lives of the heroes of Old Testament faith celebrated in the earlier part of Hebrews 11.

What doctrine of the Church and salvation does this imply? Cragg echoes the warning of those who have claimed that the traditional practice of administering isolated, individual baptism is, in the Muslim context, too 'impatient' a way. There is evidence too, that he has feared the 'impatience' of the convert desiring baptism, especially when that convert, as in the case of Daud Rahbar in the spring of 1958, might have served as a highly congenial and influential Muslim partner in dialogue. Recalling the incident Rahbar himself writes that Cragg

> was startled by my request for baptism ... He had started counting on me as a liberal participant in the dialogue between Christians and Muslims. (He said:) 'I was hoping you would take part in the dialogue as a Muslim.' The request for baptism was too sudden for his ears.[45]

The sudden conversion to Christianity of a major Muslim intellectual threw Cragg into momentary confusion, as he himself admits.[46] He was later to refer to Rahbar's spiritual and theological pilgrimage to Christian faith in considerable detail, and with obvious and intense interest, as well as contributing the Foreword to Rahbar's autobiography.[47]

Perhaps his uncertainty in this case, amply resolved later, was whether Rahbar had in fact thought through his proposed step, so that it might be 'not wholly one of abandonment but of deeper fidelity ... Let people, so to speak, persuade themselves that Christ is their own logic.' Cragg's proposals outlined above about delaying baptism for those living in the heart of Muslim communities should not be understood as arguing

45 Rahbar, Daud, *Memories and Meanings*, Boston, privately published 1985, p. 347.

46 In a personal conversation with the present author on 15 October 1986.

47 Cragg, 'Conversion and Convertibility', and foreword to Rahbar, *Memories and Meanings*, pp. i-vi.

an unconcern for the individual, as though the mission to Islam should overtake the spiritual needs of the single Muslim. On the contrary, he is anxious about the self-accusation of treachery to which that convert is liable who has not identified the genuine continuity between his old faith and his new. He may face 'a deep inner feeling of having forsaken one's past and somehow disowned one's community.'[48]

This searching out of the proper continuity between Muslim and Christian faith is a matter of careful exploration, where the head and the heart work together in assessing the new evidence of God's mercy to humanity. Characteristically Cragg calls for patience and hope in a situation where long controversy and inter-communal hostility have made mutual comprehension extremely difficult. Cragg's is a long-term view of the mission to Islam, rather than one which emphasizes the lostness of each Muslim soul and the dire necessity of saving him. A paper for a missionary conference begins typically with the New Testament phrase 'The God of patience and hope …' Yet it would be mistaken to assume that there is no intensity or passion fuelling the cool and even manner. Writing for the same audience of the 'Christian criteria for God' revealed in Jesus, he continues

> But it would be pointless to seek to bring those wondrous predicates of our faith if they did not in truth belong to Allah of Islam. What matters urgently is that they are not yet understood of him. It is that urgency which makes evangelism.[49]

It is important to grasp the turn of the argument here. Evangelism is not merely necessary and important, but urgent. (The title of the conference concerned was 'The 1978 North American Conference on Muslim Evangelization'.) But the reason for its urgency is not the common evangelical assumption of the lostness of Muslim millions, but precisely the kinship and nearness of Muslim thought and experience to that of Christians. 'God, then, the subject of all theology is one.' If that were not the case there would be no point in mission, because there would be

48 Cragg, 'Conversion and Convertibility', pp. 199, 204; Rahbar confirmed having just such feelings in a private meeting in Lahore in 1975.

49 Cragg, art. 'Islamic theology. Limits and Bridges' in McCurry, Don ed., *The Gospel and Islam*, p. 196, 198.

no possibility of conveying meaning where no relevant prior experience or thought existed, and no continuity was possible. This is the heart of Cragg's objection to Kraemer's theme of the 'discontinuity' of the Gospel and other faiths. [*World*, pp. 77-79] It bears close relationship also with his criticism of Islamic doctrines of revelation for assuming that the less a thing is human, the more it is divine.[50]

In Cragg's understanding then, mission depends on the possibility of communication, which itself assumes a relationship, and at least a potential kinship. The urgency of mission lies not in the lostness of unbelievers but in the tragedy of broken and unfulfilled relationships, human beings with one another and with God. Christians have to bear the pain of watching Islam dismiss Bethlehem and Calvary 'as "association" in the sense of idolatry! Here is the tragedy that spurs all our study and must fire all our witness.'[51]

With such thinking informing his whole concept of mission, it is natural that Cragg has felt obliged not to limit himself to enunciating general principles, but to make serious and sustained efforts to spell out the detailed implications of his understanding of Islam and of mission to every kind of Christian disciple. Some scholars have complained that his style of writing demands great effort from the reader: 'This is no bed-time reading … Cragg is just not that easy for most people'; 'His own language is not always easy'; 'His compact sentences demand sustained attention'.[52] Nevertheless he has been at pains to write not only lengthy books and articles in learned periodicals, but also several series of small pamphlets published by the Near East Christian Council (re-formed in 1974 with the addition of the Orthodox churches and in 1990 the Catholic churches as the Middle East Council of Churches), articles in publications intended for the general Christian reader interested in mission, and even occasional contributions at the level of the English parish church magazine, where no kind of previous knowledge of Islam could be assumed. It is in these shorter and more occasional publications that we might expect to find the full implications of his approach revealed

50 Cragg, *Operation Reach*, no. 2, p. 10.

51 *Ibid.*, p. 12.

52 Review of *Sandals at the Mosque* in *Bulletin of the Henry Martyn Institute* (January-March 1960), p. 49; Daniel, Norman, review of *Muhammad and the Christian* and *Jesus and the Muslim* in *The Tablet* 16 August 1986; Fitzmaurice, Redmond, review of *Muhammad and the Christian* in *Newsletter* of the Centre for the Study of Islam, Selly Oak Colleges, no. 11 (May 1984), pp. 46-7.

as he responds to daily events and to the pressures of the Muslim world on its Christian 'resident alien'.

When we turn to these publications, however, we find them unremittingly theological. Willem Bijlefeld regarded *Operation Reach* as 'the best planned attempt in the whole history of Muslim evangelism to equip and prepare a wide range of Christians for communication with Muslims'[53], but it must be said that as much is demanded of the reader in these 32-page pamphlets as from Cragg's full-length books. Much of the material in the 27 double issues of *Operation Reach* was in fact incorporated into later books, particularly *The Dome and the Rock,* whose introduction explains their genesis and raison d'être:

> ... some fifty outlines on Islamic topics ... were an effort after a surer and fuller Christian relationship to the common world of today ... They presuppose the general political and social situation but do not spell it out. Their theme is directly theological and 'religious' ... Thus the reader will find here neither special erudition in the intricacies of the Islamic heritage, nor topical reporting on its current vicissitudes. What he may find is a means of potential discoveries of service in truth and initiative in ministry. [*Dome*, p. 5]

Many of these studies were written during periods of travel, and during a political climate of Nasserite Arab nationalism following the Suez crisis of 1956 which created hazardous conditions for a British traveller. Some of his journeys must have entailed considerable courage. The dedication page of the *Dome of the Rock* speaks of 'much hospitality from Jerusalem round about unto Casablanca, Kano, Khartoum, Calcutta and Istanbul'. The consequence is that at times he is almost completely 'bookless', and unable to give detailed references. More rarely, the dedicated reader is surprised by a delightful (though entirely appropriate) aside, as in one passage on Sufi attempts to deal with the sin of self-preoccupation:

> Just as ordinary mental concentration demands firm control of the senses lest we be distracted, (Some Nigerian youngsters have just been playing soldiers outside the

53 Carman, John B, review of W Bijlefeld, *De Islam als Na-Christelijke Religie* in *Bulletin of the Henry Martyn Institute*, April-June 1960, p. 42.

> window where this is being prepared in Kano.) (But be they exonerated from all its inadequacies.) so in the coming to know God we must abate ourselves. The scholar must be disciplined to one objective study: so the soul.[54]

Despite occasional 'booklessness' Cragg is still able to recommend substantial further reading in advice where interesting personal reaction to other authors on Islam also emerges. Cantwell Smith's *Islam in Modern History* is described as 'an incisive, thorough and brilliant analysis of its theme. Some readers may find the style of writing a little taxing.'[55] *Operation Reach* maintains a steady series of meditations on Christian themes with constant references to Islamic parallels, doctrines, customs and proverbs, which any serious student of Islam would find illuminating. The later series of pamphlets, *Emmaus Furlongs,* the short-lived *The Mind of Christ,* and *Grace Cup* generally contain less Islamic material, perhaps because Cragg was not in those years daily immersed in an Islamic society. Political references, no doubt for good reasons, are rare. An exception is the issue of *Grace Cup* which reflects in November 1982 on the 'new Palestinian dispersal both of bodies and of hopes', brought about by the Israeli operation in Lebanon of that summer. One of the questions suggested for discussion at the end of the paper (Cragg's invariable custom) reveals how deeply he felt the tragedy of the total situation:

> 'Great hatred, little room, maimed me at the start,
> I bear, from my mother's womb, a fanatic heart.'
>
> How, in your view, do these words of an Irish poet apply to the legacies of bitterness in the Middle East? What is to be done about such 'maiming from the womb' and 'the fanatic heart'?[56]

So much of Cragg is in those few lines: the love of poetry, the feeling for pathos, the ability to connect diverse situations in the one human tragedy, the academic manner, the sense of hostility and antagonism as

54 Cragg, *Operation Reach*, no. 2, p. 26, no. 3, p. 11.
55 *Ibid.*, no. 3, p. 31.
56 Cragg, *Grace Cup* pamphlet series Farnham, Episcopal Church in Jerusalem and the Middle East 1979-1983, nos 16, 15.

moments of opportunity, the concern with relationship and underlying attitude rather than the details of policy and statecraft.

In general it must be said that these publications demand a considerable grasp of the English language, and a constant, serious and deep engagement with Christian themes and Muslim friends and society if they are to be made real use of. It is not that Cragg is incapable of a lighter touch. He can quote from the lyrics of John Lennon or compile brief biographies of people to be commemorated in an Anglican Calendar for the Episcopal Church in Jerusalem and the Middle East. He can reminisce, reflectively, about the history of the Anglican Church in the Middle East.[57] But he does not embark on attempts at a prophetic interpretation of current events in the Muslim world such as Samuel Zwemer delighted in offering in his editorials in *The Muslim World*.[58] It must be conceded that close comment on political affairs from 1957-1962 (the years of *Operation Reach*) and subsequently could have prevented any wide circulation of the papers and conceivably endangered their recipients. Nevertheless the difficulty which some have experienced in reading Cragg's work must lend substance to the charge that his missionary 'method' demands too much intellectual activity of the ordinary mortal—at least in the form in which it is commonly presented. It frequently happens, as we shall see, that Cragg is not properly understood.

57 *Ibid.*, nos. 17, 10, 19.

58 Lamb, Christopher A, art. 'The Editorials of *The Muslim World* 1911-68' in *The Muslim World* 71:1 (Jan. 1981), pp. 3-26.

7
THE QUESTION OF CRITERIA

1 How the Reviewers see him

Cragg's work has not passed without criticism. It is understandable, though to Cragg no doubt disappointing, that many Muslim reviewers of his books did not take up his central theological concerns but were satisfied to regard his work as simply a more sophisticated attack on Islam than the traditional missionary approach. The Palestinian Muslim scholar and educationist A L Tibawi wrote of *The Dome and the Rock* that:

> A guide for Christian missionary work among Muslims might have been a more appropriate title for this discursive work ... like the rest of this author's contributions, (it) is evidence rather of changed tactics than of changed objectives. Like his more bigoted and less informed predecessors, he still wants to change the Muslim view of Islam as a step to an acceptance not merely of Jesus but of Christ ... Nowhere does he serve his cause less than when he persists in reading Christian meaning into Islamic ideas. Ends justify the means: by 'exploring Islam' he seeks to 'arouse and inform a Muslim discovery of Christ' ... 'Islam has halted at a half-way house', the author says. He hopes to succeed, where centuries of Christian missionary effort have failed, in taking Islam to the end of the road.[1] .

The Pakistani scholar Hamidullah was rather more abrasive in reviewing *The Call of the Minaret*:

---

1 Tibawi, A L, review of *The Dome and the Rock* in *Islamic Quarterly* 12:1, 2 (January, June 1968), p. 120.

> This book gives a new look to Christian polemics against Islam, and presents a sugar-coated pill ... Mr Cragg has judged it necessary to de-Zwemerize the activities of the Hartford Theological Seminary. The method is charming ... The style is rather that of easy classroom talk: the same thing is repeated again and again.[2]

We shall note the criticism of repetitiveness again. At times the hostility of these reviewers leads them to miss Cragg's plain meaning. Hamidullah criticised Cragg for asserting 'that the rigid monotheism of Islam reflects vast expanses of the desert and the majestic sun.' What Cragg actually wrote was: 'Islam was not of desert origin, despite the persisting illusion which calls its rigid monotheism a reflection of desert vastness and the majestic sun.' [*Call*, p. 68] Hamidullah revealed similar misunderstandings of Cragg's meaning on the questions of translations of the Qur'an and Muslim beliefs about the Trinity.[3] In similar vein Isma'il al-Faruqi, reviewing *Alive to God*, stated that Cragg 'falsely accused Islam of Apartheid', of a total unwillingness to be ecumenical in faith. Yet the term does not appear in the passage Faruqi cited, nor did Cragg in this book ever couple the word 'religious' with 'apartheid', though Faruqi called the phrase a 'felicitous' coinage by Cragg.[4] Cragg only used the word 'apartheid' twice in the book.

The most antagonistic reviewer of Cragg's writing is the American Jewish convert to Islam, Maryam Jameelah, a close associate of the neo-conservative Pakistani leader Abu'l-A'la Mawdudi. Jameelah regards Cragg as 'among the most thoughtful missionary scholars of our day', and thinks his books worth 23 pages of refutation in her *Islam and Orientalism*, where he is the second scholar to receive her attention, after Philip Hitti. Others to be dealt with were Goitein, Cantwell Smith, Nadav Safran and Freeland Abbott. Some of her complaints seem difficult to understand except on the assumption of an all embracing hostility to any Christian interpretation of Islam. Thus she alleges that 'the most striking characteristic of Dr Cragg's works is their moral poverty', and refers later to 'the spiritual poverty of

---

2 Hamidullah, M, review of *The Call of the Minaret* in *Islamic Quarterly* 3:3 and 4 (January 1957) p. 245.

3 *Ibid.*, p. 248.

4 al-Faruqi, Isma'il, review of *Alive to God* in *The Journal of Ecumenical Studies* 12:2 (Spring 1975), pp. 266, 265.

these writings.'[5] Elsewhere in her books Muslim scholars are treated with the same criticism, should they be modernist in theology. So the blind Egyptian scholar Taha Husain's autobiography *Al-Ayyam* is referred to as 'a modern Arabic classic overflowing with sentimentality and self-pity', and his book on pre-Islamic poetry is said to allege 'wholesale forgery' by the *'ulama'*.[6] Albert Hourani represents a very different viewpoint on Taha Husain, calling him a 'considerable artist'.[7]

Jameelah is not, therefore, very reliable as a critic, and she seems incapable of understanding one of Cragg's major theses, the distinction between *islam* and Islam.[8] Nevertheless her significance lies in the fact that she can represent the strength of conservative Muslim reaction to Cragg, and the scale of the antipathy to be overcome from certain Islamic quarters. Cragg has not succeeded in communicating to this custodial mind. Jameelah has in addition two criticisms of Cragg which need to be taken seriously. The first relates to the vexed question of the interpretation of history. Writing of the ills of Christian history Jameelah says:

> Dr Cragg thinks that merely to condemn such events as the Crusades as fundamentally un-Christian is sufficient to disentangle himself from any responsibility for them. He does not seem to appreciate the fact that these evils were merely the natural fruits of the tree ... Since Christianity has ... had nothing but contempt for the religious law as spiritually useless, this means that there is no divine guidance for the Christian in his collective life, therefore politics ... (etc.) are guided by opportunism and expediency.[9]

As the point is expressed it seems at first very unjust to Cragg, who spares no effort to acknowledge the Crusades as 'a piece of Christian history unworthy of the name and treasonable to the cause of Christ.'[*Call*, p. 238] He rebukes any 'attitude of superior criticism of the Crusaders', and calls on Christians to become involved in the 'correction of the past', and the retrieval of its tragic mistakes. His whole theme here is of

5 Jameelah, Maryam, *Islam and Orientalism*, Yusuf Khan, Lahore, 1971, pp. 22, 38.
6 Jameelah, Maryam, *Islam and Modernism*, Yusuf Khan, Lahore, 1968, pp. 140, 141.
7 Hourani, Albert, *Arabic thought in the Liberal Age 1798-1939*, Oxford University Press, London, p. 326.
8 Jameelah, *Islam and Orientalism*, p. 27.
9 *Ibid.*, p. 18f.

retrieval. But a suspicion lingers, because, to use his own words rebuking the Muslim apologists which we have already remarked on: 'We have noted repeatedly the distinction which liberals make between the perfection of Islam and the defection of Muslims. If anything is to be criticised it is the faithful and never the faith.'[10] But is Cragg, and perhaps any committed believer reviewing the history of his own religious community, not open to the same accusation?

In Cragg's case there is an additional complication. We have already seen how Jameelah's fundamental point about the alleged Christian inability to provide guidance for political life was also made by Hamidullah. There we were examining the theological basis from which Cragg works. Here the issue is the way he interprets Islam. Cragg regards Islam as essentially superficial over sin, and content to apply external remedies, identified with the law.

> Does God undertake on behalf of our need no more than the giving of the law which identifies our failure?[11] When … man as he is in his rebellious self-assertion has defied our rules and laws and traditions, is the only answer redoubled exhortation, intensified sermonizing, renewed sanctions of warning and appeals of Paradise? … Must the diagnosis of the wrongness of society always be external? [*Sandals*, pp. 130, 131]

The comparison of any two religious traditions is always likely to proceed with the pure ideals of one's own side being held up in contrast to the shabby realities of the other. Cragg of course is never guilty of anything so crude as that. But there is clearly the danger of a complete mismatch between Christianity and Islam if one is regarded as providing only unavailing, external remedies to human problems while the other is credited with the custody of the true, because inward and spiritual, solution. Since this is very broadly Cragg's position, he does seem to lay himself open to the suggestion that he is judging Islam by its external history but Christianity by its inner spirit. Jameelah herself actually does something very similar, for she sees authentic Islam as constantly being

10 Cragg, Kenneth, *Islam in the 20th Century. The Relevance of Christian Theology and the relation of the Christian Mission to its Problems*, unpublished D.Phil thesis, Oxford University, 1950, pt 1, p. 550.

11 Cragg, Kenneth, editorial in *The Muslim World* 45:3 (1955), p. 218.

rescued from unworthy Muslims by the *mujaddids*/reformers.[12] This is of course part of the pattern of polemic writing, but it is difficult altogether to expunge it from one's work and mind. It seems at least that Cragg has not completely succeeded in doing so.

Jameelah's other criticism is of selectivity in Cragg's choice of representative Muslims. She complains that Kamil Husain, by whom he sets such store, is unknown in the Muslim world outside Egypt, and that he would have been quite unknown to anyone outside his native land if Cragg had not translated his *City of Wrong*. She has a similar complaint that a pamphlet written by Yusuf 'Ali and cited by Cragg had been out of print and unobtainable years before. The complaint about Christian history as opposed to Islamic, and the complaint about selectivity in giving voice to spokesmen for Islam belong, of course, together, and raise in acute form the issue of Cragg's interpretation of Islam. One way of articulating the issue would be to ask: Is Kamil Husain (who can stand here for all the other Muslim authors whom Cragg favours) genuinely representative of Islam? And if he cannot be said to represent the mainstream of opinion in Islam, the custodial mind, can he be thought of as representative of a sensitive, creative minority who remain faithful to the true spirit of Islam? And who is qualified to make such a judgement? The answer to this question takes us into the critical question of inter-faith hermeneutics, which we consider particularly in the next section.

Not all Muslim authors regard Cragg's work in such a critical light. The Indian Muslim quarterly *Islamic Culture* has carried a number of appreciative reviews of his books. One by Asaf A A Fyzee, about Cragg's *The House of Islam* (part of a series on different religions), judged that 'No better man could be selected to deal with Islam in the English speaking world; and the result is a very perceptive and thought-provoking volume.'[13] It is worth noting that Maryam Jameelah selects Asaf Fyzee as one of her targets for attack in her *Islam and Modernism*.[14] Syed Vahiduddin, one of the principal reviewers for *Islamic* Culture, reckoned that Cragg's books.

> are marked by a sincere attempt to understand the spiritual content of Islam. His views need not always be ours and

12 Jameelah, *Islam and Orientalism*, p. 19.

13 Fyzee, Asaf A A, review of *The House of Islam* in *Islamic Culture* 50:1 (January 1976), p. 48.

14 Jameelah, *Islam and Modernism*, pp. 75-83.

> we have sometimes differed from him on his interpretation of certain specific aspects of Islam. But whatever he says deserves to be heard with respect and to be thought about.[15]

Vahiduddin is an Indian Muslim philosopher trained in Germany, and, unlike many of Cragg's other Muslim critics, is fully competent linguistically, theologically and especially philosophically to assess his work. His family has strong links with Sufism. His own writings, moreover, reveal several important points of agreement with Cragg. He shares, it seems, at least one of Cragg's deepest convictions about Islam, that it lacks any real contemporary theology. In spite of the traditional Muslim unease about theology's association with philosophy, Vahiduddin is prepared to say that 'In fact there is no living Islamic theology today at all.' On *The Event of the Qur'an* he wrote: 'Works such as these have an importance for Muslims which they cannot overestimate. They may at last shake them in their dogmatic complacency and force them to develop a critical self-awareness which has been sadly lacking hitherto.' He believes Muslims would benefit by taking a keen interest in the ferment of Christian theology—precisely Cragg's argument in the thesis. He also has a serious place for suffering in his understanding of theology, and though remaining Islamically orthodox about the death of Christ, writes:

> What greater ignominy and disgrace could there be than which Christ suffered. But here it is that Christ appears in all His glory, and the world and all that it stands for is exposed in all its vanity ... What strikes me most, is not the suffering through which he passes but his triumph through suffering.

With this he shares something of Cragg's own misgivings about argument in which religious truth is regarded as confirmed by worldly success:

> Success in history is by no means a decisive criterion for judging events. It is rather modern man, whose ultimate concern is earthly success, who places a disproportionate emphasis on history as a judge of events.[16]

---

15 Vahiduddin, Syed, review of *The Wisdom of the Sufis* in *Islamic Culture* 51:1 (January 1977), p. 70.

16 Vahiduddin, Syed, review of *The Privilege of Man* in *Islamic Culture* 44:1 (January

With such evident common ground between himself and Cragg, the criticisms Vahiduddin makes of Cragg are all the more telling. '*The Mind of the Qur'an*,' he says:

> has all the qualities and limitations of the writer's earlier works. Eloquent in exposition, rich in information and clever in argument as the distinguished scholar is, he is often tempted to oversimplify issues and become unnecessarily repetitive in his critical observations. However, even though one may disagree with his conclusions and feel unhappy at his approach to the Qur'an situation it is still a joy to read his elegantly written works.

Vahiduddin finds both repetitiveness and oversimplification in the treatment of Islamic 'militancy', which he believes Cragg allows to overshadow everything else in 'the personal religion as envisaged in the Qur'an.' Vahiduddin is provoked to ask: 'Is it really so exceptionally Qur'anic to think that Truth shall prevail and that adversity must be transitional?' 'Are we given to understand that religion can only be authentic in its sense of failure and God-forsakenness?'[17] Fazlur Rahman made a similar complaint that Western writers seemed incapable of understanding why Muhammad attacked the Meccans by force.

> They say they fail to understand the Prophet at this juncture: how can a preacher become pugnacious? We must confess we fail to understand this failure, prejudice apart, except on the hypothesis that so addicted are these writers to pathetic tales of sorrow, failure, frustration and crucifixion that the very idea of success in this sphere seems to them abhorrent.[18]

Vahiduddin felt that in introductory material like *Islam and the*

1970), p. 66; review of *The Event of the Qur'an* in *Islamic Culture* 47:2 (April 1973), p. 178; *The Islamic Experience in Contemporary Thought*, Vol. 3 of C W Troll ed., *Islam in India. Studies and Commentaries*, Chanakya Publications, Delhi, 1986, pp. 59, 185, 63.

17 Vahiduddin, Syed, review of *The Mind of the Qur'an* in *Islamic Culture* 48:1 (January 1974), p. 62; review of *The Event of the Qur'an*, p. 177; review of *Islam and the Muslim* in *Islamic Culture* 54:4 (October 1980), p. 244.

18 Fazlur Rahman, *Islam*, 2nd edn, University of Chicago Press, Chicago, 1979, p. 19.

Muslim Cragg's assumptions about the Prophet's 'quest for success' was allowed to falsify his account of the origins of Shi'ism, just as his books on the Qur'an were dominated by the sense of the failure of the Qur'an to reckon with the tragic quality in humanity. He is uneasy too with Cragg's handling of the theme of forgiveness and how the 'divine response is in no way pledged' in Islam, and the contention that in Islam no comparison may be allowed between human and divine forgiveness. Vahiduddin finds this seriously oversimplified, ignoring the theological and metaphysical problems involved. Cragg's demands on God in terms of liability for humanity, and human power to 'impugn God' call forth the term 'Promethean' from Vahiduddin:

> However Promethean a man may aspire to be, he must not forget the dust he is in his alienation from his source … How has then the awareness of Man's tragic quality suddenly left our writer and a 'pagan' sense of man's defiance taken hold of him?

He is clearly uneasy that Cragg in *The Privilege of Man* is tempted to give too much ground before the 'secularist onslaught', and contrasts him unfavourably in this respect with Catholic thinkers, though he does not develop the comparison in detail.[19]

The most extensive Muslim critique of Cragg has come from the philosopher Shabbir Akhtar (b.1960), the author among other writings of a book on *Paul's Letter to the Galatians*. In his *Islam as Political Religion: The Future of an Imperial Faith* (2011) Akhtar devotes some 36 pages to Cragg, concentrating his fire mainly on Cragg's *Muhammad and the Christian,* and *Jesus and the Muslim.* This is in itself an impressive tribute to Cragg, that Akhtar finds him worth so much attention, and in a measure, praise. To come to a proper assessment of Muhammad, he writes,

> we must command intellectual patience, inter-faith courtesy and skills of conceptual analysis. These virtues are partly present in the work of the Anglican missionary-scholar and Arabist Kenneth Cragg … His provocative but courteous

---

19 Vahiduddin, review of *Islam and the Muslim*, p. 244; review of *The Mind of the Qur'an*, pp. 59, 60-1; review of *The Privilege of Man*, p. 67f.

> criticisms enable us to sketch the contours of Islam as a politically aware religion.[20]

He acknowledges that Cragg's critique of Islam is 'largely didactic and objective, not polemical or propagandist', but like Fazlur Rahman, Vahiduddin and other Muslims he rejects Cragg's contention that Medina and all it stood for in the victorious use of force was an abandonment of the prophetic vocation. For Akhtar Islam is 'an ineradicably political faith', and 'Muhammad's career began and ended as a political tale.'[21] He dismisses Cragg's 'wistful Christian musings' as 'irresponsibly pious', and alleges that:

> Cragg wants to Christianize Islam by introducing accents of pathos and tragedy so that Muslims became more reflective in their piety and less hasty in their militancy. Thus he wants Muslims to develop their minimalist theology, not their extensive jurisprudence … A more Christianized Islam would be a liberal Islam which the West can accommodate and one which would not, presumably, threaten Western political hegemony and economic interests.[22]

His fundamental charge is that 'Cragg presents us with a false dichotomy between spiritual authenticity and political success … If a cause must fail in order to be authentic, only then is Cragg right to accuse Muhammad, the successful politician, of unpardonable compromise.'[23] Neither Shi'ism, nor faiths such as Sikhism under Guru Gobind Singh, nor 'self-respecting Christian nations' have renounced the use of force when it could serve their ends. The unpopularity of the pacifist ideal cannot be regarded 'as a sign of its supposed nobility. Muslims reject the view that impracticality and widespread lack of appeal are the hallmarks of genuinely religious ideals.'[24]

Akhtar's characteristic Muslim views are presented with particular skill and cogency, and together with those of Vahiduddin offer us shrewd

20 Akhtar, Shabbir, *Islam as Political Religion: The Future of an Imperial Faith*, Routledge, London, 2011, pp. 88, 89.
21 *Ibid.*, pp. 89, 99.
22 *Ibid.*, p. 108.
23 *Ibid.*, p. 114.
24 *Ibid.*, p. 112.

and perceptive criticisms, some of which we have anticipated earlier in this work, and some which must be taken up in a final assessment of Cragg later. But it is interesting that Vahiduddin makes no mention of 'Christianising' Islam, and Akhtar does only briefly. Tibawi, as we saw, seemed angered that Cragg 'persists in reading Christian meaning into Islamic ideas.' Others, Christians like Marshall Hodgson and Charles J Adams among them, have made similar criticisms. Hodgson, from a Quaker background, acknowledges both the value and the problems posed by scholastic pre-commitment, but is essentially opposed to the approach taken by the apologists to another faith. 'A view of Islam as a Christianity manqué, or the reverse, however elegantly formulated, must be received with great scepticism.'[25] He seems to be saying that faiths are simply different. In a similar way Henry Victor has said that 'the quest of Cragg is a quest for Christian Islamics rather than for the Islam of the people who are Muslims.'[26] Cragg has felt bound to reply to the accusation. [*Muhammad*, p. 12] Accused of failing to respect the genuine 'otherness' and autonomy of Islam, he responds with the conviction that the differences between faiths exist within a human race which is essentially the same. Christian witness must demonstrate 'the utmost respect for such autonomy. But it will also be a refusal to allow that the autonomies of religions have other than one humanity.'

> It is one thing—a necessary one—to avoid 'Christianizing' what is properly and vigorously distinctive in Islam. It is another to conclude that, therefore, the disparate faiths are incommunicado … Doing so would effectively terminate all relationship. Each would then be left in impenetrable self-congratulation or delusion. [*Ibid.,* pp. 123, 12, 13]

This seems to be very much Vahiduddin's own view, and though he notes in his reviews of Cragg's books that at times there is a certain failure in 'methodological detachment from (his) own tradition', he is not threatened or surprised by it, because each person has to make his own response to the demands he perceives from God on his understanding and obedience.

---

25 Hodgson, Marshall, *The Venture of Islam*, 3 vols, University of Chicago Press, Chicago, 1974, p. 29.

26 Victor, Henry, 'A Critique of Kenneth Cragg's Response to Muslims', unpublished MTh thesis, Serampore University, 1984, p. 13.

> The Christian accent which is discernible everywhere does not detract in any way from the value of his contribution, but rather enhances it as the authentic expression of a profound personal commitment.[27]

If Muslims are divided about whether Cragg 'Christianises' Islam, so too are Christians. The Iranian (and former Muslim) bishop, H B Dehqani-Tafti, made a vigorous defence of Cragg from the charge.[28] For Norman Daniel 'he is merely quicker than most to recognise (usually across the barrier of unfamiliar concepts) the real points of resemblance, often in unexpected places.'[29] Since Daniel's seminal work was in the documentation of Christian misunderstanding and defamation of Islam, this is a considerable tribute. But has Daniel been led astray by his appreciation of Cragg's determination to speak positively and not negatively about Islam? Albert Hourani, reviewing *Sandals at the Mosque,* felt that 'From sheer desire to be fair, to put the case for Islam at its strongest, he does sometimes seem to come near to reading Christian meanings into Islamic concepts.' 'Is there room', asks Hourani doubtfully, 'for ... an ideal Islam which has a Christian soul but nevertheless is not Christianity?'[30] Cragg has no doubts:

> It may happen that the Christian endeavour to understand Islam to the full will result in Christian expositions of Islam that many actual Muslims would not recognize as familiar ... But there is nothing surprising in this possibility: nor inappropriate. To see anything through Christian eyes is to see it in the light of Christ, and from the standpoint of 'the God of hope' revealed in Christ. [*Sandals*, p. 90]

Bijlefeld, quoting this, calls it 'one of those stimulating and provoking passages in Kenneth Cragg's writings, a passage which immediately appeals to some as much as it antagonizes others.' He does not tell us

27 Vahiduddin, review of *The Event of the Qur'an*, p. 177; review of *The Privilege of Man*, p. 68.
28 Dehqani-Tafti, H B, review of *The Dome and the Rock* in *The International Review of Missions* 54 (April 1965), p. 209.
29 Daniel, Norman, review of *Muhammad and the Christian* and *Jesus and the Muslim* in *The Tablet* 16 August 1986.
30 Hourani, Albert, 'Christians and Muslims' in *Frontier* 3:2 (Summer 1960), p. 129.

his own reaction, but Cragg clearly does not fall into the category of the unreflecting 'Christianisers of Islam' cited in Bijlefeld's article.[31] But neither Bijlefeld nor Cragg explore in any depth the question of how one judges when a Christian exposition of Islam *is* inappropriate. Cragg simply says: 'What matters is that the exposition should be seen on reflection to have conveyed a true picture.' [*Sandals*, p. 90] But the question of who is qualified to reflect accurately remains.

We have already raised the question of the separation, which Cragg appears to reject, of 'scientific' observation of the life and texts of another faith, from the theological evaluation of it. If we concentrate on the textual study alone, leaving aside the history and contemporary life for the moment, it may be that certain discussions in another academic discipline will help to throw the issues into sharper focus.

2 Techniques of Interpretation

The criticism of 'Christianising' Islam is a crucial issue in any assessment of Cragg's work, but few of those who have voiced it have explained in any detail what they mean. It is also noticeable that his critics contradict each other in the way they frame the accusation. Muslims criticising Cragg for 'Christianising' Islam generally accuse him of a fundamental lack of sympathy for Islam and of attacking it on unreasonable grounds.[32] Christians criticising Cragg for 'Christianising' Islam, on the contrary, tend to accuse him of an unrealistically sympathetic account of it which does not do justice to its real difference from Christianity.[33] The latter is the view of Harry Partin, who, in his review of *Christianity in World Perspective,* was unusually explicit about what he meant by the term 'Christianising':

> This reviewer has the uneasy feeling that Dr Cragg gives a somewhat Christianized reading of other religious faiths. In other words, that the author's view of the 'core of their seriousness' is not necessarily that of adherents of the religious community. This suggests that one ought more

31 Bijlefeld, Wim, art. 'The Danger of "Christianizing" our Partners in Dialogue' in *The Muslim World* 57:3 (July 1967), p. 174.

32 For example, Tibawi, review of *The Dome and the Rock*, p. 120.

33 For example, Victor, 'A Critique of Kenneth Cragg's Response to Muslims', p. 17.

> properly to begin with Jewish, Muslim, etc, expressions of religious self-understanding. If one proceeds as Cragg does he is able, having formulated 'Christian' questions in interpreting the religions, to give Christian 'answers'. Does one really 'concede' the other faiths until he has fully granted their distinctiveness? This 'concession' is inhibited by, as it turns out, Cragg's *praeparatio evangelica* position. He writes that:
>
> > *there is truth enough, within Christian premises, in seeing a 'preparation' for Christian faith in the meaning of other religions, provided we see that they have the right not to view it that way, and provided we explore and serve this understanding of ours with a properly sensitive humility.*
>
> One ought to begin with the proviso rather than the proposition, for the latter enables the author to evade the full measure of the dilemma.[34]

The criticism is worth full quotation because it is well formulated and carries potential damage to Cragg's whole enterprise. Zaehner is one who has pointed out that different faiths actually ask different questions and are concerned with different issues.[35] Later, in ideas which resemble Cragg's understanding of the working of the Spirit in other faiths, he spoke of a kind of self-correcting mechanism whereby faiths in their development quietly shed embarrassing elements and borrow or develop new elements for which a need is felt. Judaism and Islam in their 'Semitic transcendentalism' develop a mystical tradition, and Hinduism and Buddhism in their 'Indian immanentism' find room for a social conscience. In an article written at the very end of his life, however, Zaehner seemed to be recommending Islam as a purer monotheism than Christianity, and he and Cragg decisively parted company.[36] The disagreement of these two Christian scholars throws into even sharper relief the real question of how any interpreter of a faith other than his own is to proceed, and indeed, how we understand the process of interpretation itself.

---

34 Partin, Harry B, review of *Christianity in World Perspective* in *The International Review of Mission* 58 (October 1969), p. 333f.

35 Zaehner, R C, *At Sundry Times*, Faber, London, 1958, pp. 16-20.

36 Zaehner, R C, art. 'Religious Truth' in J Hick ed., *Truth and Dialogue in World religions: Conflicting Truth-Claims*, Westminster Press, Philadelphia, 1974, p. 13f; art. 'Why not Islam?' in *Religious Studies* 11:2 (June 1975), pp. 167-79; cf. Cragg, Kenneth, art. 'How not Islam?' in *Religious Studies* 13:4 (1977), pp. 387-94.

Hermeneutical theory, developed as philosophical reflection on the procedures used equally in literature, theology and law, has traditionally spoken of three tasks; the task of understanding, the task of explaining, and the task of applying the interpretation. Some used the terminology of 'subtilitas intelligendi, subtilitas explicandi, and subtilitas applicandi', where the 'subtilitas' was a word deliberately used to avoid the suggestion of 'method', since it was rather 'a talent that requires a particular finesse of mind.' Much of what follows here is dependent on Gadamer's book *Truth and Method,* and it has been pointed out that the use of the word 'method' in the title is ironical, since Gadamer's argument is that there is no method which can simply be 'applied' in hermeneutics.[37]

The third task, of application, tends to attract less attention than the other two, in spite of the fact that in both law and theology the purpose of understanding is the application of that understanding to a particular concrete situation. Consequently the interest focussed on the other two tasks has tended to create an artificial distinction between them and to obscure their real inner unity. For as Gadamer and his many followers see it, understanding is not a separate process which is followed, once completed, by explanation, but rather understanding itself begins with an attempt at explanation, which will generally be discarded in favour of a better, because a more satisfying and coherent explanation, accounting for a larger range of phenomena. Hence

> A person who is trying to understand a text is always performing an act of projecting. He projects before himself a meaning for the text as a whole as soon as some initial meaning emerges in the text. Again, the latter emerges only because he is reading the text with particular expectations in regard to a certain meaning.

Gadamer calls this kind of expectation a 'prejudice', attempting to rescue that word from its negative associations and endow it with a more neutral sense. Naturally, however, he is concerned to warn that 'the important thing is to be aware of one's own bias.' 'How', asks Gadamer,

37 Gadamer, Hans-Georg, *Truth and Method*, 2nd edn, Eng. tr., Sheed and Ward, London, 1979, p. 274; Thiselton, Anthony, *The Two Horizons: New Testament Hermeneutics and Philosophical Description with special reference to Heidegger, Bultmann, Gadamer and Wittgenstein*, Paternoster, Exeter, 1980, p. 293.

'can we break the spell of our own fore-meanings?' (or prejudices). His answer seems to be that the problem cannot be solved in advance.

> (The interpreter) is not able to separate in advance the productive prejudices that make understanding possible from the prejudices that hinder understanding and lead to misunderstandings.

Nevertheless Gadamer is clear that interpretation cannot be limited to a reproduction of the original meaning in the historical context in which the text arose.

> Not occasionally only, but always, the meaning of a text goes beyond its author. That is why understanding is not merely a reproductive, but always a productive attitude as well ... (In contrast to the beliefs of the Romantics) Time is no longer primarily a gulf to be bridged, because it separates ... This was, rather, the naive assumption of historicism, namely that we must set ourselves within the spirit of the age, and think with its ideas and its thoughts, not with our own, and thus advance towards historical objectivity. In fact the important thing is to recognise the distance in time as a positive and productive possibility of understanding.[38]

The work of Gadamer, and the thinking of other philosophers like Dilthey, who aimed to understand his author better than he understood himself, and Heidegger, who spoke about the 'word-event' which changed history, obviously carry great significance for the question of Cragg's techniques of interpretation. We begin to see that what appear in analysis to be the two procedures of observing and then evaluating are not necessarily two procedures at all. It is clear therefore that the charge of reading Christian meaning into Islamic concepts is by no means a straightforward issue, if the 'fore-meanings' or 'prejudices' of a particular tradition of thought are inevitably and properly a considerable element in the interpretation of a text. How is any reader supposed to eliminate his own 'fore-meanings' from his understanding of the text? The older, naive understanding of objectivity supposed that only the historical context of the text itself was significant and

38 Gadamer, pp. 236, 238, 237, 263, 264.

not that of the interpreter, and that the latter had only to immerse himself in the data of the text and its world to arrive at its 'objective' meaning. The grappling with those data cannot, indeed, be sidestepped, but theological interpretation, like all hermeneutics, has much more in common with art than with science. As Thiselton says, following (and quoting) Gadamer:

> The work of art can never be reduced to the level of the consciousness of any one individual in history, but always transcends it. For it may yet disclose 'something more' to subsequent generations. 'The experience of art acknowledges that it cannot present the perfect truth of what it experiences in terms of final knowledge … There is … no final exhaustion of what lies in a work of art.'[39]

Gadamer and especially Thiselton's work is focussed on Christian theological language, and does not consider the case of theological language being interpreted outside the community which formulates it or holds it sacred, except in the case of Christian interpretation of the Old Testament. Clearly within the relevant community tradition can act as a filter both to eliminate inappropriate interpretation and to refine what is of permanent value. Is it then a disqualification for interpreting Islam that Cragg does not belong to the community of Islam? If it be judged that it is, then we are faced with a proposition which would disallow the work of almost all Western scholars on Muslim, Hindu or Buddhist traditions, not to mention massive achievements by historians, anthropologists and literary critics.

In the view of hermeneutics developed by Gadamer and Thiselton the distinction characteristic of phenomenological religious studies between understanding and evaluation begins to break down. (Gadamer talks about 'explanation' rather than 'evaluation', but the terms are obviously very closely related in hermeneutics.) A third process, that of application, emerges as part of the interpreter's task. All this seems to cohere well with Cragg's own approach, which, as we have seen, rejects the concept of study of another faith 'in a neutrality, or abeyance, of belief', and continually stresses the 'due relationships' to be developed between Christian and Muslim individuals and communities. Few, perhaps, have done more in the attempt to 'apply' a Christian interpretation of Islam. Secondly, Gadamer's analysis (broadly accepted by Thiselton) of

39 Thiselton, p. 296f.

the processes of 'understanding' and 'explanation' seems to legitimate the bringing of Christian questions to Islamic material, at least in the first instance, and until they are shown to be inappropriate. No mind can become a *tabula rasa* on which Islamic data may be imprinted for subsequent explanation or evaluation by external criteria, for the process of understanding simply does not work that way.

Thirdly, if the meaning of a text goes beyond its author, and acquires, as it were, a 'career', as Paul Ricoeur calls it, of its own, then can that career be shaped not only by the religious community which holds the text precious but also by outsiders? If literary criticism is the model here it would seem that the only qualification for the interpreter is a serious engagement with the text itself. Just such an engagement with the text seems to be sought by the very Qur'an: 'Do they not then earnestly seek to understand the Qur'an, or are their hearts locked up by them?' [47:24 cf. *Muhammad* p. 119f.] Such 'permission' to interpret can be strengthened into positive invitation if another insight of Gadamer be developed in a particular way. In his view, the historical distance between the composition of the text and the time of the interpreter is not a liability but an asset, for time reveals more of the meaning of a great work, which is never finally exhausted. Gadamer presupposes a continuity of community among the interpreters, who develop their own tradition. But if historical distance can become an asset in this way, is it possible that a sympathetic outsider to the tradition may also turn that cultural and communal 'distance' into an asset? The practice of Scriptural Reasoning since the mid-1990s suggests that engaging together in close attention to sacred texts by believers of different faiths can bring mutual respect and illumination. Can religious traditions themselves be fostered and refined by those who are not ideologically and existentially committed to the community shaping, and shaped by them? Cragg's contention is that they can.

> The belief of these chapters is that the Qur'an is truly open to more than its formal community of institutional allegiance. Given the quality of sympathy that keeps them always in mind, there may well be a capacity of penetration that is the better for its being the outsider's search. [*Event*, p. 20]

Cragg argues that non-Muslim interpretation of the Qur'an can set aside certain Muslim attitudes and traditions of exegesis which in his opinion 'have in part obscured and impeded its fullest relevance.' *[Ibid.]* But this freedom from the restrictions of Muslim interpretation has to be accompanied by a serious engagement with the text at the heart of the tradition, and a genuine respect for the community which lives by it. 'A scholarship,' says Cragg, 'that exempts itself from the patient toils of due relationships is liable to forfeit in real intellectual achievement what it may attempt in bare analysis.' *[Ibid.]*

Here Cragg is following a well-respected modern hermeneutical insight in emphasizing the significance of the personal and historical context of the interpreter, but how far such 'patient toils' should or can extend will be a matter for much debate. We have already noted a certain impatience with the classical tradition of exegesis on the part of Cragg, and this is echoed in the passage under discussion when he refers to it as 'an intricate and tedious subject.' *[Ibid.]* If Cragg aims to develop and refine the Islamic, here specifically the Qur'anic, tradition by passing it through the filter of a Christian mind, is that filter adequately hospitable to all the potential material, and will the final residue be recognisable as Islam? We have seen that both Muslims and Christians are divided in their judgement. We may also question whether Cragg has been able to abide by his own principles when it comes to faiths and faith-communities other than Islam.

Two warnings also seem to emerge from theoretical studies of hermeneutics. One concerns the temptation to aim at a premature reconciliation, or 'fusion of horizons', between the interpreter and his text. Thiselton quotes Ebeling on the danger as seen by Christians in relation to Biblical studies:

> According to Luther, the word of God always comes as *adversarius noster,* our adversary. It does not simply confirm and strengthen us in what we think we are, and in what we wish to be taken for … This is the way, the only way, in which the word draws us into concord and peace with God.

The text must not merely 'mirror back' the thoughts and attitudes of the interpreter to him. It is arguable that this is actually less of a danger in interpreting a strange text from outside one's own community—e.g. for a Christian reading the Qur'an, or a Muslim reading the Bible—than for the 'native' reading his own text, when its familiarity may suggest to him only ideas already in his mind.

The second warning, drawn especially from the work of Wittgenstein, concerns the danger of developing a private language which is not publicly intelligible, which does not therefore serve the function of language at all. Wittgenstein used the analogy of words for colour to emphasize the necessity of regularity in human speech for mutual intelligibility. 'A child must learn the use of colour words before it can ask for the name of a colour.'[40] The point at issue in hermeneutics is whether terms with a particular history and common use are being used in a special and idiosyncratic way which is not merely novel but actually inaccessible to ordinary readers and listeners. Here Cragg's treatment of Islamic themes may be more vulnerable. We have noted his distaste for fixed dogmatic statements, and we have seen some dissatisfaction with his clarity of expression, though others have delighted in his 'elegantly written works'. But it is time to turn from these general considerations to see whether he does in fact avoid these dangers, and find a valid way of interpreting the 'text' of Islam starting from Christian premises. It is proper to begin with his treatment of the Qur'an.

3 Cragg's Interpretation of the Qur'an

More than in any other faith, interpretation of the foundation document of Islam is central to any understanding of the religious life and thought of Muslims. Cragg calls the intense preoccupation of Muslims with their scripture 'perhaps the largest and most sustained expression of what might be called documentary faith.' [*Event*, p. 13] He is deeply conscious that, in Kraemer's words, 'The foundation of Islam is not, The Word became flesh. It is, The Word became book.' But unlike Kraemer he does not believe that in the Qur'an 'the whole drama of salvation between God and the world … is entirely absent', or that the relation between God and humanity that characterizes Islam is 'strangely eventless'.[41] On the contrary it is precisely the 'event of the Qur'an' in the encounter of Muhammad with his native Arab paganism which gives Cragg the title of a major book on the Qur'an, and impels him to search for the sense of that event for Christians. [*The Event of the Qur'an*, 1971]

40 Thiselton, pp. 319, 379-85, 381.

41 Kraemer, Hendrik, *The Christian Message in a non-Christian World*, Edinburgh House Press, London, 1938, p. 217f., 218f.

The opening pages of the book make clear the intention of his Qur'anic exegesis. He addresses his writing primarily to a Christian, rather than an academic or a Muslim audience, as is made clear by the explanation of 'our silence here on Old and New Testament matters'. But unlike some other Christian writers on the Qur'an he intends to examine the 'pagan direction of Muhammad's calling and of the Qur'an' [*Event*, p. 15], in a whole-hearted recognition that the vocation and therefore significance of Muhammad was in the first instance not to Islam's monotheistic precursors Judaism and Christianity, but to the polytheism of Mecca and the Quraish. It was 'a mission to retrieve idolaters for a true worship.' *[Ibid.]* So the age-old controversy between Islam and Christianity is not here in mind. Rather there is a definite assurance of 'the deep relevance of the Qur'an to contemporary man ... Our purpose is to take the measure, in its own context, of a phenomenon which bears urgently upon our own age.' [*Ibid.,* p. 16] The Qur'an is religiously significant for the contemporary world irrespective of its relationship with the Biblical record, and even apart from its current meaning for the lives of Muslims.

The intention of Cragg then is to take the Qur'an in its own significance, 'to reflect on the book within itself and assemble its own implications about the nature of what happened in its genesis as a religious experience'. [*Ibid.*, p. 18] If Cragg is accused of reading Christian meanings into the Qur'an, he is certainly not guilty of doing so in the style of Basetti-Sani, for whom the 'mother of cities' is Jerusalem rather than Mecca, the 'people of the Book' are rabbis and scribes rather than Jews and Christians, and the Night of Destiny of Surah 97 is Christmas Eve. Cragg and Basetti-Sani may be agreed that the Qur'an records 'the progress of a religious experience', and even that it needs to be read with a 'Christian key', but they differ fundamentally about how that key is to be used. Basetti-Sani's belief is that Islam was intended to be a 'catechumenate for the sons of Ishmael', and that, partly through Christian negligence and hostility, its development was arrested, and there was no-one to help it 'continue on the right path to the house of the Father'. Basetti-Sani's 'Christian key' really involves a view of Islam as a 'Deuteronomic religion', needing 'development and enrichment',[42] not quite a Christian heresy, but only to be properly understood within the framework of the full-blown Catholic faith.

42 Basetti-Sani, Giulio, *The Koran in the Light of Christ: A Christian Interpretation of the Sacred Book of Islam*, Franciscan Herald Press, Chicago, 1977, pp. 120, 139, 153, 27, 36, 32, 30.

Basetti-Sani's approach to Islam is not unique, but rather forms part of a tradition which stretches back into the nineteenth century with scholars like Forster, Carlyle, F D Maurice and Bosworth Smith and continues into this century with those scholars like Asin Palacios and Margaret Smith who saw the origins of Sufism in Christianity. Bijlefeld notes more recent examples in di Matteo and Ledit.[43]

Basetti-Sani's understanding depends upon accepting the Qur'an as revelation: 'Let us suppose that the Koran is actually a revealed book …'[44] Cragg, on the other hand, while fully acknowledging the status of the Qur'an for Muslims, and noting, in a way that Basetti-Sani does not, the way its use shapes their lives, is able to sidestep the issue of the status of the Qur'an for those outside the Islamic community. Whatever the answer to that ontological question, the Qur'an still carries real existential significance as a document addressed to humanity. It is evident here that Cragg has a more developed and discriminating natural theology than either the Reformed theologian Kraemer or the Franciscan Basetti-Sani. The latter seems to have aimed at a Christianising of Islam, or in Gadamer's language, at a 'fusion of horizons' which turns out to be altogether premature, ignoring the proper objectivity of the Qur'anic text.

Cragg handles the Qur'an essentially as literature recording religious experience. Islamic revelation, he says, is fourfold: 'the prophetic, the literary, the political and the spiritual', but there is little doubt that it is religion as art which more than anything engages his attention in the Qur'an. 'Throughout we have to do with revelation as literature and with literature as revelation.' [*Event*, p. 13] In order to demonstrate the parallels he begins the first chapter of *The Event of the Qur'an* with an eight-line quotation from Wordsworth's *Prelude*. He wants to rescue the understanding of Muhammad's call to Prophethood from 'the prose of historians' and 'the terms of dogma', by the provocation of a poet's sensibility to dream and vision. [*Ibid.*, p. 25] Other books begin in similar fashion: *Alive to God* with *Measure for Measure, The Privilege of Man* with Ernest Hemingway, *Christianity in World Perspective* with a Northumberland ballad, and *The Christ and the Faiths* with Wilfred Owen. After a few pages of *The Event of the Qur'an* Henry Vaughan is pressed into service 'to register

43 Bijlefeld, p. 176, referring to di Matteo, *La Divinita di Cristo e la Dottrina della Trinita in Maometto e nei Polemisti Musulmani*, Rome, 1938; Ledit, Ch J, *Mahomet, Israel et le Christ*, Paris, 1952.

44 Basetti-Sani, p. 39.

the mood' of the early surahs, and Cragg is talking of 'the rugged native Semitic genius that speaks in the Qur'an.' [*Ibid.*, pp. 31, 35] For in spite of the Qur'an's own passionate declaration that there was no connection between the words given to Muhammad and those of the poets and professional soothsayers, Cragg insists that.

> the Qur'an, in its power and quality, is a thing of surpassing poetical worth, and ... its genesis must be understood in terms of literary inspiration. The mystery of its origins cannot be fathomed without sounding the depths of language. [*Ibid.*, p. 41]

The depths of language are symbolised for Cragg in the mystical letters, the Arabic letters which prefix many of the surahs of the Qur'an, and which have defied innumerable attempts to decode them. [*Ibid.*, p. 50f.].

We have seen how the artistic theme, in the form of drama, is for Cragg the controlling image of theological understanding, and that the Biblical story is a 'theatre for the world'. Here we must ask how appropriate the literary or artistic model of interpretation is for dealing with the Qur'an. True, the Islamic assessment of the Qur'an emphasizes continually its *i'jaz* or 'matchlessness', the miracle of its incomparability. (see Surahs 28:49, 17:90, 11:16, 10:39) 'Abduh wrote:

> The mighty Book was vindicated (before the Meccans) as being speech *par excellence,* and its judgements superior to all others. Is not the appearance of such a book, from the lips of an illiterate man, the greatest miracle and clearest evidence that it is not of human origin? [*Unity*, p. 119]

But Cragg is always reluctant to admit that things are in any literal sense incomparable, whether they be the Qur'an or Kraemer's 'Biblical realism', and he cannot resist linking the theme of Qur'anic 'matchlessness' with a couplet of Dryden's about the inimitable magic of Shakespeare. [*Event,* p. 42] We might expect some Muslim reaction to this treatment, and Vahiduddin takes up the point. In a very irenic manner he wants to quarrel with Cragg's claim that 'It may be doubted whether, in the last analysis, prophecy has ever been other than poetic and poetry, at its truest, ever other than prophetic.' [*Ibid.*, p. 45] For Vahiduddin

> if the Qur'an is taken to be poetry and appreciated mainly as such it will remain nothing but poetry and will lose the revelationary character which it claims. It will, therefore, not allow the quality of its expression to eclipse its transcendental reference.[45]

Vahiduddin has a related criticism which is more vigorously expressed. Towards the end of his book Cragg draws attention to medieval Muslim estimates of Muhammad which abandoned the picture of an illiterate prophet simply receiving the scripture totally from above, for assessments which credited him with superlative qualities of reason and spirit, and, by implication, the natural capacity for contributing, at least, to the formulation of the Arabic text of the Qur'an. In pursuit again of relatedness, and to avoid the suggestion of literal incomparability, Cragg notes that

> The way was then open for men of reason to hold the significance of the Qur'an in easy relation with the activities of reason in other spheres of culture and history ... This allowed the great names, Socrates, Plato, Aristotle and the rest, to be in some sense conjoined with the Quranic ultimacy of truth. [*Event*, p. 184]

Cragg does not go beyond this general description to specify whom he means, but he must be referring to the Mu'tazilite thinkers and those philosophical commentators on the Qur'an whose approach to the Qur'an equating revelation and reason was condemned by the *ijma'* consensus of the Islamic community, led by the Ash'arites. Whatever his precise meaning the passage triggers an explosion in Vahiduddin the professional philosopher:

> It drives one really to despair to see a man of the writer's religious sensitivity hailing the efforts to 'conjoin', in whatever sense it may be, the charismatic figures of the prophetic religion with the great means of philosophical speculation. If this process of assimilation is allowed to drift, the claims of other great names may well be pressed and

45 Vahiduddin, review of *The Event of the Qur'an*, p. 175.

> Islam will be hard put to it in finding a place in its category of unmentioned prophets for many an associate member.[46]

It is plain that for Vahiduddin there must be a clear and unambiguous distinction between such things as poetry and philosophy, and the transcendent dimension of revelation. He fears that the Qur'an will come to be regarded as 'nothing but poetry'. Cragg, however, would expand the categories and blur the distinctions. Admitting that 'all parallels in this exciting sphere are treacherous', Cragg uses Blake as his model for the inspiration which also gripped Muhammad in an 'unpredictable, and even uncontrolled, eruption in heart and pen together, in their strange community.' For like all poetry, 'the Qur'an is understood to say *what* it says in an inseparable identity with *how* it says it.' [*Event*, pp. 47, 46—emphasis original] Here Cragg is at one with other Western writers who see revelation primarily in literary terms. Paul Ricoeur, reflecting on Biblical models, asks whether we do not

> too often and too quickly think of a will that submits and not enough of an imagination that opens itself? … For what are the poem of the Exodus and the poem of the Resurrection … addressed to if not to our imagination rather than our obedience? … If this is true, we must say that the imagination is that part of ourselves that responds to the text as a Poem, and that alone can encounter revelation no longer as an unacceptable pretension, but a nonviolent appeal.[47]

Cragg's handling of this theme is itself a flowing passage of great power and originality [chapter 2 of *The Event of the Qur'an*: 'A Luminous Arabic Language'], as befits his fascination with words and his sense of their mystery. But one short paragraph exposes the limitations of the poetic model in his hands, and at the same time enables us to see once again how hard Cragg finds it to muster imaginative sympathy for Muhammad's later career.

> The poetic prophecy passed into phases of argumentative and political 'prophecy', where prose was the more accordant

46 *Ibid.,* p. 178.
47 Ricoeur, Paul, *Essays on Biblical Interpretation*, SPCK, London, 1981, p. 117.

> form. Deliverances turned into directives, ordinances and documents of law and community ... Muslim faith sees an undifferentiated status of authority throughout. But the feel and fervour of the Qur'an, by the literary criteria, are evidence enough that there is a transition, a change of key. It is clearly in the poetry, where it lives in its strength, that we must locate the essential meaning of 'an Arabic Qur'an'. [*Event*, p. 49]

Prophecy for Cragg cannot be political, and so the word must be used in inverted commas for the later Qur'anic material. Although he will not talk, as others have, about a marked deterioration in the character of Muhammad in the Medinan years, it is only because 'that is probably too simple, mistaking a symptom for its source.' [*Call*, p. 85] So the literary hermeneutic applied to the Qur'an confirms what Cragg believes on other grounds, that 'later development ... did not sustain the pattern of these beginnings.' [*Event*, p. 49] He conveys the sense of a decline in the whole response of Muhammad to his prophetic vocation.

Yet one is bound to ask whether the model of 'poetry' is adequate here, since definition of the term is notoriously difficult. Certainly the Qur'an does not fit the definition of Arabic poetry, having neither regular rhymes nor strophes, and being marked rather by assonance and disjointedness both in the earlier and the later passages. Bell and Watt's judgement is that it is more fruitful to look for 'didactic rather than poetic or artistic forms' in the Qur'an.[48]

Cragg's characteristic judgement on the later Qur'an does not, however, inhibit him from detailing the colour and eloquence of the Qur'anic language of metaphor in such chapters as 'The Landscape of the Hijaz', and 'Markets of the City', drawing his material from every part of the Qur'an. When he turns to what might be called Qur'anic theology in *The Mind of the Qur'an* we find the same recognition of the capacity of the Qur'an to reflect things of the earth as signs and settings of God's gracious provision and the continual reminder of himself (see especially chapter 9 'The Sacramental Earth'). Cragg, of course, is well aware that the stress on literary excellence in the Qur'an implies 'an active human factor'. He quotes Sayyid Qutb of the Muslim Brotherhood using such expressions

48 Bell, R and Watt, W M, *Introduction to the Qur'an*, Edinburgh University Press, Edinburgh, 1970, pp. 69, 75.

as 'allegory is often employed', and 'the intended musical effect', in a way that, though Qutb would deny it, imputes the normal human process of creativity to the 'artistry' of the Qur'an. As Cragg comments: 'Were such a partnership of the divine Spirit and the human self to be conceded in respect of artistry, a like partnership in respect of content could hardly be excluded.' [*Pen*, pp. 56, 57]

Elsewhere Cragg is similarly anxious to find Muslims acknowledging the historical setting of Qur'anic revelation, and not, as so often, reluctant to pursue the full implications of the *asbab al-nuzul* or 'occasions of sending-down.' Other observers of Islam have had the same concern. Jansen notes Suyuti (died 1505) discouraging such study and comments on the paucity of modern Egyptian books on the subject.[49] Fazlur Rahman, however, calls for it in his *Islam and Modernity* [1982]. Cragg admits that classical motivation was to avoid an antiquarian attitude to the Qur'an, and a determination to assert its living relevance, but alleges that the result has been an insensitivity to the history involved.

In such ways Cragg might well be regarded by some as subversive of Muslim attitudes to the Qur'an. Occasionally the reader senses a distaste born perhaps of an over-spiritual approach to scripture. Writing of the 'markets of the city' and the Qur'anic metaphors drawn from commerce, Cragg comments that

> the religious and the human … fit all too readily into the commercial criteria. The robust assurance of the metaphors is never in doubt nor their fitness for the issues. It is this, perhaps, more than any other consideration, which measures how deeply the ethos of Mecca penetrated the Islamic world … Morality itself may be seen as a transaction in profit … Unbelief is the bad bargain. [*Event*, p. 107]

Yet one may find a very similar emphasis on the lips of Jesus in the Gospels, where prudential motives and financial imagery have their place in inviting people into the Kingdom. (e.g. Matthew 13:44-46, Luke 14:28, 16:9)

---

49 Jansen, J J G, *The Interpretation of the Koran in Modern Egypt*, Brill, Leiden, 1974, p. 2.

Occasionally Cragg is conscious of the temptation to 'a private exegesis'. [*Ibid.*, p. 134] But does this amount to a 'Christianising' of the Qur'an? Does he attempt a 'fusion of horizons' between Qur'anic revelation and Christian faith, or relapse into a 'private language' of interpretation which no-one else can share? As far as his interpretation of the Qur'an is concerned, and this after all is the focus of his major attention in some 13 books and a translation of much of the Qur'an, it is difficult to find him guilty. He is too deferential to standard Muslim exegesis, too diffident (though always immensely fertile) about his own understanding of a text, too aware of the impropriety, as an outsider, of proposing something which goes against the grain of Muslim sentiment or doctrine, and above all too critical of what he sees as the fundamental 'power-assurance' of Islam, and so of the Qur'an, to mistake its message for his own understanding of Christianity. Basetti-Sani might well be so accused, but it is noticeable that Muslim reviewers of his books on the Qur'an do not so accuse Cragg. Where he is vulnerable to criticism is not so much in the style or substance of the interpretation of the Qur'an which he gives, as in the areas which he does not touch. His quintessence of the Qur'an, hallowed, he believes by long Muslim tradition, consists of Surahs 1, 112, 113 and 114. [*Event*, p. 73] Others would have preferred Surah 2 as 'the Qur'an in little', but as already observed, Cragg's choice is significant in emphasizing the oracular, 'poetic' Qur'an in preference to the prosaic, prescriptive one. In his books on the Qur'an Cragg does not attempt exegetical comment on the directions for prayer, fasting or pilgrimage, marriage and family or economic life. In his *Readings in the Qur'an* [1988] translated excerpts totalling about two-thirds of the total text are grouped into sections entitled

God and His Praise (7 pages).
God in Creation: Man and Nature (20 pages).
Prophets and Messengers from Adam to Jesus (64 pages).
Muhammad: The Prophet-Preacher and the Meccan Years (49 pages).
Muhammad: The Prophet-Ruler and the Medinan Climax (50 pages).
Faith and Religion (20 pages).
Society and Law (33 pages).
Unfaith, Judgement and the Last Things (22 pages).

Fazlur Rahman, not translating but commenting on Qur'anic themes, chooses for his titles: God, Man as Individual, Man in Society, Nature, Prophethood and Revelation, Eschatology, Satan and Evil, and the Emergence of the Muslim Community. Jomier's themes are comparable: the nature of the Qur'an, Mecca, 'Hymnes au Dieu Créateur', Adam, Abraham, the Prophets, Jesus, the Muslim Community, and Reason and Persuasion.[50]

Cragg's Qur'an is then an intense call of God to a human race in crisis, calling it into responsive relationship with himself, and through that relationship into gratitude and responsibility for the whole created order, and a keen awareness of its beauty and coherence. It asserts no merely arbitrary divinity or scheme of obedience, but gathers everything into one overarching unity of purpose, in which Islam itself and the Prophet of Islam are only instruments to secure submission to the divine claim. In principle religion itself is subordinated to God as all in all, and, as Cragg sees it, this is something strikingly relevant for modern minds.

> The Islamic trust of the greatness of God … is surely rightly seen as the ally, even the anticipation, of the current charge that much religion is not really about God, but about comfort, or illusion, or security, or cultural identity and that the God of a true worship is, and ought to be, greater than all these. [*Mind*, p. 140]

Here again is Cragg's theme that every protest against religion is in effect a cry for more adequate religion. The grounds for such a conviction can be found at least as far back as Amos ('I hate, I spurn your pilgrim-feasts … ', 5:21), but Cragg has been able to recruit the Qur'an itself to promote it. As he sees it, the Qur'an is not the charter for obscurantism that some in the West presume, but a document of urgent importance for contemporary humanity. This is particularly evident in the emphasis he perceives in the Qur'an both upon the *istighna'* or attempt at independence from God, and the proper dominion of humanity over the world as *khalifah*.

Cragg has then retrieved the Qur'an for Christian attention not merely as a document of Muslims, to be studied and valued as a phenomenon belonging to Islamic life and community, but as a call addressed to all humanity. The advantage of his psychological distance from the Muslim

50 Fazlur Rahman, *Major Themes of the Qur'an*, Bibliotheca Islamica, Minneapolis, 1980; Jomier, Jacques, *Les Grands Thèmes du Coran*, Centurion, Paris, 1978.

community is that it makes this universal relevance of the Qur'an all the more convincing. In terms of the hermeneutical discussion of our previous section we may say that Cragg's cultural and communal distance from the text has become an asset to him as an interpreter. However, it is as a document of theology, prophecy and poetry that Cragg presents it. There is an instructive contrast here with Fazlur Rahman, who also complains of the misreading of the Qur'an in the classical period, but in terms of a failure to establish Islamic law on 'a systematic intellectual working out of the sociomoral values of the Qur'an.' 'A vibrant and revolutionary religious document ... was buried under the debris of grammar and rhetoric.'[51] The significance of the Qur'an to this modern Muslim is then quite distinct from its significance for Cragg, as Cragg himself recognises in his essay on Fazlur Rahman, where he refers to

> his insistent view of the Qur'an as wholly 'functional', a Book which has to do, not with personal devotion and the inner life of the human spirit, but with a concrete programme for a socio-political order in human society ... . The Qur'an must be read and pondered as a living campaign for a just and ethical socio-political order on earth, a campaign intelligently reproduced in every generation by its light. [*Pen*, pp. 91, 103]

For Cragg such concepts set all kinds of alarm bells ringing about the use of power in the service of religion, as we saw earlier.

Cragg himself, however, acknowledges that 'we are only at the beginning of this kind of reading of the Qur'an outside its own community.' [*Mind*, p. 194] There is clearly more to be done, and the gaps in his own account of the Qur'an seem to point to a very powerful, but also very particular and personal vision of Islam.

4 How Cragg anthologises Islam

No one scholar can attempt to do original work in the whole range of Islamic studies, or make a genuinely new contribution to more than a very

51 Fazlur Rahman, *Islam and Modernity. Transformation of an Intellectual Tradition*, University of Chicago Press, Chicago, 1982, pp. 29, 36.

small field. But the one who sets out to interpret Islam, or any other faith, to those who do not share it, is under some obligation to convey the whole range and thrust of the faith, not as he would have it be, but as it is. We have noted that some doubt on this score arises with Cragg's handling of the Qur'an. How does the rest of his work rate in the completeness of its account of Islam?

We noted that Cragg's initial interest was in the modernists of Islam. This interest has been sustained especially through the translation of works from 'Abduh, Kamil Husain and Taha Husain, the examination of eight modern Muslim writers in *The Pen and the Faith* (though these were contemporary writers rather than 'modernists' in any ideological sense), and another four Muslim contemporaries in *Troubled by Truth*. An earlier and broader survey was contained in *Counsels in Contemporary Islam*. Five books have dealt with the general theme of the Christian understanding of other faiths (*Christianity in World Perspective, The Privilege of Man, The Christian and Other Religion, The Christ and the Faiths*, and *To Meet and to Greet*), and fourteen have aimed to foster Christian understanding and responsibility towards Islam (*The Call of the Minaret, Sandals at the Mosque, The Dome and the Rock, The Event of the Qur'an, The Mind of the Qur'an, Muhammad and the Christian, Jesus and the Muslim, Returning to Mount Hira', Muhammad in the Qur'an, Am I not your Lord?, The Tragic in Islam, The Qur'an and the West, A Christian-Muslim Inter-Text Now, and Mosque Sermons*). He has published a translation of selected passages of the Qur'an (*Readings in the Qur'an*), an anthology of Sufi writers (*The Wisdom of the Sufis*), and a collection of Christian and Muslim prayers (*Alive to God* and *Common Prayer*). Three books (*Next Year in Jerusalem*, *The Arab Christian* and *Palestine: the Prize and Price of Zion*) deal with history and contemporary issues in the Middle East.

In none of these can the reader reasonably expect a total treatment of Islam. In writing for a Christian audience it may be right to indulge in an 'intelligent neglect … in respect of the Qur'an's more desolating areas'[52], for the aim is not to render a complete account—whatever may be meant by that—but to enable a new kind of relationship, both to the faith and to the people. Here, to be sure, 'the goal of study is an open country of relationship. ' [*Event*, p. 187] Nor should we expect a total abeyance of personal judgement in writings designed for a general rather than a specific audience. Nevertheless the purpose of three of Cragg's book-length

52 Cragg, Kenneth, 'Temple Gairdner's Legacy' in *International Bulletin of Missionary Research* 5:4 (Oct. 1981), p. 166.

publications seem to require the broadest and least idiosyncratic view of Islam which the author can present. These are the two anthologies *The House of Islam* and *Islam from Within* (with Marston Speight), both written for a series called *The Religious Life of Man*, and the university student textbook *Islam and the Muslim*, written for the Open University.

The House of Islam has chapters entitled, 'Lord of the Worlds', Muhammad and the Rasuliyyah, Qur'an, Law, Liturgy, Ummah and Questions of Time—the last dealing with questions of historical and contemporary issues rather than eschatology. There is a useful Table of Dates, a glossary and bibliography. Although the Christian vocation of relationship with Muslims cannot be assumed from the readers of these publications, Cragg still wants to put the personal before the academic, and chapter one begins with the words: 'To enter into Islam it is better to go to the mosque than to reach for the dictionary.' [*House*, p. 5] It seems also that he still wants to present Islam with the accent on contemporary issues and on those thinkers within Islam whom he sees as responding most appropriately to them. The bibliography, arranged according to the chapter headings, contains surprisingly few Muslim authors, although some have naturally been introduced in the text itself. Out of 51 titles listed only nine are by Muslims, who include Fazlur Rahman, S H Nasr and A A A Fyzee.

In this 1969 publication there is no real attempt to present radical or revivalist Islam, with its accent on *shari'ah* and eschatology. A brief reference to the Muslim Brotherhood elicits the judgement that the 'intractability of the human world to the religious ideal seems to many Muslims today to require a more modest philosophy about the actualization of Islam in the contemporary world.' [*Ibid.*, p. 94] That 'modesty' has not been much in evidence in the intervening years when Muslims of radical mind have made their mark all over the Muslim world, notably in Iran, and devastatingly in acts of terrorism, as Cragg implicitly acknowledged in *Faith at Suicide* (2005). A second edition of *The House of Islam* in 1975 added some new titles to the bibliography (two by Muslims), and a stronger historical element, but in the updated text the shattering of Pakistani unity in 1971 is taken as proof of the judgements of the earlier edition. 'The mood of disillusion, or at least of greater realism, is unmistakable.' [2nd ed. p. 113]

Islam from Within was produced in 1980 as a companion anthology to the above, again in a series of comparable publications. In this book Cragg made the selections on the Qur'an, Worship and Religion,

Art and Architecture, Mystics and Saints and Contemporary Issues. Cragg's co-author Marston Speight was responsible for Tradition, Law and Theology. [*Within*, p. xiv] The opportunity is taken here to underline the hospitality theme implied in the title of the companion volume, and in contrast to the rather orientalist bibliographies of that work, the only non-Muslims quoted here are Rudyard Kipling, Alan Villiers and Lawrence Durrell, in descriptions of Muslims at worship. Here too Mawdudi and Sayyid Qutb find a place, but otherwise the interpretation is as before, with the unexpected addition of the chapter on art and architecture. The comment of a conservative Muslim on the text is instructive. Noting that 'the anthologists' own understanding, preferences, priorities, even inner dispositions' are an integral part of the anthology, Khurram Murad complains particularly about the absence of any treatment of 'The Hereafter, *al-Akhira*' either in the extracts from the Qur'an or elsewhere. 'An outsider who is not allowed a full glimpse of it will find it difficult to receive a true understanding of Islam.' We noted a similar gap in Cragg's writing about the Qur'an compared with that of Fazlur Rahman in the last section. Murad is uneasy that Tradition and Law together rate only forty pages, while Mystics and Saints receive thirty-five, and Contemporary Issues forty. Readers, he feels, have not been allowed to hear the contributors speak without intrusive, even impatient comment. It is not difficult to see where the anthologists' sympathies lie.[53]

Islam and the Muslim, together with its companion section in *Man's Religious Quest. A Reader*, are comparable texts published in 1978 for the Open University and its students. The two texts are intended to be used in close conjunction. In the brief space available in the *Reader* there is little room for more than Qur'anic passages, several pages of meditations on the Beautiful Names by Ghazzali, and brief sections on Hadith, Law, Mysticism and a contemporary statement on Islam (a conservative view from the Islamic Council of Europe). The ninety pages of *Islam and the Muslim* broadly follow the divisions of the previous books, but with particular sections on pilgrimage and Islamic sects. Familiar patterns emerge: an early section distinguishes between Islam and *islam* [*Islam*, p. 5]; the *Hijrah* is the 'hinge of the Muslim story' [*ibid.*, p. 18], by which Muhammad made 'the transition from prophethood to rulership' [*ibid.*, p.

53 Murad, Khurram, review of *Islam from Within* in *Muslim World Book Review* 2:3 (Spring 1982), pp. 4-7.

22]; the *Shari'ah* is introduced as 'the imperative mood in Islam' [*ibid.*, p. 49], and Shi'ite Islam under the title 'the mystery of suffering'. [*Ibid.*, p. 64]

'It is understandable', writes Vahiduddin reviewing this work, 'that the recurrent themes of the writer's critique of Islamic consciousness should not fail to appear in the little manual, though marginally and as if by the way.'[54] Cragg's writing is in fact remarkably consistent, and the demands made upon him by publishers testify to the acceptability of his work as an interpreter of Islam for the general public as well as for those who share his Christian commitment. The criticisms made of the one are to be made equally of the other.

One has to question, in relation to these anthologies, why the gaps occur, and whether the neglect is in fact 'intelligent'. The Psalmists' attitude to the *Torah* of Israel might have been one way of appreciating the comparable Muslim understanding of *Shari'ah*. Scholars like Goldziher and Gibb seem to have been more ready to see the Muslim theological mind operating in that framework of detailed guidance about daily affairs. Norman Anderson, a contemporary who shared Cragg's conservative evangelical origins, was widely respected and consulted by Muslims for his knowledge of Muslim law. Similarly with *kalam*/Islamic philosophy, there are close affinities with 'Ash'arite texts in Aquinas or other Christian scholastic writers. The eschatological dimension can easily be found in Christian writers.

Such considerations suggest that Cragg's silences in respect of Islam reflect reservations and a lack of sympathy in wider areas, and in expressions of Christian faith where he does not feel sufficiently at home to set pen to paper about them. To the wider areas we must now turn.

54 Vahiduddin, Syed, review of *Islam and the Muslim*, p. 243.

8
VOCATIONS BEYOND ISLAM

1 Encountering Judaism

Cragg's understanding of and writing about Islam was his major contribution to the Christian interpretation of other faiths. The question to be asked now is how the principles in operation there are available for use in relation to faiths other than Islam. Cragg's engagement with Islam has been so broad in scope and long in years that it has naturally left him little room for engagement with other faiths. However, he has left us certain writings which range outside Islam, and reveal a particular concern for Judaism and for Buddhist thought.

It is inevitable that a Christian theologian, particularly from a tradition which prides itself on its faithfulness to Biblical norms, should be brought to engage in some way with Judaism. This will be all the more so in one who has lived in Beirut and Jerusalem, and seen with his own eyes the conflict in Lebanon between Maronite and Muslim over the establishment of the state of Israel. Given the history of Muslim/Jewish relations in the Middle East, can such a man as Cragg set aside his Muslim sympathies and see the Jewish experience for what it is, or does the whole nature of his own Islamic experience disqualify him from making or even commending a parallel approach to Judaism? Is the character of his theological method, formed in the crucible of Islam, capable of adaptation to the other Semitic faith?

Cragg's major writing about Judaism is contained in *The Privilege of Man* (1968), a book about the doctrine of humanity in the three Biblical faiths; in *This Year in Jerusalem* (1982), a book about Israel and Palestine; in a major section of *The Christ and the Faiths* (1986) under the title of 'Messiah and Jewry'; in reflections on three writers on Judaism in *Troubled by Truth* (1992), and in *Palestine: the Prize and Price of Zion* (1997). There are also extensive chapters on 'Judaica' (*The Order of the Wounded Hands*

2006), and on 'Palestine in Israel: Israel in Palestine. The Lie of the Wall' (*A Christian-Muslim Inter-Text Now* 2007). Two of the books listed were written in the shadow of Israeli incursions deep into Lebanon, in 1982 and 2006. He refers to the latter as 'the grim summer of 2006 (when) the crime of the devastation of Lebanon unfolded to arouse "the dreadful astonishment of God".' [*Hands*, p. 1] It is plain that Cragg was deeply disturbed by these events. [*Inter-Text*, p. 197]

As we read these publications certain familiar accents are at once apparent. There is the search for common ground even, and especially within the most controverted issues of theology. In Islam this is seen in the way Cragg handles the crucifixion of Jesus, where he stresses the intention to crucify, which Muslims do not deny. With Judaism the most vexed issue is the coming of the Messiah: has he or not? Again Cragg looks for the common ground, acknowledging the obstacles in the path of finding it. In the face of the Holocaust, especially as presented by a writer of the power of Elie Wiesel, he admits that it may well seem that Christian theology is marked by 'easy, romantic, hollow Messianic pretensions.' [*Troubled*, p. 79] Cragg in response asks of the Messianic hope of Israel: 'can concept never be event? ... One cannot rule out at least the possibility of "the Messianic event" and intelligibly retain "the Messianic idea".' [*Ibid.,* p. 86] He fixes on the fact that the Messianic hope, however understood, has sustained Jewish identity in their long history and given its very name to Christianity. This he sums up in the phrase 'He that was to come', which Christians will gladly refer to Jesus, and Jews, while of course rejecting its application to Jesus, might possibly also accept as an expression of their historic hope. [*Christ*, p. 97] 'He that was to come', however, does not seem a phrase calculated to arouse Jewish enthusiasm, since its immediately obvious meaning fits Christian assumptions too well.

Cragg might have done better to emphasize the future coming of Jesus the Messiah, as in the remarkable German radio debate between Hans Küng and Pinchas Lapide, in which the Orthodox rabbi declared:

> Professor Küng, you are waiting for the *parousia*; with you too the fullness of redemption is still in the future; I await its coming, but the second coming is also a coming. If the Messiah comes and then turns out to be Jesus of Nazareth, I would say that I do not know of any Jew in this world who

> would have anything against it. Thus a legitimate awaiting of his advent or second coming—and the distinction here is really secondary—would not only be our common expectation of salvation, but in the meantime would enable both of us to concentrate on what can be known.[1]

Lapide is by no means typical of Jewish thinkers, as his later book *The Resurrection of Jesus. A Jewish Perspective* shows. (In this he argues for the historic reality of Jesus' Resurrection, but against his being the Messiah or divine.[2]) But such considerations have not generally worried Cragg in his search for the 'creative minority' in a community of faith. In this theological crux Lapide's handling of the issue seems both more pertinent and more incisive than Cragg's, though the method is the same. The nearest Cragg approaches to Lapide's argument is the suggestion that 'Jesus was Messiah-designate as well as Messiah-actual' and pointed to a future still to be fulfilled. [*Christ*, p. 116]

Cragg is compelled to take this question of fulfilment further in answer to the Jewish claim that the Messiah cannot have come and redeemed the world, as Christians claim, since it (and they) remain so manifestly unredeemed. [*Ibid.,* p. 113ff.] Cragg acknowledges the force of the Jewish argument and the pain of Jewish history behind it, but calls Christians and Jews to a realism which rejects both the romanticism of which Jews accuse Christians and the despair which sees only a world of unredeemed evil. Christians who know themselves to be redeemed 'must in turn become redeemers,' taking up their cross. [*Ibid.,* p. 115] But Cragg offers more than an ethical and existential answer, though his talk about 'the redemptive principle' might be read exclusively in those terms. There is a fact—the Cross—on which hope can be based. He notes the Exodus as the great fact of the past which has justified the continuing hope of the present and future for Jews, and asks whether the Cross of God's Messiah might not properly be a similar factual basis for continuing hope. 'Such faith does not romanticize away the unredeemedness of the world but reads it as the measure of the Messiah there had to be.' [*Ibid.,* p. 117] The parallel with the Exodus comes of course from Luke 9:31,

---

1 Küng, Hans and Lapide, Pinchas, *Brother or Lord? A Jew and a Christian talk together about Jesus*, Eng. tr., Collins, Glasgow, 1977, p. 43.

2 Lapide, Pinchas, *The Resurrection of Jesus: A Jewish Perspective*, Eng. tr., SPCK, London, 1984.

and 1 Corinthians 5:7, but one might have expected a greater stress on the Resurrection as an integral part of it.

Other familiar accents are also heard. There is the emphasis on the powerlessness of the prophets; the ministry of Jesus 'heading into crisis'; the sin of the world expressed in the 'collective mechanisms of obduracy, timidity, prejudice or folly'; 'how in any and every evil situation love must suffer'; and the welcome to 'critical scholarship alive' to the pressures of communities on it. [*Ibid.,* pp. 101, 106, 108, 109, 111] Cragg finds his most congenial Jewish writer in Abraham Heschel, to whom he devotes a chapter in *Troubled by Truth.* Cragg warms to Heschel's emphasis on the 'divine pathos', 'the relation between God and man, the correlation of Creator and creation, the dialogue between the Holy One of Israel and His people'. [*Troubled,* p. 114] The prophets share and live this costly sympathy, developing an interior life which, formed by the pathos of God, is actually theomorphic. [*Ibid.,* p. 121] Cragg delights to point out how close this comes to the language of incarnation, but regrets Heschel's reluctance to deal with the person of Jesus himself, and seems saddened by his insistence that divine pathos is not of the divine essence, being functional not substantial. Here he sees the Gnostic and Marcionite heresy of understanding God's disclosure, whether in pathos or in Christ, as somehow less than God. Again we find Cragg's concern for a valid worship rejecting the idea that God is unknowable. [*Ibid.,* p. 122]

We have seen how with Islam Cragg's ultimate critical focus rests on the allegation of the 'power-assurance', the political aspiration of the faith-community in the name of God. This central trait reflects negatively for Cragg on the Muslim understanding of the God whom they worship. With Judaism there is a similar central focus, that of 'peoplehood' (or sometimes 'Moses and peoplehood'). [*Jesus,* p. 287] Cragg points to the conjunctions characteristic of all three Semitic faiths: 'God *and* ... ' 'God *and* his Prophet' in Islam; 'God *and* his Christ' in Christianity; 'God *and* his People' in Judaism. [*Christ,* p. 121] In Judaism, Cragg maintains, the division between Jew and Gentile is central. Despite Jewish talk about universalism, and some embarrassment, Jews are different in their own eyes. 'Conceptually and practically, the otherness exists and is decisive'. [*Ibid.,* p. 123] But the 'otherness', he complains, is not merely the 'antiseptic' otherness of salt, which must preserve its saltness if it is to do its job of preservation. In this case the job would be that of preserving the proper humanity of the world by a necessary Jewish distinctiveness, following the will of God as revealed to the Jewish people. But this particular 'otherness' fails its antiseptic rôle and becomes also a rejection of non-Jewish humanity. Despite the

> splendid universalism of an Isaiah … extend(ing) a common and deeply sacramental humanism … there remained an abiding ambivalence. Any 'towards them' about 'the Gentiles' was conditioned by the perception that for their very sake the distinction from them was vital. Only via a people that remained 'apart' could their ministry 'bless the nations … Their 'mission' could never be shared, since they held the copyright.' [*Hands*, p. 56]

Such an attitude tragically invites an answering rejection. This is not merely an ethnic distinction between Jews and others:

> It is a unilateral dissociation from *all* others who, by that dissociation alone, are denominated 'Gentiles'. Is there any other corporate self-consciousness which requires the whole human family to be defined by a single contradistinction? [*Christ*, p. 127, emphasis original]

Yet Cragg himself goes on to instance just such comparable 'contradistinctions', in the ideology of *apartheid* and the 'Russianism' of Ivan the Terrible and Dostoevsky. Here too are chosen peoples, in their own eyes. But these, he claims, wore Biblical dress and justified themselves from the Scriptures because they were generated, 'however distortedly', from Judaic conviction. It was the Jewish nation that 'originated exceptionality'. [*Ibid.,* p. 135] But can it really be said that all forms of racial and ethnic exclusivism must be laid ultimately at the Jewish door? Cragg comes close to saying so, yet there are surely many examples which owe nothing to historic Jewish or Biblical influences. Cragg retrieves the accusation, half-made, by examples from Ben-Gurion and others of a secularized sense of Jewish chosenness in which it is the people who choose God, and so their destiny, rather than the passive case. Such a vocation could be adopted by any virile and self-confident group of people. Cragg cites Dow Marmur's 'painful book', *Beyond Survival. Reflections on the future of Judaism*,[3] to suggest that in contrast to the secular version, or the preferable 'open peoplehood'

3 Marmur, Dow, *Beyond Survival: Reflections on the Future of Judaism*, DLT, London, 1982.

concept of the Church, the exclusive peoplehood-by-birth conviction of Judaism leads only to neurosis and self-preoccupation. [*Christ*, p. 139f.]

This theme persists into Cragg's later writing. Reflecting on Elie Wiesel's lifelong engagement with 'the long and bitter tangle of Anti-Semitic crimes and horrors', he comments '"Gentiles" are the issue that Jewishness has never yet resolved.' [*Troubled*, p. 82] James Parkes, he notes in the same book, tried to resolve the issue from the Christian side by the doctrine of the two covenants, Sinai and Christ being equally acts of God, one for Jews, the other for Gentiles. Parkes, says Cragg, has thereby rewritten the New Testament and the Creed, making the latter say 'who for us non-Jews came down from heaven and was made man.' So the 'entire accessibility of Christian faith' is compromised, and Jews exempted from its universal relevance. [*Ibid.,* p. 106] Cragg applauds Parkes' motive and intention to reconcile, but finds him guilty of 'disloyalty' to both faiths. 'James Parkes missed the logic of Jesus' ministry.' [*Hands*, pp. 71, 72] In one of his last books (*Dying Daily. Quotidian Living* [2010]) he continues to refer to the 'exclusivity of Jewishness', 'the separatist principle at the heart of Jewry', Jewish 'exceptionality'. [*Dying*, p. 33]

The missionary concern with universal relevance is bound to meet with particular problems in the case of Judaism and its tortured relationship with Christianity, but has Cragg handled the issue adequately in suggesting so often that ethnicity is the clue to Judaism? Breiner commented on a passage in *The Privilege of Man* [p. 54f.] that 'despite a remarkably sympathetic Christian response to Judaism … (the reference) remains a good example of how deeply entrenched this attitude to Judaism is in Christian thinking.'[4] There are Jewish voices which explicitly disavow any fundamental distinction from the rest of humanity. Rabbi Norman Solomon asks pointedly

> Is it really too much for Jews to expect Christians to meet them as *normal human beings* rather than as peculiar theological objects? … Surely the foundation of prejudice lies in looking at the other as something *different in some deep way from everybody else.*[5] [Emphasis original]

4 Breiner, Bert, 'Abraham in Judaism, Christianity and Islam: Faith and Encounter', unpublished PhD thesis, Birmingham University, 1985.

5 Solomon, Norman, art. 'A Commentary on "The Common Bond: Christians and Jews"', in *Christian-Jewish Relations* 18:3 (September 1985), p. 69f.

Why are such voices not given more centrality in Cragg's critique of Judaism? Where is his response to the Islamic view of Jewish exclusivism which takes its authority from the Qur'an? 'Say (O Muhammad): O ye that are Jews! If ye claim that ye are favoured of Allah apart from (all) mankind, then long for death if ye are truthful.' (62:6 in Pickthall's translation) Surah 2:94-96 expresses the same sentiment, with the explanation that these people do not desire to die and be with God, as his sincere friends would, because of their sins. The Palestinians can be seen as living evidence of the consequences of Jewish exclusivism.

Cragg has devoted two entire books to the historical reality of Israel, the astonishing triumph of its achievement and the tragedy of its effects on the Middle East as a whole and the Palestinians in particular, whereby 'homecoming means displacement.' [*Jerusalem*, p. 89f.] All Cragg's eloquence in registering the tragic paradox of the human situation are deployed in telling the story of Israel. In particular he notes how the very success of the Israelis, combined with the conviction of their own uniqueness, tended to blind them to the lessons their own history held for people in the situation that the Palestinians were now reduced to.

> A Jewish analysis which misses the power of despair and the tenacity of the powerless is strangely negligent of its own long history and of the land-fidelity behind its own success ... It would be odd to imagine that Palestinians would forget in three decades what Jews remembered for eighteen centuries. [*Ibid.,* pp. 58, 59]

He sees both Arab and Jew locked in absolutist interpretations of their historical situation which allow no shades of grey and no admission of guilt except from the enemy. 'History itself is not rightly told unless it makes absolute reports of denunciation and legitimacy.' [*Ibid.,* p. 94] In a typical approach to the 'mind' behind the attitudes Cragg recommends the need for a sense of the ironical, and regrets that Arabic appears to have no word for 'paradox'. [*Ibid.,* p. 95] (The dictionaries give *tanaqud zahiri* or literally 'outward contradiction'.)

However, it is Judaism that, from Cragg's account of it, abounds in paradox. Zionism springs 'from a deep reading of the Jewish past' but results only in 'another cycle of the same haunting paradox.' [*Christ*, p. 152] For the people that is intended to be different, and different because they are to be a blessing to the nations, wants to be a nation like all other nations, with passports and frontiers and guns to protect them. If Auschwitz and Oxford, representing the extreme Jewish experiences of persecution and assimilation, both menaced Judaism [*ibid.*, p. 151], security seemed to lie in a national refuge which dispossessed another innocent people and made them refugees in their turn. Cragg tells in some detail the story of the heroism and the tragedy of the Zionist achievement of Israel, not omitting the moral ambiguity of the 'ratchet' process, whereby political and military decisions regretted by Israelis of more tender conscience nevertheless become, once successful, the starting-point for new advances. [*Jerusalem*, pp. 28, 30] He is clear that the Arabs, by political and military ineptitude, were their own worst enemies, but insists that 'minority status for Palestinians was basic to the whole Zionist ideal.' [*Ibid.,* p. 53] Both Palestinians and Israelis must abandon the comforting myth of their own innocence. In a later book he wrote 'If it could be said that "the Arabs are victims of their fictions", it could be said that Israelis are the beneficiaries of their larcenies.' [*Iron*, p. 98] Beyond abandoning the 'folly of retaliation' Cragg's prescription is twofold: a mutual recognition by Palestinians of the reality and permanence of the Jewish state, and by Jews of the legitimate peoplehood and consequent civil rights of the Palestinian people.

> If Israel is to avail for Jewry's fulfilment as Zion, the Palestinian case and cause must be able to rise to the human quality and the tragic realism which will allow that fulfilment. If that is to be, Israel, for its part, must share that tragic realism and offer human community to those whose consent alone can save her from jeopardy and frustration. [*Jerusalem*, p. 163]

This Year in Jerusalem was published only a matter of months before the Israeli invasion of Lebanon in 1982, which can have done nothing to reconcile Cragg to the Israeli refusal to admit Palestinian opponents to 'the human community'. As already suggested, this probably underlies the focus on Jewish exclusivism in his recent writing. But it seems to have had another effect also. *The Christ and the Faiths*, for the first time in Cragg's immense literary output, questions Christian use of parts of the Old Testament, especially in worship. Even in the New Testament, passages like Luke 1:68-79, the *Benedictus* of the Anglican liturgy, have been an embarrassment to Arab Christians of the Middle East ever since 1948.[6]

> There is, for Arab Christians, an almost unbearable ambiguity in singing: 'Blessed be the Lord God of Israel … ' Israelis themselves are not agreed about him and if his 'visiting and redeeming his people' has to be read in terms of contemporary Palestinian history, how is he to be called 'blessed'? [*Christ*, p. 334]

But the problem is not simply an Arab and Middle Eastern one, though no doubt Cragg was first alerted to it there. The effect of the use of many of the psalms and much Old Testament history in many national churches' worship has been, he claims, to feed the

> tendency to recruit God … and ally his providence to their designs. Even the loveliest of psalms have this sad ambivalence. There is scarcely one rich *vade mecum* of the heart before God which may not link its piety with enmity and its praise with its animadversions about others as foes. [*Ibid.,* p. 331]

The effect is to accentuate 'ethnic, political, even tribal, pride' at the expense of the true meaning of the Church accessible to all, or even to identify the two. Cragg makes clear that he is not advocating an abandonment of the Canon of Scripture, but asking how it is to be used. Has the Church 'too readily assumed the unity of its double-testamented Bible?' [*Ibid.,* p. 134] Christians who describe themselves as 'Bible-believing' and who can see no evil in Israeli policies because the Jewish state is the fulfilment of prophecy are a case in point. [*Ibid.,* p. 334]

Exclusivism then, is a many-facetted thing, but in Cragg's understanding deeply characteristic of historic and contemporary Judaism, and deeply disturbing. His later writing no longer uses terms like 'spiritual imperialism', which can be found in some of the earlier. In *Sandals at the Mosque* he wrote that 'The making of proselytes to Judaism was a kind of spiritual imperialism in that the central announcement was

6 BCC (British Council of Churches), *Towards Understanding the Arab-Israeli Conflict: the Report of a BCC Delegation to the Middle East*, BCC, London, 1982.

an offer of naturalization into Jewry.' [*Sandals*, p. 142], and in *Christianity in World Perspective*:

> The opening up of the faith in Christ, on equal terms, to Gentile as well as Jew was the abandonment of a kind of imperialism of the Spirit by which Jewry, despite its magnificent potential universalism, interpreted election as a human privacy of its own and made accession to truth a sort of naturalization to itself. [*World*, p. 33]

The older language of supersession and displacement of the Jewish people by the Church, 'the new Israel', has also been refined, though it still appears in the revised edition of *The Call of the Minaret.* [*Call* 1956 edn, p. 244 = *Call* 1986 edn, p. 218] But it is a refinement and not an essential change. In some respects his language becomes sharper. Cragg is clearly ill at ease with certain responses to the Holocaust, notably the 'passionate partisanship with Jewry' of some Christians like Rosemary Ruether. Her saying: 'Anti-Judaism is the left hand of Christology' is vigorously rejected along with similar statements from others as 'wild and facile dicta ... quite wanting in the discipline of either spiritual perception or intelligent scholarship. ' [*Christ*, p. 158] The attempt in some Jewish circles to equate anti-Judaism and anti-Zionism, so that hostility to Zionism is understood as enmity to all Jews, is also roundly dismissed as 'either stupid or malicious', given the extent of Jewish reservations about Zionism both historic and even contemporary. [*Ibid.,* p. 159]

It is entirely understandable that his writings on Judaism do not reflect the same grasp of communal sentiment as his writings on Islam, and appear to be based more on reading than personal encounter. It seems dubious, for example, that he has fully appreciated the defensiveness Jews feel about Israel, and the consequent equation of anti-Zionism with anti-Judaism. In the light of left-wing student attacks on British university Jewish Societies for alleged 'racism', it seems unwarranted to say that the equation is 'either stupid or malicious', since such attacks themselves presume it. It may be guessed also that some terms offensive to Jews, like 'ethno-theology' [*ibid.*, p. 148] would not be likely to survive the process of bi-lateral dialogue. It is true that the Jews whose thinking justifies such language are the less likely to enter into dialogue. Comparable Muslim attitudes, however, have received gentler treatment from Cragg's pen.

2 Hinduism and Buddhism

Cragg's personal engagement as a resident amid cultures shaped by other world faiths was limited to the Middle East, and more briefly, Nigeria. Though he travelled extensively throughout Asia his cultural and religious experience was Semitic and Western rather than non-Semitic and Indian. He shows no knowledge of the further Eastern cultures of China and Japan, or the Pacific. His understanding of religious cultures outside the Middle East is therefore gained primarily from literature. We might in consequence expect some disclaimers of his competence to write about them, especially considering the emphasis put in the case of Islam on developing personal relationships rather than mere study, but none are forthcoming. Buddhism in its Theravada form (described in a rare slip as the 'northern' form in *Christ* p. 259) did catch his attention.[7] He makes only scattered references to Mahayana Buddhism, though curiously he tends to use a vocabulary which is more characteristic of the Mahayana than of the Theravada tradition. For example he consistently uses the name 'Sakyamuni' for the Buddha, and makes much of the concept of *sunyata* or voidness.[8] He has three chapters on Hinduism and three on Theravada Buddhism in *The Christ and the Faiths,* which contains his most substantial writing on these subjects. All three, together with Islam would have formed part of his responsibilities as Reader in Religious Studies in the University of Sussex.

Again we have to ask whether the approach and techniques of interpretation developed in the case of Islam prove adequate for other faiths, and here particularly for faiths which do not share the same monotheistic and creationist basis that Christianity enjoys with Islam and Judaism. If the doctrines of God and humanity cannot, as in the Semitic faiths, be plausibly understood as reciprocal, is it possible to find some other common ground on which a constructive dialogue can proceed?

The difference in Cragg's handling of Hinduism and of Buddhism is instructive both in regard to the extent of the historical encounters between these faiths and Christianity, and also to the respective philosophical and religious gulfs between them. In the Indian context Cragg is familiar with the life and writings of C F Andrews, A G Hogg,

7 Cragg, Kenneth, art. 'Buddhism and Baptism' in *Theology* LXXXII: 688 (July 1979).

8 Parrinder, G, art. 'Shakyamuni' in *A Dictionary of non-Christian Religions*, Hulton, Amersham, Bucks., 1971.

Raimundo Panikkar, Chenchiah, Chakkarai, Sadhu Sundar Singh and Gandhi. All these figures, except Hogg, form an integral part of his developing argument, and others like Bede Griffiths, M M Thomas and Paul Devanandan make brief appearances. In the Buddhist case Cragg quotes virtually no Buddhist writing except the Pali Canon. His other authorities are Western scholars of Buddhism, and innumerable Western poets, especially, in this context, Traherne and Keats as celebrants of the goodness of the created order. Of indigenous Christian writing in the Buddhist context he has only single references to the Sri Lankans Aloysius Pieres and Lynn de Silva, (the latter in criticism). This imbalance no doubt reflects the long association of Britain with India (and Sri Lanka), and the consequent ease and familiarity of Indian thinkers with the English language. He does not quote the extensive German or American literature on Buddhism. The imbalance also reflects the relative strength of the Church in India compared with Buddhist lands. But primarily it means that Cragg is able to report a vigorous ongoing debate in the Hindu context, where the term 'Indian Christian theology' has real meaning, whereas in the case of Buddhism he has to conduct his argument alone, with the help of his poets.

Hinduism

Cragg's principal focus in his discussion of Hinduism is the simple issue of whether the Incarnation of Christ can in any sense be regarded as replicated by the *avatars* of Hinduism, the issue often termed 'the uniqueness of Christ'. He also returns to the theme of the definition and knowability of God in handling the non-dualistic tradition within Hinduism. He finds these questions most sharply posed not by Hindus but by the Indian Catholic theologian Raimundo Panikkar, who attempts 'to think Christology from within Hinduism' [*Christ*, p. 187], and who with C F Andrews is made the representative of the Indian religious tradition in *Troubled by Truth*. Panikkar, as interpreted by Cragg, believes that 'we may locate in Hinduism the living presence of the mystery which Christians call Christ.' Cragg believes that if Panikkar's view is accepted

> It is as if a Christ of concept or of contemplation is replacing the Christ of actuality, with a readiness to equate

> the two by dispensing with the event-character which in Christianity defines it. [*Ibid.,* p. 186]

In other words the historic Christ has ceased to be significant, and the historic parameters of Christhood do not matter. 'Christ' can be equated with the Krishna who appears as Arjuna's charioteer in the *Bhagavad Gita,* and with many other human encounters with the reality which defy definition, and for which 'Christians have no other name than Christ.' [Panikkar in *ibid.,* p. 185] Cragg responds to this in a number of ways. He questions the moral significance of the appearance of Krishna as the charioteer compared with Jesus. He asks what will prevent the elaboration of such Hindu 'Christologies' to include 'the lurid Puranic tales or the antics and lusts of the other Krishnas'. [*Ibid.,* pp. 191, 190] But most of all he responds by rehearsing, at some length, the 'happenedness' of Jesus the Christ. This is ground familiar to readers of *Paul and Peter. Meeting in Jerusalem* (1980), some of which is reprinted in his last book *Bent to Literary Event* (2011, pp. 75-82).

Cragg is convinced that the significance of Jesus was not immediately grasped by the New Testament Church, but that the development of exalted language about him did take its origins essentially from the genuine character of the events of his life and teaching. It was not an invention of the early Church in compensation for an otherwise failed Messiah. It was not the illegitimate product of an enthusiasm for Jesus which found no warrant in his own understanding of himself. Cragg clearly feels that it is not only Hindus who are adrift in this issue, for he patiently expounds his philosophy of history, which is also a kind of epistemology.

> There is what happened and what what happened meant. Without the latter, noted, pondered, stored and probed in mind, the former never becomes history and is, as it were, unhappened into oblivion. It is thus the historian who 'makes' history, given the 'history' (as yet unrecorded) which makes him historian. [*Christ*, p. 199, cf. *Paul*, p. 31ff. and *passim*]

The last qualification is vital, for it is by the 'given history' that religious communities live and shape their own history. The difficulty for Cragg, sharply posed in Panikkar's proposals about Christology, is that Hinduism is religion of a different sort, for which human history is little better than illusion. Other Western theologians determined to retain the centrality of the historic record of Jesus have encountered the same difficulty as Cragg, in that Hinduism encourages a 'gnosticising' tendency to all Scriptures.[9]

Cragg is not, however, left simply in opposition to Hinduism. He is able to determine a number of parallels between Hindu and Christian thought, such as the suggestion, taken from Sadhu Sundar Singh, that the concept of *karma*, described as 'the entailing of evil out of a past into a future' resembled the New Testament meaning of the wrath of God. [*Christ*, p. 229] He also suggests that the struggle of Gandhi against untouchability was a witness against Hinduism from within Hinduism, and as such it had something of the moral passion of the Hebrew prophets. Consequently Gandhi might in some sense be counted among them. [*Ibid.,* p. 235] Cragg might also have reminded us that Gandhi was assassinated by a Hindu extremist.

Cragg's conclusion about Hinduism is that the witness of India shows that 'Jesus may indeed be known in a "following" which is not a "confessing",' and that the warning of Jesus not to prevent those who cast out devils in his name (Mark 9:38f.) can remind us not to forbid the association of any gracious, prophetic action with his name. For God's grace operates by its own laws, unrestricted by human religious frontiers, and once identified in its perfect form in Jesus can be recognised everywhere. This is the abiding truth behind all the attempts to 'Indianise' Christology. 'Divine revelation is consummated in the historical Jesus and his cross but is everywhere refracted in the human search.' [*Ibid.,* pp. 238, 232] The key question is that of the criteria by which we may recognise, in the endless diversity of myths and alleged experiences of God, what is authentically divine. And how can the non-dualist tradition make room for that in God which is 'more than, though not alien to, the human relation', and for the human waywardness which rejects that relationship? [*Troubled*, p. 215]

Buddhism

As already noted, Cragg has to pursue his argument in the case of Buddhism without the help of a strong indigenous tradition of Christian

9 For example Robinson, J A T, *Truth is Two-Eyed*, SCM, London, 1979.

interpretation, though, as we shall see, he does not always accept what help there is. The consequence is that the discussion becomes rather rarified at some points, and at others digresses to engage related themes in Western existentialism. He does note Buddhist warnings that Buddhism is not understood in the West [*Christ*, p. 246], and might have enlivened his work by quotations from Western Buddhist authors, as done in a somewhat comparable book by Stephen Neill.[10] His reason for not doing so is unstated, but was probably connected with the wish to avoid an eclectic account from a variety of Buddhist traditions, such as that given by Christmas Humphreys,[11] in favour of focussing exclusively on the Theravada tradition with its uncompromising and allegedly original non-theism.

This gives him the opportunity of making the whole thrust of his discussion of Buddhism the question of the reality of the Self, and the desire or craving (in Pali *tanha*), which according to Theravada teaching sustains the illusion of the Self. Against some Christians like Lynn de Silva who credit Theravadins with a kind of functional equivalent of theism in the Buddhist sense of the transcendent, the ineffable, Cragg wants to insist that there is no place for 'intentionality' or any sense of purpose in that system, and therefore no genuine theism, however shadowy. For Theravadins we cannot be 'guests within divine hospitality' for 'the fact is that Buddhism, or at least its Theravada form, has never wanted to be theological.' [*Christ*, p. 310] Cragg accuses Buddhism of social unconcern, of a focus on the individual psyche and the means of its repair which excludes any significance for the whole of the natural and human environment. Yet what we have called 'the individual psyche' has no real existence, and is only posited for the sake of convenience in speaking, sometimes being referred to as 'the conventional self'. Cragg makes the most of the contradiction inherent in this:

> Will, clearly, is here involved. Even 'undesiring' has to be desired. Though the self may be in theory an illusion it belongs, in some sense, with the enterprise that aims at its surcease … Theory may demand that this be called 'the conventional self' to safeguard the doctrine that it is not

10 Neill, Stephen, *Crises of Belief: The Christian Dialogue with faith and No Faith*, Hodder, London, 1984, pp. 125-58.

11 Humphreys, Christmas, *Buddhism*, Penguin, London, 1951; cf. De Silva, Lynn A, *The Problem of the Self in Buddhism and Christianity*, Macmillan, London, 1975, p. 60.

> ultimate. But, conventional or not, it is in some sense a self exercising a will about itself. [*Ibid.,* p. 291f.]

These sharp contrasts might suggest a thoroughgoing polemical approach. But in fact they emerge only at the end of Cragg's treatment of Buddhism, while earlier passages, though never failing to distinguish the Christian and the Buddhist teaching, see many 'meanings' in Buddhist doctrine which run parallel to Christian thought. Despite the later comments about the contradictions in the Buddhist understanding of the Self, Cragg is prepared for paradox about it, on the grounds that no faith escapes paradox, least of all Christianity. 'There is this strange paradox about the Buddhist thesis of the self, namely that the loss of the self is almost self-fulfilling.' [*Ibid.,* p. 249] Yet one is compelled to ask whether Cragg has not taken unfair advantage of the English language here, and whether such a term as 'self-fulfilment' is ever used as a Buddhist expression in Buddhist languages. The question is extremely complex.[12]

As always Cragg's concern is to 'retrieve' the Buddhist concept. In outlining the Buddhist understanding of death Cragg sees in it 'a clue which Christian faith retrieves and enlarges.' The whole of Buddhist discipline can be regarded as a parable of what Christian discipleship means. [*Ibid.,* p. 285] Like other parables it has no one-to-one correspondence, and can mislead, but in general should be read positively for the truths it may illumine. As Cragg sees it, the Buddhist confuses the elimination of selfishness, which is desirable, with the elimination of selfhood, which is not. Nevertheless

> It would certainly be a Christian's duty to maximize whatever in Buddhism would allow one to speak of 'selfless persons' in whom personhood was real and the selflessness was that of character, not of extinction. [*Ibid.,* p. 293]

So Cragg finds many points at which, to use a photographic image, the Christian understanding is the positive picture of the Buddhist negative. He discovers Thomas Traherne, for example, using the vocabulary of Buddhism, fire, flame, discernment, emptiness, but all with the opposite sense, celebrating instead of turning away from existence. Cragg maintains that the question of which is right must remain open. 'Existence leaves to us whether to read it as annunciation or renunciation.' [*Ibid.,* p. 263] Again

12 See De Silva, *op. cit.*, ch. 6, 'The Quest for Self-Identity'.

he finds in Keats' idea of 'negative capability', or the ability to sustain doubt and uncertainty without requiring premature solutions, something in positive mode of what Buddhism conveys negatively through its concepts of *anicca, anatta* and *dukkha.* [*Ibid.,* p. 267f.]

The inevitable question is whether Cragg has rightly assessed the Buddhist meaning, whether the negative language is indeed the positive in another mode and therefore can be 'maximized', or something quite different. Conversely, has Cragg correctly perceived real difference, as in the question of theism and 'intentionality' behind the universe? Some Christians who have lived much closer to Buddhism for much longer than Cragg appear to have made different judgements. De Silva, for example, uses the well-known *Udana* passage which refers to 'an unborn, unbecome, unmade, uncompounded' and maintains that it clearly implies an 'Ultimate Reality' other than *Nirvana.* For '*Nirvana* is an experience related to the Absolute and not the Absolute in itself.' He quotes Romans 11:33—'How unsearchable are his judgements and how inscrutable his ways!'—to suggest that Christian theology has attempted to analyse God in minute detail, and consequently obscured him with its formulations.[13] Even Cragg himself suggests that *sunyata*, 'emptiness', or 'no-thing-ness', is properly understood as 'a silence to halt improper questions' [*Christ*, p. 252], and appears to accept Panikkar's acquittal of the Buddha as an agnostic. [*Troubled*, p. 213] William Johnston, a Jesuit scholar long resident in Japan, and so, admittedly, speaking from a Mahayana context, has written

> Some (Western philosophers) have not hesitated to call Buddhism atheistic.
>
> I believe … that this is a misunderstanding: we must not blind ourselves to the extremely positive elements which lie behind the negative language. First of all we must remember that Buddhism is above all a religion of salvation.

Johnston goes on to quote the same *Udana* passage from the Pali Canon used by the Theravadins, and to draw the same conclusions from it as Lynn De Silva.[14] But Cragg does not accept that Buddhism is about 'salvation' in the accepted sense. [*Christ*, p. 312 n. 4]

13 De Silva, *op. cit.*, pp. 123, 124, 125f.

14 Johnston, William, *The Inner Eye of Love. Mysticism and Religion*, Fount, London, 1981, pp. 113, 114.

We have noted earlier Cragg's difficulties with negative language in his strictures on the knowability of God in Islam. With Theravada Buddhism, on the other hand, it must be admitted that some Buddhists themselves hold an explicitly atheist view.[15] There are clearly great varieties of Western interpretation of Buddhism, and many problems arise because of the enormous contrast in philosophical assumptions and the sheer difficulty of understanding.[16] It is interesting, however, to note that Cragg appears not to have observed the similarity of both De Silva and Johnston's general approach to Buddhism to that which he has pioneered in relation to Islam. Nor has he shared their conclusions. This must raise doubts about the value of his interpretation of Buddhism.

15 Dharmasiri, Gunapala, *A Buddhist Critique of the Christian Concept of God*, Lake House, Colombo, 1974.

16 Johnston, *op. cit.*, p. 106f.

9
A VOCATION FOR ALL?

The main lines of Cragg's understanding of Christianity and other faiths are now clear. The case of Buddhism reveals a mind to some degree made up before a close examination is undertaken, and unwilling to be surprised. Perhaps the most remarkable thing about Cragg's writing is its revelation of a mind settled and even characteristic formulations evolved in the thesis of 1950. The same themes emerge in manifold variety: the God who undertakes for his creation the task of restoration for which the original decision to create has made him liable; how this restoration was worked for through the prophets and eventually brought about by the love that suffers; how Jesus became the Christ in whom this suffering love was finally and decisively made plain and effective for all; how that single event once recognised and accepted finds echoes or refractions everywhere. These have to be retrieved, in the exercise of hospitality to unfamiliar and alien ways of thought and life. For we are ourselves at all times recipients of the divine hospitality. Then it will be clear that God can be known, not merely by the elite engaging the ineffable in mystic trance, but by the most ordinary person untrained in prayer or contemplation. Cragg wrote remarkably little about mysticism for so prolific a writer. He regarded it as an escape, an evasion of the real religious issues.

His preference was to search for signs of God where one might least expect to find them, and even where religion itself is neglected or denied outright. He engaged consistently with secular voices. The work of Albert Camus continually recalled him to ask 'Why should the loss of meaning be so meaningful? Why should absurdity command such integrity in its defence?', and to feel beneath the literature of despair for the impulse of faith and hope on which every venture into literature depends. [*Privilege*, p. 166f.] He quotes Camus saying that 'A literature of despair is a contradiction in terms.' [*Other*, p. 12] Cragg's greatest gift is perhaps the ability to search out from the most unpromising material the unexpected evidence which indicates that the Spirit of God is never inactive. He is prepared to risk the bathos which could result from beginning a chapter entitled 'The Holy Spirit' with a quotation from Steinbeck's *Grapes of Wrath*: 'Can't you stick on somepin from Scripture so it'll be religious?' The scene finds the migrant Joads, too poor for funerals but fearing the authorities, writing out an explanation over Grandpa's makeshift grave. Cragg picks up, or using his characteristic vocabulary we could say 'retrieves', the word 'religious' and asks what the text requested could be thought to add. For the 'religiousness' is already there

> in the mortal pathos, in the dumb tragedy of social wrongs stoically borne, in the dignity of human courage in lowly quarters, in reverence for the dead, in the will to come clean, in the integrity that anticipates and cares about justification, in the family unity, in the patience of grief. With these, has the psalmist or the evangelist anything more to say? [*Other*, p. 103]

Cragg concludes that he has, though it is not something more in the sense of something other, but something which expresses what is already there, and seals it as a kiss or an embrace makes outward and visible the inward reality of love. The inner reality requires the outer expression. 'We might almost make the paradox that if the Joads had not wanted the text it would not have been necessary.' [*Ibid.*, p. 104] Here is a magnificent 'retrieval' for faith of an incident at first sight merely pathetic. The question that lingers, as we ask below, is whether everything is therefore religious? Is there, as he declares in connection with Elie Wiesel, 'a will to faith in the very passion of unbelief'? [*Troubled*, p. 75]

The artistic illustration and the metaphor of expression are characteristic, and provide the clue and even the justification for much of Cragg's writing. It explains not only the intricacy of his literary style but also the apparent, and in one sense real, circularity of thought. Many Craggian sentences return at their end to the phrase they began with, as a composer may complete his work by restating the opening theme—'A living religion calls for study on the part of those whose religion is alive.'[1] Sometimes, taken out of context, such sentences seem simply tautologous:

1 Cragg, Kenneth, art. 'The Christian church and Islam Today' in *The Muslim World* 42 (July 1952), p. 217.

'It is thus the historian who "makes" history, given the "history" (as yet unrecorded) which makes him historian.' [*Christ*, p. 199] Yet, as we have tried to show in that particular case, a real point is being made, and a genuine development of the argument created. Logic and mathematics, after all, are essentially tautologous and in them everything depends upon the force and elegance of the reasoning. That reasoning begins from a stated premise, and must reach its conclusion in consonance with it, without that conclusion covertly being made part of the premise in the first place. For that would be to sabotage the adventure of thought.

Cragg's writing may seem to some to be so constrained by its Christian premises that it does not embark on any real adventure. Such a view appears fortified by the very absence of any significant change of viewpoint in the years of literary production. But this would be to ignore another fundamental feature of his writing which is symbolized by the love of paradox and irony. Stimulated originally by readings in F D Maurice and Kierkegaard, this feature actually grew with Cragg until he needed to coin one of his neologisms to express the incidence of it. 'The fact of paradox does not, of course, disqualify the faith that clings to them. There is no religion exempt from paradoxicality. Christians should be least minded of all to urge against it.' [*Ibid.*, p. 249] For the contradictions expressed in paradox and irony are not, in Cragg's understanding, weaknesses in the formal structure of a faith's reflections on the way things are, but rather warnings not to rest too much faith on any given formulation. So he had found contemporaries doing in his youth. 'It is not seldom that faith erects a dogma where it would better hold a confidence.' [*Event*, p. 21] For mere loyalty to a dogma cannot deal with the contradictions that the faith will be faced with: contradictions intellectual from those who perceive flaws in the sense of the proposition, contradictions practical in the failures of the faithful to live according to it, and contradictions moral in the self-preserving instincts of the religious community.

There is another reason for Cragg's distrust of dogma, which does not spring merely from the personal experience recounted earlier, but from a particular understanding of the Christian faith which we have called dynamic. 'At least in our time, whatever may have earlier been true, relevance is not, first, to be realized by dint of proposition, but only of participation—ours with men.' [*World*, p. 215] Cragg's argument at that point concerns the inviting of humanity to faith in the Incarnation, and therefore the exercise, on the part of those who invite, of an Incarnational faith, one which shares the life and thinking of those invited. This is a stance, one might say a policy, well geared to deal with the explicit contradictions of opponents to the Christian faith, and the proponents of alternatives, both religious and secular. Cragg speaks of the harshness of the Muslim response to Christian convictions, and says,

> Yet the harshness has to be transcended, for much of it is well intentioned. And in any event the story to be told is only safe in the custody of those for whom every antagonism is an opportunity. For that, precisely, is the heart of the story itself. [*Call*, p. 164]

The commending of the faith must be in accordance with its own character, because there is an inner coherence of word and deed in Jesus himself which forms the core of the faith to be commended, and if that is lost nothing is left. The heart of the matter is reconciliation, and the restoration of unity.

The mention of coherence raises the question of whether Cragg has done justice to the intellectual and spiritual problems inherent in a religiously plural world. Does the character of his thought about other faiths offer real promise of the reconciliation he aims at? We have noted the eirenic nature of his intentions towards other faiths, particularly, in the context of ancient enmity, Islam. We have seen the highly appreciative comments of some Muslim reviewers towards his books, and the expected hostility of others. Even his critics have had to concede the extent of his knowledge of the Qur'an. Yet he does not by any means cover all aspects of Islam in his writing, and makes significant omission of most aspects of *Shari'ah*. Nor does he, like many Christian writers, focus on Sufism, but rather takes a special interest in contemporary Muslim apologetic. His concern here is therefore theological, but he does not always indicate an awareness that for many Muslims theology, or right thinking about God, is of little interest or importance compared with discovering the right conduct which God requires. Muslims lean to orthopraxy rather than to orthodoxy, and as people with a strong sense of God-given community think naturally in what Westerners would call 'political' terms, though all political life has a religious basis in Islam. (In the Christian case it would be truer to say that the faith has strong political implications.)

This causes Cragg considerable problems. Even among Muslims most positive towards him there is a feeling that he over-emphasizes the tragic element in life, and sometimes writes as though a successful outcome to corporate moral and spiritual struggle can never be authentic. More hostile reviewers have asked whether his sensitivity towards the abuse of power by Muslim leaders should not be applied to Christian parallels. Perhaps the limitations of his sympathies are most evident in the brief references to Christian liberation theology, which he identifies with the 'power-assurance' and legalism that he repeatedly criticises in Islam. [*Muhammad*, p. 157, 158; cf. *Pen*, p. 74f.] Cragg's 'reservation about Muhammad' is precisely his reservation about the Mexican theologian José P Miranda, and about Marx, whom Miranda couples with the Bible in the title of his book.[2] But as Cragg's discussion of Miranda makes clear, more is at stake for Cragg than a theology of law or of liberation. The question arises: can God be known or only obeyed?

For the dominant 'imperative mood', as Cragg calls it, the prescriptive power of the Qur'an and of some Christian theologies can be used, as in Miranda's case, to forbid any 'indicative' theology which speaks descriptively of God. Miranda fears that a pre-occupation with ontological descriptions of God evades the prophetic call to obedience and social justice. So Cragg is moved to ask:

> Is revelation only for obedience, or can it be also for fellowship? Is the divine related only as commanding us? Or also as 'desiring' us? Is there a meaning in 'transcendence' which truly descends into our knowledge, and dependably so, without ceasing to surpass all knowing?[3]

In the common tendency to discount or radically qualify all such knowledge Cragg finds threatened the reciprocal relationship between humanity and God which is at the heart of his theological understanding, and which alone makes sense of his hope for universal reconciliation. But this leads him into considerable difficulties, as we have seen, with negative language about God, whether its source is al-Ghazzali, Aquinas

2 Miranda, José P, *Marx and the Bible. A Critique of the Philosophy of Oppression*, Eng. tr., Orbis, New York, 1974.

3 Cragg, Kenneth, art. 'Tadabbur al-Qur'an: reading and meaning' in A H Green ed., *In Quest of an Islamic Humanism: Arabic and Islamic Studies in Memory of Mohamed al-Nowaihi*, American University in Cairo Press, Cairo, 1984, p. 189.

or the Buddha. He does not seem to have benefited as he might have done from contact with Christian Orthodox theology, with its strong apophatic tradition, and its openness to mysticism.

The same influences might have placed a question mark over his fondness for 'kenotic' language about God, and the ideas of Bushnell and Wheeler-Robinson which place such emphasis on Calvary. The Orthodox tradition balances the Cross with the Resurrection, which features surprisingly little in Cragg's presentation of Christianity. It also fights shy of any suggestion of passibility in God, and would have grave reservations about Wheeler Robinson's 'Kenosis of the Spirit'. For Orthodoxy 'Pentecost is not a "continuation" of the Incarnation. It is its sequel, its result … Pentecost is thus the object, the final goal, of the divine economy upon earth.'[4] In the light of this Cragg emerges as a man still firmly identified with his Protestant background, despite an eclectic cast of mind. Is his also too human an account of Christian faith? For this is clearly the danger, as it is the fascination, of his doctrine of reciprocity between God and humanity, and the doctrine of 'divine liability' which goes with it. Can human beings really call God to account? Cragg would say Yes, because of the faithfulness God keeps with himself and his venture in humanity. So Camus and others can be seen as secular prophets calling for a purer understanding of the character of God, in the confidence that every protest against religion is at heart a demand for better religion. The trouble with this very skill in observing religious significance everywhere, is that if everything is religion the word ceases to have useful meaning. We have simply made God in our own image.

This is merely the negative aspect of Cragg's powerful concept of retrieval. As he uses the term, retrieval is the work of God in mending the broken creation. Christ is his chosen instrument, and those who become his followers share in his work of retrieval, knowing themselves called to be redeemers in their turn. But the work of the Spirit of Christ is not limited to the Church, and others can share in it too. Cragg does not use and will not approve the idea of 'anonymous Christians' or 'anonymous Christianity'. Yet his positive assessment of so many elements in Islam and to lesser degree other faiths does in other respects suggest a Rahnerian approach, in which all that is good in other faiths must be claimed as the work of Christ. At the same time he retains a Barthian suspicion

4 Lossky, Vladimir, *The Mystical Theology of the Eastern Church*, Eng. tr., James Clarke, Cambridge, 1957, p. 159.

of religion in its established forms, though this is directed more at the institutions of religion, and the morality of religious (like other) collectives, than at the enterprise of religion in itself. Cragg is then both positive and negative towards religion as a human phenomenon, though he is most positive towards the tentative, fragile expression, and most hostile to the exercise of religious coercion on the part of governments. But Cragg never abandoned the aim of 'recruitment' to Christian understanding and loyalty. Though he questioned the policy of administering baptism to individuals in some circumstances, his position as regards mission did not fundamentally change from that of the young missionary who wrote in 1943 that

> our Christian evangelism must go on battering by thought and literature, by speech and service, by lip and life at those ears and minds and hearts which are so fortified, till the fortifications begin to crumble and to fall. And fall they must, for they are false.[5]

Even the quotation from *Hamlet* which begins that article and provides its controlling image is used and re-used later: *Sit down awhile, and let us once again assail your ears which are so fortified against our story*. [*Call*, p. ix] *Absent thee from felicity awhile And in this harsh world draw thy breath in pain To tell My story,* from the final scene of *Hamlet* prefaces a book from 2006.[*Hands*, p. xv] The later books are just as insistent as the earlier that 'The Christian Gospel is conversionist through and through.' [*Christ*, p. 17]

It is for this reason that, in spite of early experiences at their hands, Cragg was still acceptable to conservative evangelical thinkers about mission, and frequently called into their counsels. They were aware that he owed much to the tradition of Protestant missionary venture towards Islam, with his acknowledged debt to Temple Gairdner and Constance Padwick, and distinct resemblances to Duncan Black Macdonald, Gairdner's teacher. He shared Macdonald's fascination with the Muslim mind and his determination to let Islam speak for itself, while struggling to relate that speech to Christian faith and Western culture. Nor would Cragg repudiate entirely the tradition which focussed on controversy with Islam, because 'for all our revision of their methods, the great

5 Cragg, Kenneth, art. 'A Moslem Stronghold' in *Under Syrian Skies* (April 1943), p. 45.

Lulls and Martyns of the past still serve as our exemplars … From such "controversy" there is no loyal escape.'[6] He even sympathised with the central contention of men like Kraemer, with whom in other respects he disagreed, that Islam is fundamentally superficial on the question of sin, and that the hinge-event of Muhammad's career, the *Hijrah*, reveals the spiritual inadequacy of the faith.

It is perhaps in his traditional Christian view of the *Hijrah,* with all that goes with it of regret for the campaigns and policies of Medina, that he most clearly loses Muslim sympathy. He argues repeatedly in his later writings for the 'priority of Mecca', the preaching that Medina fought to defend, but can find little Muslim support for such 'reverse abrogation'. Shabbir Akhtar, vigorously opposed to what he regards as Cragg's extreme pacifism, gently notes his status as 'a bishop sympathetic to the travail of ordinary people, (who) remains nonetheless … insulated by layers of privilege. He is a white male ensconced among the religious and educational elite of an important nation.'[7] It is true that Cragg, like every Western Christian has benefited from the forceful imposition of Christianity on Europe by Constantine, and by the centuries of Anglican hegemony in England. Cragg himself notes the parallel in saying that 'Muhammad was his own Constantine.' His lack of sympathy for Miranda is significant.

A related feature of his later writing, the insistent attack on retaliation and the *lex talionis*, is less controversial, and his major book on the subject, *The Iron in the Soul. Joseph and the Undoing of Violence* (2009) is a creative study of a neglected figure. Intriguingly the cover is a picture of Israeli soldiers at the Western (Wailing) Wall in Jerusalem. Perhaps a powerful passage in a previous book (*A Christian-Muslim Inter-Text Now* 2007) stimulated the focus on Joseph.

> The folly of retaliation is closely tallied with the fact of suffering … What did Palestinian suiciders gain from their self-immolation vested in the griefs of Israelis unless the rearing of the Wall as a countering policy? … What did Israel gain from sundry invasions or incursions into Lebanon except a mounting of legitimate resentment … That of

6 Cragg, Kenneth, art. 'The Christian Church and Islam Today' in *The Muslim World* 42 (October 1952), p. 281.

7 Akhtar, Shabbir, *Islam as Political Religion: The Future of an Imperial Faith*, Routledge, London, 2011, p. 122.

> 2006 was grimly counter-productive doing the utterly folly-laden thing of no 'endearing', reconciling, healing sense at all. [*Inter-Text*, p. 197]

His treatment of faiths other than Islam, beneath its sophistication, is firmly in the traditions of Western Protestantism, though some in those traditions will be uneasy with his insistence on the 'exceptionality' of Jewish people-hood as the central problem of Judaism. But he did not simply leave that Protestant tradition where he found it. He developed a theology of mission to Islam, and not simply to Muslims, which takes with profound seriousness the self-definition of those believers, while probing its real adequacy as a vehicle for the worship of a God able to deal with the world as we know it. So he was able to ask persistently not *whether* Islam is to be adopted, or retained, but *how* a true *islam* can be offered. He thus avoided both negativity towards other faiths, and an uncertain Christian anchorage, where Christ is no longer, or not pre-eminently, definitive of God. He is one of the elder statesmen of what has been known as Inclusivism, boldly hospitable to other faiths, and ready to learn from them, but secure in the Christian home from which such hospitality is offered.[8]

What then did Cragg achieve? There is no doubting the depth of his engagement with the Qur'an and with Muslim apologetic. The manner of his treatment of other scriptures and religious traditions is open, positive, humane and perceptive. He commends by precept and example an approach to other faiths which continually struggles to keep open the channels of communication while never evading the controversial questions. He attempted new and important refinements of these questions which offer real liberation to minds clouded with historic misunderstandings. His consistent emphasis on personal relationships is of particular value to the newly plural societies of the West, where historic prejudices threaten the growth of mutual acceptance. At the same time there is a certain evasiveness on the major questions of the Christian theology of religion, and a deep reluctance to pronounce on the status of other faiths in relation to Christianity.

This can be understood in terms of his personal history, and as missionary method, but does not assist Christians deeply puzzled by the Church's empirical acceptance of other religious traditions as it makes the

---

8 Cf. D'Costa, Gavin, *Theology and Religious Pluralism. The Challenge of Other Religions*, Blackwell, Oxford, 1986, p. 122.

daily policy decisions of its social witness. Here his repeated reminders of the immorality of collectives, while passionate and pertinent, do not make for clarity of thought about the religio-political issues of the day. Both his literary style and his unease in handling questions of political theology indicate a rather private, even idiosyncratic, mind whose fertility is easier to appreciate than to transpose into specific decisions. His theology, in short, is admirably adapted to inspire and invigorate a struggling minority of Christian believers. It has not been shaped by the current situation of many Western countries, where Christians made deeply uncertain of the value of their own historic Western culture are nevertheless representatives of the dominant religious tradition, and so compelled to make or influence decisions profoundly affecting the lives of the adherents of other faiths. 'We do not here take up the politics of inter-religion,' he warns in the opening pages of his most complete statement on Christian faith and other faiths. [*Christ*, p. 7] So, unlike his fellow-Anglican bishop and Islamic scholar David Brown, he explicitly declined to construct a detailed Christian vision of a plural society.[9]

We cannot, however, leave Cragg's massive and enduring contribution there. The nearest equivalent figure is perhaps Louis Massignon, with his own lifelong service to Islamic scholarship on Sufism and his intense desire to serve the cause of Muslim-Christian reconciliation for Christ's sake. Though, unlike Cragg, Massignon was from the beginning an Orientalist, like Cragg he believed he had found 'Islamic reasons for being Christian'. Cragg's influence in his Anglican and Protestant circle has been as extensive as Massignon's in the Roman Catholic Church. He would want to be assessed first as a missionary to Islam rather than as an Orientalist, and in this respect his concept of retrieval does in a Protestant context what Massignon's more sacramental idea of *badaliyya* does in a Catholic. We have noted that as a theologian he refused to be drawn on the question of the status of faiths relative to Christianity, and in that respect declined to join the current debate with its religio- and socio-political implications. However, his missionary concepts are thoroughly theological, not merely pragmatic, and offer, with the qualification already noted, a coherent and Biblically-grounded Christian theology of inter-faith relations. As scholar and Arabist he concentrated on the Qur'an and contemporary Muslim writers and hardly at all on historic Islam. The result is deeply-held and

9 Brown, David, *All Their Splendour. World Faiths: The Way to Community*, Collins, London, 1982.

somewhat idiosyncratic views on Islam, and to a degree on other faiths. However, we have noted that some criticisms of his work are mutually contradictory, especially on the issue of 'Christianising' Islam. As writer and poet he had immense skills to make the alien and bewildering suddenly familiar and attractive, though the richness and density of his writing does not always carry the reader with him.

Cragg stands firmly in the succession of missionaries to Islam, but in no clear intellectual tradition. His instincts intellectually are eclectic, guided more by artistic than logical considerations. The range and richness of his work constitutes a call to the missionary, the theologian and the ordinary Christian with neighbours of another faith, a call to retrieve ignorance, misunderstanding and alienation in a Christ-like hospitality to the world, and a Christ-like embassy resident within it. It is a call to which contemporary Christians must respond if they are to be faithful to the Gospel in a world grown suddenly small and yet bewilderingly diverse.

GLOSSARY

The meanings given are those appropriate to this text. Many of the terms explained here have much fuller and richer meanings than those given.

'abada	to serve, worship
abrogation	cancellation of a law by a later revelation
'adl	justice
al-akhira	the Hereafter
amanah	the Trust
amr	matter, affair
anthropomorphism	ascribing human characteristics to God
apophatic	denying that human categories apply to God
'aql	intellect
Arian Logos	a secondary divinity in the manner of Arius (250-336)
avatar	earthly manifestation of a Hindu deity
al-Azhar	ancient Sunni mosque and university in Cairo
asbab al-nuzul	the circumstances of revelation
badaliyya	Massignon's idea of 'exchange' where Christians pray for Muslims
balagh	preaching, warning
Barth, -ian	Karl Barth (1886-1968) stressed God's initiative and opposed metaphysics
bi-la kaif	without (asking) how
deus ex machina	an artificial solution to a problem
Fiqh Akbar	an early codification of Muslim law
furqan	criterion, a title of the Qur'an
ghaib	the unseen world
Gnostic	emphasizing (often secret) knowledge and mythology
hadith	a tradition attributed to Muhammad
hadith qudsi	Muhammad's report of God's words not in the Qur'an
Hanafite	one of the four Sunni law schools
Hijrah	migration from Mecca to Medina in 622
Hira'	the cave in which Muhammad first received the Qur'an
hululi	Incarnation, incarnationists
Iblis	the Devil, Satan

Ihya' 'ulum al-din	'The Revival of the Religious Sciences', Ghazzali's major work
i'jaz	the miracle or uniqueness of the Qur'an
ijma'	consensus on a point of law
ijtihad	individual striving to solve a question
al-insan al-kamil	the Perfect Man, identified as Muhammad
istighna	self-sufficiency, independence of God
islam	submission, surrender to God
Isma'ili	a sect of Shi'ism, followers of the seventh Imam
jahiliyya	time of ignorance before the Qur'an was revealed
jihad	struggle in the way of God to establish good
jinn	beings created of fire
kalam	the speech of God, theology
kenosis, -otic	the 'emptying' of his divine status by Christ in taking human form (Philippians 2.7)
khalifa/ khilafa	vice-gerent, vice-gerency
khalil	friend (Abraham was a friend of God)
khaliqa	created beings, creation
Kharijite	7th century Muslim dissidents, rejecting rulers judged immoral
kufr/ kafir	ingratitude, unbelief, unbeliever
lahut	divine
Liberal Catholicism	a movement in Anglicanism open to the results of critical scholarship
liqa'	meeting
madhab pl. *madhahib*	school of thought in Muslim law
Madina	the City of the Prophet (formerly called Yathrib)
mahmud	praised, lauded
Makka	preferred spelling of Mecca
makhluq	created
mala'ika	angels
malakuti	angelic
Marcionite	Marcion (d. 160) rejected the Old Testament and much of the New, accepting only the letters of Paul and a version of Luke's Gospel
minbar	mosque pulpit
Mishkat al-anwar	'The Niche for Lights' by Ghazzali
mufassir	commentator on the Qur'an
mujaddid	one who renews, reforms the Muslim community
munafiqun	hypocrites pretending loyalty to Islam
munajah	relationship
munasabah	resemblance, conformity
Mu'tazilite	Muslim rationalist
mutakallim	Muslim theologian, dialectician
ontology	what underlies appearance, what really is
nafs pl. *anfus*	the inner self, soul
nasut	human

passibility	the idea that God can be affected by human events and so change
praeparatio evangelica	a situation prepared for the preaching of the Christian Gospel
qadar	power, capacity
qadim	ancient, eternal
qalam	pen
qiblah	the direction to face in canonical prayer
qist	justice, equity
rabb	Lord (used only of God)
Rahner, -ian	Karl Rahner (1904-1984) taught that all people participate in the grace of God and so are 'Anonymous Christians'
rasul	apostle, messenger
reification	treating as real and concrete what is only an abstraction or an idea
ruh pl. *arwah*	spirit
Shafi'i	ninth-century jurist, founder of Shafi'i school of law
shaikh	teacher of Islam
shari'ah	the codified law of Islam
shaytan	a devil, evil spirit
shibboleth	originally a test of pronunciation to identify foreigners, so an in-language
Shi'ism	the party of 'Ali, minority group in Islam
shirk	polytheism, associating partners with God
sifaat	the attributes of God
soteriology	concerning salvation
Stygian	from the Styx, in Greek mythology the river at the boundary of earth and the underworld
sufism/tasawwuf	the mystical dimension of Islam
sunna	the path, or practice of Muhammad
sunyata	literally 'emptiness', the absence in Buddhism of a controlling self in the individual or the universe
tajalli	appearing in glory, a theophany
taqlid	faithful following of an earlier legal ruling
tafsir	commentary on the Qur'an
theodicy	concerning the justice of God
theomorphic	being in the shape of God
Theravada	the 'teaching of the elders', the dominant form of Buddhism in Sri Lanka and SE Asia
Udana	sayings of the Buddha in the Pali canon
umma	the worldwide community of Muslims
Umayyad	first Muslim Arab dynasty 661-750
wali	a friend, patron or person of great piety
zandaqa	dualism
zulm	injustice, tyranny, wrong-doing

GENERAL BIBLIOGRAPHY

ADAMS, Charles: 'Islamic Religious Tradition' in BINDER, L: *The Study of the Middle East: Research and Scholarship in the Humanities and Social Sciences*. New York, 1971.

AKHTAR, Shabbir: *Islam as Political Religion. The future of an imperial faith.* Oxford: Routledge, 2011.

ALLARD, Michel: *Le Problème des Attributs Divins dans la doctrine d'al-Ash'ari et de ses premiers grands disciples* Beirut. Éditions de l'Imprimerie Catholique, 1965.

ANDERSON, Norman: *Christianity and World Religions*. Leicester: IVP, 1984.

ANDERSON, Gerald H and STRANSKY, Thomas F: *Mission Trends number 5: Faith Meets Faith* New York/Grand Rapids: Paulist Press/Eerdmans, 1981.

ANSARI, Md Abdul Haq: *Sufism and Shari'ah. A Study of Shaykh Ahmad Sirhindi's Effort to Reform Sufism*. Leicester: The Islamic Foundation, 1986.

ASAD, Muhammad: *The Message of the Qur'an*. Gibraltar: Dar al-Andalus, 1980.

AYOUB, Mahmoud M: *Redemptive Suffering in Islam. A Study of the Devotional Aspects of 'Ashura' in Twelver Shi'ism*. The Hague: Mouton, 1978.

——*The Qur'an and its Interpreters*. volume 1 Albany: State University of New York Press, 1984.

BALJON, J M S: *Modern Muslim Koran Interpretation (1880-1960)* Leiden: Brill, 1961.

BASETTI-SANI, Giulio: *The Koran in the Light of Christ. A Christian Interpretation of the Sacred Book of Islam*. Chicago: Franciscan Herald Press, 1977.

BELL, R and WATT, W M: *Introduction to the Qur'an*. Edinburgh: Edinburgh University Press, 1970.

BIJLEFELD, Wim: art. 'The Danger of "Christianising" our Partners in Dialogue" in *The Muslim World* vol. 57:3 (July 1967), pp. 171-7.

BODINE, J J: The Romanticism of Duncan Black Macdonald, unpub. Ph.D thesis for the Hartford Seminary Foundation, USA, 1973.

BOYD, R H S: *An Introduction to Indian Christian Theology*. Madras: CLS rev. ed., 1975.

BREINER, Bert: *Abraham in Judaism, Christianity and Islam: Faith and Encounter.* Unpublished Ph.D. thesis, Birmingham University, 1985.

BREWSTER, D P: *Al-Hallaj: Muslim Mystic and Martyr*. Christchurch: University of Canterbury, 1976.

BRITISH Council of Churches: *Towards Understanding the Arab-Israeli Conflict. The Report of a BCC Delegation to the Middle East.* London: BCC, 1982.

BROWN, David: *All Their Splendour. World Faiths: The Way to Community*. London: Collins. 1982

BROWNE, E G: *A Year Amongst the Persians. Impressions as to the Life, Character and Thought of the People of Persia received during Twelve Months' Residence in that Country in the Years 1887-1888.* London: Century edition, 1984.

al-BUKHARI: *Al-Jami' Al-Sahih*, vol 4 [ed. Juynboll] Leiden: Brill, 1908.

CARMAN, John B: art. 'A New Assessment of the Christian Encounter with Islam' in *The Bulletin of the Henry Martyn Institute* LVIII:2 (Apr-June 1960), pp. 38-51, and LIX:1 (July-Sept 1960), pp. 13-32 [a review of W Bijlefeld: *De Islam als Na-Christelijke Religie*, Utrecht, 1959].

CHADWICK, Owen: *The Victorian Church.* (Part One) London: Black, 1966.

——*The Victorian Church.* (Part Two) London: Black, 1970.

——*Hensley Henson. A Study in the Friction between Church and State.* Oxford: Clarendon, 1983.

CHAPMAN, Colin: *Whose Promised Land?* Tring, Herts: Lion Publishing, 1983.

CORM, Charles: *La Montagne Inspirée. Chansons de Geste.* Beirut: Editions de la Revue Phénicienne, 1964.

CRACKNELL, Kenneth: *Towards a New Relationship. Christians and People of Other Faith.* London: Epworth, 1986.

DANIEL, Norman: review of *Muhammad and the Christian* and *Jesus and the Muslim* in *The Tablet* 16 August 1986.

D'COSTA, Gavin; *Theology and Religious Pluralism. The Challenge of Other Religions.* Oxford: Blackwell, 1986.

DEHQANI-TAFTI, H B: review of *The Dome and the Rock* in *The International Review of Missions* 54 (April 1965), pp. 206-209.

DE SILVA, Lynn A: *The Problem of the Self in Buddhism and Christianity*. Colombo: SCRS 1975 [also London: Macmillan/New York: Barnes, 1979].

DHARMASIRI, Gunapala: *A Buddhist Critique of the Christian Concept of God.* Colombo: Lake House, 1974.

DILLISTONE, F W: *Into All the World. A Biography of Max Warren.* London: Hodder and Stoughton, 1980.

DI MATTEO: *La Divinita di Cristo e la Dottrina della Trinita in Maometto e nei Polemisti Musulmani.* Rome, 1938.

DODGE, Bayard: *The American University of Beirut.* Beirut: AUB, 1958.

ed DOUGLAS, J D: *New International Dictionary of the Christian Church.* Grand Rapids: Zondervan, 1974.

Encyclopaedia of Islam. 1st edition Leiden: Brill, 1913-1934.

EDMONDS, P: review of *Paul and Peter* in *The Heythrop Journal* 23 (1982), pp. 187-188.

ELKHOLY, Abdo: art. 'The Concept of Community in Islam' in eds. AHMAD, K and ANSARI, Z I: *Islamic Perspectives. Studies in Honour of Mawlana Sayyid Abul 'Ala Mawdudi.* Leicester: Islamic Foundation/Jeddah: Saudi Publishing House, 1979, pp. 171-181.

FAKHRY, Majid: *A History of Islamic Philosophy*, 2nd ed. London: Longman, 1983.

al-FARUQI, Ismail: review of *Alive to God* in *The Journal of Ecumenical Studies* 12:2 (Spring 1975), pp. 265-267.

FAZLUR RAHMAN: *Islam.* Chicago: University of Chicago Press 2nd ed., 1979.

——*Major Themes of the Qur'an.* Minneapolis: Bibliotheca Islamica, 1980.

——*Islam and Modernity. Transformation of an Intellectual Tradition.* Chicago: University of Chicago Press, 1982.

FITZGERALD, Michael: review of *The Hallowed Valley* in *Islamochristiana* 5 (1979), pp. 260-261.

FITZMAURICE, Redmond: review of *Muhammad and the Christian* in the *Newsletter* of the Centre for the Study of Islam, Selly Oak Colleges, no. 11 (May 1984), pp. 46-47.

FYZEE, Asaf A A: review of *The House of Islam* in *Islamic Culture* 50:1 (January 1976), pp. 48-49.

GADAMER, Hans-Georg: *Truth and Method.* ET, London: Sheed and Ward 2nd ed., 1979.

GAIRDNER, W H T: *The Reproach of Islam.* London: CMS, 1909.

——art. 'Al-Ghazali's *Mishkat al-Anwar* and the Ghazali-Problem' in *Der Islam* 5 (1914), pp. 121-153.

——tr. with introduction of Al-Ghazzali: *Mishkat al-Anwar.* London: Royal Asiatic Society, 1924.

GÄTJE, Helmut: *The Qur'an and its Exegesis. Selected Texts with Classical and Modern Muslim Interpretations.* ET, London: RKP, 1976.

GEERTZ, Clifford: *Islam Observed. Religious Development in Morocco and Indonesia.* Chicago: Chicago University Press 2nd ed., 1971.

al-GHAZZALI: *Ihya Ulum id-Din*, 4 vols. ET, Lahore: Sind Sagar Academy, 1971.

GIBB, H A R: *Islam. A Historical Survey.* 2nd ed. London: OUP, 1953.

GOLDZIHER, Ignaz: *Introduction to Islamic Theology and Law.* ET (German ed. 1910) Princeton: Princeton University Press, 1981.

GORE, Charles: *The Incarnation of the Son of God.* London: John Murray, 1891.

——ed.: *Lux Mundi. A Series of Studies in the Religion of the Incarnation.* London, 1889.

HAMIDULLAH, M: review of *The Call of the Minaret* in *The Islamic Quarterly* 3:3 and 4 (Oct. 1956 and Jan. 1957), pp. 245-249.

HASAN, Ahmad: *The Doctrine of Ijma' in Islam. A Study of the Juridical Principle of Consensus*. Islamabad: Islamic Research Institute, 1978.

HEWITT, Gordon: *The Problems of Success. A History of the CMS 1910-1942*. Vol. 1 London: SCM, 1971.

HICK, John: *God and the Universe of Faiths*. London: Macmillan/New York: St Martin's Press, 1973.

——ed: *The Myth of God Incarnate*. London: SCM, 1977.

——*God Has Many Names. Britain's New Religious Pluralism*. London: Macmillan, 1980.

eds HICK, J and HEBBLETHWAITE, B L: *Christianity and Other Religions. Selected Readings*. Glasgow: Collins, 1980.

HODGSON, Marshall: *The Venture of Islam* (3 vols). Chicago: Chicago University Press, 1974.

HOURANI, Albert: art. 'Christians and Muslims' in *Frontier* 3:2 (Summer 1960) pp. 127-132 [reprinted in HOURANI: *Europe and the Middle East*. London: Macmillan, 1980, chapter 3.

——*Arabic Thought in the Liberal Age 1798-1939*. London: OUP, 1962.

HUJWIRI: *The* Kashf al-Mahjub, *the Oldest Persian Treatise on Sufism*, tr R A Nicholson Gibb Memorial Series (1st ed. 1911) London, 1959.

HUMPHREYS, Christmas: *Buddhism*. London: Penguin, 1951.

IBN AL-'ARABI: *The Bezels of Wisdom*. ET, tr. with intro. by R W J Austin. London: SPCK, 1980.

IBN KHALDUN: *The Muqaddimah. An Introduction to History*. ET, F. Rosenthal. 3 vols London: RKP, 1958.

IQBAL, Allama Md: *The Reconstruction of Religious Thought in Islam*. Lahore: Ashraf, 1971.

IZUTSU, Toshihiko: *The Structure of the Ethical Terms in the Qur'an. A Study in Semantics*. Tokyo: Keio University, 1959.

JAMEELAH, Maryam: *Islam and Modernism*. Lahore: Yusuf Khan, 1968.

Islam and Orientalism. Lahore: Yusuf Khan, 1971.

JANSEN, J J G: *The Interpretation of the Koran in Modern Egypt*. Leiden: Brill, 1974.

JOHNSTON, William: *The Inner Eye of Love. Mysticism and Religion*. London: Fount, 1981.

JOMIER, Jacques: *Les Grands Thèmes du Coran*. Paris: Centurion, 1978.

KRAEMER, Hendrik: *The Christian Message in a non-Christian World*. London: Edinburgh House Press, 1938

KÜNG, Hans and LAPIDE, Pinchas: *Brother or Lord? A Jew and a Christian Talk together about Jesus*. ET, Glasgow: Collins, 1977.

LAMB, Christopher A: art. 'The Editorials of the Muslim World 1911-1968' in *The Muslim World* 71:1 (January 1981), pp. 3-26.

LAMBTON, A K S: art. 'Quis Custodiet Custodes. Some Reflections on the Persian Theory of Government' in *Studia Islamica* V (1956), pp. 125-148, and VI (1956), pp. 125-146.

LANDAU, Rom: *The Philosophy of Ibn 'Arabi.* London: Allen and Unwin, 1959.

LAPIDE, Pinchas: *The Resurrection of Jesus. A Jewish Perspective.* ET, London: SPCK, 1984.

LECOMTE, Gerard: *Le Traité des Divergences du Hadit d'Ibn Qutayba* (annotated tr. of *Kitab Ta'wil Mukhtalif al-Hadith*). Damascus: Institut Français, 1962.

LEDIT, Ch. J: *Mahomet, Israel et Le Christ.* Paris, 1952.

LINDBECK, George: *The Nature of Doctrine. Religion and Theology in a Post-Liberal Age.* London: SPCK, 1984.

LOSSKY, Vladimir: *The Mystical Theology of the Eastern Church.* ET, Cambridge: James Clarke, 1957.

ed McCURRY, Don: *The Gospel and Islam. A 1978 Compendium.* Monrovia, California: MARC, 1979.

MACDONALD, Duncan Black: *The Religious Attitude and Life in Islam.* Chicago: University of Chicago Press, 1909.

——art. 'The Development of the Idea of Spirit in Islam' in *The Muslim World* 22:1 and 2 (Jan and Apr 1932) pp. 25-42, 153-168.

MAHMASSANI, S: *Falsafat al-Tashri fi al-Islam. The Philosophy of Jurisprudence in Islam.* ET (Arabic ed. 1946) Leiden: Brill, 1961.

MAIMONIDES, Moses: *The Guide of the Perplexed,* 2 vols. ET, Chicago: Chicago University Press, 1963.

MALIK, Charles: art. 'The Near East: The Search for Truth' in ed. HAIM, Sylvia G: *Arab Nationalism. An Anthology.* Berkeley, Losangeles 1964, pp. 189-224.

——art. 'The Orthodox Church' in ed. ARBERRY, A J: *Religion in the Middle East,* vol 1. Cambridge: Cambridge University Press 1969, pp. 297-346.

——ed. *God and Man in Contemporary Christian Thought.* Beirut: American University of Beirut, 1970.

MANWARING, Randle: *From Controversy to Co-existence. Evangelicals in the Church of England 1914-1980.* Cambridge: CUP, 1985.

MARMUR, Dow: *Beyond Survival. Reflections on the Future of Judaism.* London: DLT, 1982.

Bulletin of the HENRY MARTYN INSTITUTE: review of *Sandals at the Mosque,* Jan-Mar. 1960, pp. 48-53.

MASSIGNON, Louis: *Kitab al-Tawasin par al-Hallaj.* Paris: Guenther, 1913.

——*Le Lexique Technique de la Mystique Musulmane.* Paris: Guenther, 1922.

——*Les Trois Prières d'Abraham*. Paris, 1935.

——*The Passion of Al-Hallaj, Mystic and Martyr of Islam*, 4 vols. ET, H Mason, Princeton: Princeton University Press, 1982.

MAWDUDI, S Abul A'la: *Fundamentals of Islam*. ET, Lahore: Islamic Pubs, 1975.

The Meaning of the Qur'an, volume 1. Lahore: Islamic Pubs 2nd ed., 1971.

MAURICE, F D: *The Religions of the World and their Relations to Christianity*. 6th edition London: Macmillan, 1886.

MIRANDA, José P: *Marx and the Bible. A Critique of the Philosophy of Oppression*. ET, London, 1977.

MOZLEY, J K: *Some Tendencies in British Theology: From the Publication of* Lux Mundi *to the Present Day*. London: SPCK, 1952.

MUDGE, Lewis: art. 'Hermeneutics' in eds. RICHARDSON, Alan and BOWDEN, John: *A New Dictionary of Christian Theology*. London: SCM, 1983.

MULDER, D C: review of BIJLEFELD, W: *Islam als Na-Christelijke Religie* in *The International Review of Missions* 49 (1960), pp. 357-360.

MURAD, Khurram: review of *The House of Islam* in 'Hira and Madina: the West's dilemma' in *Muslim World Book Review* 1:3 (Spring 1981), pp. 3-9.

——review of *Islam from Within* in *Muslim World Book Review* 2:3 (Spring 1982), pp. 4-7.

MUSLIM, Imam: *Sahih Muslim, Being Traditions of the Sayings and Doings of the Prophet Muhammad*. ET, 4 vols, Lahore: Ashraf, 1976.

NASR, Seyyed Hossein: *Ideals and Realities of Islam*. London: Allen and Unwin 2nd ed., 1975.

——*Islam and the Plight of Modern Man*. London: Longman, 1975.

NEILL, S C: *Christian Faith Today*. London: Penguin, 1955.

——*Anglicanism*. London: Penguin, 3rd edition, 1965.

——*Crises of Belief. The Christian Dialogue with Faith and No Faith*. London: Hodder, 1984.

NEWBIGIN, Lesslie: *The Finality of Christ*. London: SCM, 1969.

The Open Secret. Sketches for a Missionary Theology. London: SPCK, 1978.

NIEBUHR, H Richard: *Christ and Culture*. London: Faber, 1952.

NIEBUHR, Reinhold: *Moral Man and Immoral Society. A Study in Ethics and Politics*. London: SCM, 1963 (1st ed. 1932).

al-NUWAIHI, Md: art. 'The Religion of Islam. A Presentation to Christians' in *The International Review of Mission* 65:258 (Apr 1976), pp. 216-225.

O'SHAUGHNESSY, Thomas: *The Development of the Meaning of Spirit in the Koran*. Rome: Pontifical Inistitute of Oriental Studies, 1953.

PADWICK, Constance: *Temple Gairdner of Cairo*. London: SPCK, 1929.

——art. 'North African Reverie' in *The International Review of Missions* 27:107 (July 1938), pp. 341-354.

——*Call to Istanbul.* London/New York: Longmans/Green, 1958.

——*Muslim Devotions. A Study of Prayer-Manuals in Common Use.* London: SPCK, 1961.

PARRINDER, G: *A Dictionary of Non-Christian Religions.* Amersham, Bucks: Hulton, 1971.

PARSHALL, Phil: *The Fortress and the Fire. Jesus Christ and the Challenge of Islam.* Bombay: Gospel Literature Service, 1975.

——*New Paths in Muslim Evangelism. Evangelical Approaches to Contextualization.* Grand Rapids: Baker, 1980.

PARTIN, Harry B: review of *Christianity in World Perspective* in *The International Review of Mission* 58 (October 1969), pp. 332-334.

PATTERSON, R L: *The Conception of God in the Philosophy of Aquinas.* London: Allen and Unwin, 1933.

PICKTHALL, M M: *The Meaning of the Glorious Koran. Text and Explanatory Translation.* Karachi: Taj n.d.

RACE, Alan: *Christians and Religious Pluralism. Patterns in the Christian Theology of Religions.* London: SCM, 1983.

RAHBAR, Daud: review article on *The Call of the Minaret* in *The Muslim World* 48:1 (January 1958), pp. 40-51.

RAHIM, Md 'Ata ur-: *Jesus. A Prophet of Islam.* London: MWH, 2nd ed., 1979.

RAISÄNEN, Heikki: art. 'The Portrait of Jesus in the Qur'an: Reflections of a Biblical Scholar' in *M W* 70:2 (April 1980), pp. 122-133.

RAMSEY, A Michael: *F D Maurice and Modern Theology.* Cambridge: CUP, 1951.

——*From Gore to Temple.* London: Longmans, 1960.

REARDON, B M G: *From Coleridge to Gore: A Century of Religious Thought in Britain.* London: Longman, 1971.

RICOEUR, Paul: *Essays on Biblical Interpretation.* London: SPCK, 1981.

RICHARDSON, A and Bowden, J: *A New Dictionary of Christian Theology.* London: SCM, 1983.

ROBINSON, J A T: *Truth is Two-Eyed.* London: SCM, 1979.

SAID, Edward W: *Orientalism.* London: RKP, 1978.

SALIBI, Kamal: *The Modern History of Lebanon.* New York: Caravan, 1977.

SCHACHT, Joseph: art. 'Theology and Law in Islam' in ed. von Grunebaum: *Theology and Law in Islam.* Wiesbaden: Harrassowitz, 1971, pp. 3-23.

SCHIMMEL, Annemarie: *Mystical Dimensions of Islam.* Chapel Hill: University of North Carolina Press, 1975.

——*And Muhammad is His Messenger. The Veneration of the Prophet in Islamic Piety.* Chapel Hill: University of North Carolina Press, 1985.

SCHUON, Frithjof: *Understanding Islam.* London: Allen and Unwin, 1963.

SCOTT, Frances E: *Dare and Persevere. The Story of One Hundred Years of Evangelism in Syria and Lebanon, from 1860 to 1960.* London: Lebanon Evangelical Mission, 1960.

SHARPE, Eric J: *Faith Meets Faith. Some Christian Attitudes to Hinduism in the 19th and 20th Centuries.* London: SCM, 1977.

SHEHADI, Fadlou: *Ghazali's Unique Unknowable God. A Philosophical Critical Analysis of some of the Problems raised by Ghazali's view of God as utterly unique and unknowable.* Leiden: Brill, 1964.

ed. SMART, Ninian et al: *Nineteenth Century Religious Thought in the West*, volume 2. Cambridge: Cambridge University Press, 1985.

SMITH, Wilfred Cantwell: *Modern Islam in India.* Lahore: Minerva Bookshop, 1943.

——review of *Christianity in World Perspective* in *Journal of American Academy of Religion* 37 (Summer 1969), pp. 305-306.

SMITH, J I and HADDAD, Y Y: *The Islamic Understanding of Death and Resurrection.* Albany, NY: State University of New York Press, 1981.

SOLOMON, Norman: art. 'A Commentary on "The Common Bond: Christians and Jews."' in *Christian-Jewish Relations* 18:3 (Sept. 1985), pp. 67-73.

SWEETMAN, J W: *Islam and Christian Theology.* London: Lutterworth, 4 vols, 1947-1967.

SYKES, Stephen W: *The Integrity of Anglicanism.* London: Mowbray, 1978.

THISELTON, Anthony: *The Two Horizons. New Testament Hermeneutics and Philosophical Description with special reference to Heidegger, Bultmann, Gadamer and Wittgenstein.* Exeter: Paternoster, 1980.

THOMAS, DAVID and AMOS, CLARE: *A Faithful Presence. Essays for Kenneth Cragg.* London: Melisende, 2003.

TIBAWI, A L: *American Interests in Syria 1800-1901. A Study of Educational, Literary and Religious Work.* Oxford: Clarendon, 1966.

——review of *The Dome and the Rock* in *Islamic Quarterly* 12:1,2 (Jan., June 1968), p. 120.

VAHIDUDDIN, Syed: review of *The Privilege of Man* in *Islamic Culture* 44:1 (January 1970), pp. 66-68.

——review of *The Event of the Qur'an* in *Islamic Culture* 47:2 (April 1973), pp. 175-178.

——review of *The Mind of the Qur'an* in *Islamic Culture* 48:1 (January 1974), pp. 59-62.

——review of *The Wisdom of the Sufis* in *Islamic Culture* 51:1 (January 1977), pp. 70-71.

——review of *Islam and the Muslim* in *Islamic Culture* 54:4 (October 1980), pp. 243-244.

——*The Islamic Experience in Contemporary Thought* being vol. 3 of ed. CW TROLL: *Islam in India. Studies and Commentaries.* Delhi: Chanakya Publ., 1986.

VICTOR, Henry: *A Critique of Kenneth Cragg's Response to Muslims.* Unpublished M.Theol. thesis, Serampore University, 1984.

VIDLER, Alec: *The Church in an Age of Revolution: 1789 to the Present Day.* London: Penguin, 1961.

Von DENFFER, A: *'Ulum al-Qur'an. An Introduction to the Sciences of the Qur'an.* Leicester: Islamic Foundation, 1985.

Von GRUNEBAUM, G: art. 'Observations of the Muslim Concept of Evil' in *Studia Islamica* 31 (1970), pp. 117-134.

WARREN, Max: *A Theology of Attention.* Madras: CLS/ISPCK, 1971.

WATT, W Montgomery: *The Formative Period of Islamic Thought.* Edinburgh: Edinburgh University Press, 1973.

——art. 'Suffering in Sunnite Islam' in *Studia Islamica* 50 (1979), pp. 5-19.

——*Islam and Christianity Today. A Contribution to Dialogue.* London: RKP, 1983.

WENSINCK, A J: *The Muslim Creed. Its Genesis and Historical Development.* Cambridge: Cambridge University Press, 1932.

WHALING, Frank: review of *The Christian and Other Religion* in *The Scottish Journal of Theology* 31:5 (1978), pp. 498-499.

WHEELER ROBINSON, H: *Redemption and Revelation in the Actuality of History.* London: Nisbet, 1942.

WOOTTON, R W F: *Jesus. More than a Prophet.* Leicester: IVP, 1982.

YUSUF 'ALI, A: *The Glorious Qur'an. Translation and Commentary.* Leicester: Islamic Foundation, 1975.

ZAEHNER, R C: *At Sundry Times.* London: Faber, 1958.

——art. 'Religious Truth' in ed. HICK, J: *Truth and Dialogue in World Religions: Conflicting Truth-Claims.* Philadelphia: Westminster Press, 1974, pp. 1-19.

——art. 'Why not Islam?' in *Religious Studies* 11:2 (June 1975), pp. 167-179.

ZWEMER, S M: *The Moslem Doctrine of God. An Essay on the Character and Attributes of Allah according to the Koran and Orthodox Tradition.* Boston: American Tract Society, 1905.

——*Studies in Popular Islam.* London: Sheldon, 1939.

A BIBLIOGRAPHY OF KENNETH CRAGG: BOOKS

References to these books in the text is to the abbreviated title and page number.

1956 *Call*

The Call of the Minaret. New York: OUP. 2nd ed. (rev. and enlarged) Maryknoll, New York: Orbis 1985/London: Collins 1986: 3rd edition Oxford 2000 (References in the text are to the 1986 edition.)

1959 *Sandals*

Sandals at the Mosque. Christian Presence amid Islam. London: SCM/New York: OUP

1959 *City*

(tr.) *City of Wrong. A Friday in Jerusalem* by M Kamel Hussein. Amsterdam: Djambatan and Oxford: Oneworld 1994

1964 *Dome*

The Dome and the Rock. Jerusalem Studies in Islam. London: SPCK

1965 *Counsels*

Counsels in Contemporary Islam. Islamic Surveys 3. Edinburgh: Edinburgh University Press

1966 *Unity*

(tr.with Ishaq Musa'ad) *The Theology of Unity by Muhammad 'Abduh.* London: Allen and Unwin

1968 *Privilege*

The Privilege of Man. A Theme in Judaism, Islam and Christianity. London: Athlone Press

1968 *World*

Christianity in World Perspective. London: Lutterworth/New York: OUP

1969 *House*

The House of Islam. California: Dickenson (2nd ed.1975)

1970 *Alive*

Alive to God. Muslim and Christian Prayer. London and New York: OUP
Revised as *Common Prayer. A Muslim-Christian Spiritual Anthology.* Oxford: Oneworld 1999

1971 *Event*
The Event of the Qur'an. Islam in its Scripture. London: Allen and Unwin (re-issued 1994)

1973 *Mind*
The Mind of the Qur'an. Chapters in Reflection. London: Allen and Unwin

1976 *Wisdom*
The Wisdom of the Sufis. London: Sheldon/New York: New Directions

1976 *Passage*
(tr.). *A Passage to France* by Taha Husain (Autobiography vol.3). Leiden: Brill

1977 *Other*
The Christian and Other Religion. The Measure of Christ. London: Mowbrays

1977 *Valley*
(tr.) *The Hallowed Valley. A Muslim Philosophy of Religion.* Cairo: American University

1978 *Islam*
Islam and the Muslim. Milton Keynes: Open University [used in conjunction with ed. Foy, W: Man's Religious Quest. A Reader London: Croom Helm/Open University 1978. pp 467-535]

1980 *Within*
Islam from Within. An Anthology of a Religion. (With Marston Speight) Belmont, California: Wadsworth

1980 *Paul*
Paul and Peter. Meeting in Jerusalem. London: Bible Reading Fellowship

1982 *Jerusalem*
This Year in Jerusalem. Israel in Experience. London: DLT

1984 *Muhammad*
Muhammad and the Christian. A Question of Response. London: DLT/New York: Orbis

1985 *Pen*
The Pen and the Faith. Eight Modern Muslim Writers and the Qur'an. London: Allen and Unwin

1985 *Jesus*
Jesus and the Muslim. An Exploration. London: Allen and Unwin

1986 *Christ*
The Christ and the Faiths. Theology in Cross-Reference. London: SPCK

1987 *Christmas*
Poetry of the Word at Christmas. Worthing: Churchman (revised and expanded 1996)

1988 *Readings*
(tr.) *Readings in the Qur'an.* London: Collins (republished Brighton 1999)

1989 *Decided*
What Decided Christianity. Event and Experience in the New Testament. Worthing: Churchman

1991 *Arab*
The Arab Christian. A History in the Middle East. London: Mowbray/Cassell

1992 *Meet*
To Meet and to Greet. Faith with Faith. London: Epworth

1992 *Troubled*
Troubled by Truth. Life-Studies in Inter-Faith Concern. Edinburgh: Pentland

1994 *Hira'*
Returning to Mount Hira'. Islam in Contemporary Terms. London: Bellew Publishing

1994 *Negotiate*
Faith and Life Negotiate. A Christian Story-Study. Norwich: The Canterbury Press

1995 *Credentials*
The Lively Credentials of God. London: DLT

1996 *Christmas* (revised)
Poetry of the Word at Christmas. Brighton: New Millennium

1997 *Defending*
Defending (the) Faith. The Matter of the Article. London: New Millennium

1997 *Zion*
Palestine: The Prize and Price of Zion. London: Cassell and Herndon, Virginia

1998 *Secular*
The Secular Experience of God. Harrisburg, Pennsylvania: Trinity Press International

1999 *Trust*
With God in Human Trust. Christian Faith and Contemporary Humanism, A meeting of Minds. Brighton: Sussex Academic Press

1999 *Weight*
The Weight in the Word. Prophethood: Biblical and Quranic. Brighton: Sussex Academic Press

1999 *Common*
Common Prayer. A Muslim-Christian Spiritual Anthology. Oxford: Oneworld
A revised and re-titled edition of *Alive to God* OUP, Oxford 1970

2000 *Education*
The Education of Christian faith: critical and literary encounters with the New Testament. Brighton: Sussex Academic Press

2000 *Oxford*

Islam among the Spires. An Oxford Reverie. London: Melisende

2001 *Task*
Muhammad in the Qur'an: the Task and the Text. London: Melisende

2002 *Lord*
Am I not Your Lord? Human Meaning in Divine Question. London: Melisende

2002 *Pronouns*
Faiths in their Pronouns: Websites in Identity. Brighton: Sussex Academic Press

2003 *Christian Jesus*
The Christian Jesus: Faith in the Finding. Brighton: The Alpha Press.

2004 and 2005 *Sympathy*
A Certain Sympathy of Scriptures Biblical and Quranic. Brighton: Sussex Academic Press

2004 *Tragic*
The Tragic in Islam. London: Melisende

2005 *Semitism*
Semitism: The whence and whither "How dear are your counsels". Brighton: Sussex Academic Press

2005 *Suicide*
Faith at Suicide Lives in Forfeit- Self–Bombed and Self-Betrayed. Brighton: Sussex Academic Press

2006 *West*
The Qur'an and the West. Some minding between. London: Melisende

2006 *Hands*
The Order of the Wounded Hands. Schooled in the East. London: Melisende

2006 *Wrong*
God's Wrong is most of all. Divine Capacity—Per Necessitatem Christianus. Sussex Academic Press

2006 *Lintel*
The Lowly Lintel. London: Melisende (privately published)

2007 *Inter-text*
A Christian-Muslim Inter-text Now. From Anathemata to Theme. London: Melisende

2008 *Mosque*
Mosque Sermons. A Listener for the Preacher. London: Melisende

2009 *Globe*
The Compass of the Globe. Shakespeare's Drama, Mind and Faith. London: Melisende

2009 *Iron*
The Iron in the Soul. Joseph and the Undoing of Violence. London: Melisende

2009 *Transaction*
Trans Action in Biblical Society. London: Melisende

2010 *Dying*
Dying Daily: Quotidian Living. London: Melisende

2010 *Bread*
The Breaking of the Bread. London: Melisende

2011 *Bent*
Bent to Literary Event. Masters in their Masterpieces. London: Melisende

62.

A BIBLIOGRAPHY OF KENNETH CRAGG: ARTICLES

CONTRIBUTIONS TO BOOKS

1956 ed. Sands,W: *Tensions in the Middle East.* Washington, DC: Middle East Institute (10th Annual Conference on Middle East Affairs): art. 'Decisions in Men's Minds. (Some ideological issues in the Middle East)', pp. 43-49.

1957 ed. Frye, R: *Islam and the West.* 's-Gravenhage: Mouton: art. 'The Modernist Movement in Egypt', pp. 149-178.

1966 ed. Anderson, G H: *Sermons to Men of Other Faiths and Traditions.* New York: Abingdon: art. 'To the Muslim: Man and Empire—God and Forgiveness', pp. 90-102.

1969 ed. Arberry, A J: *Religion in the Middle East.* Cambridge: Cambridge University Press vol.1: art. 'The Anglican Church', pp. 570-579.

1969 ditto. vol.2 art. 'Doctrine' (under the name 'Abd al-Tafahum,), pp. 365-412.

1969 ed. Archbishop of Canterbury: *Lambeth Essays on Faith.* London: SPCK: art. 'Dialogue with Other Faiths' pp. 32-39.

1971 ed. Samartha, S J: *Dialogue Between Men of Living Faiths.* Geneva: World Council of Churches: art. 'Dialogue and Devotion', pp. 99-103.

1972 ed. Samartha, S J: Christian-Muslim Dialogue. *Papers from Broumana.* Geneva: World Council of Churches: art. 'In the Name of God', pp. 137-144 [also printed in Islam and the Modern Age 4:1 Feb. 1973, pp. 1-10].

1974 ed. Hick, John: *Truth and Dialogue in World Religions: Conflicting Truth Claims.* Philadelphia: Westminster Press [US edition] *Truth and Dialogue. The Relationship between World Religions* London: Sheldon [British edition]: art. 'Islam and Incarnation', pp. 126-139 (both editions).

1974 Jomier, J: *Jesus. The Life of the Messiah.* Madras: CLS. Preface by Kenneth Cragg, pp. vii-xii.

1974 *New Encyclopaedia Britannica.* 15th ed. Chicago: Benton art. HADITH.

1975 ed. Hurley, M: *Beyond Tolerance. The Challenge of Mixed Marriage.* London: Chapman: art. 'Interfaith Marriage. 2 A Christian-Muslim Perspective', pp. 9-20.

1979 ed. McCurry, D: *The Gospel and Islam. A 1978 Compendium.* Monrovia, California: MARC: art. 'Islamic Theology. Limits and Bridges', pp. 196-207.

1979 ed. Falaturi, A and Schimmel, A: *We Believe in One God. The Experience of God in Christianity and Islam*. London: Burns and Oates, Introduction by Kenneth Cragg, pp. vii-ix.

1979 ed. Welch, A T and Cachia, P: *Islam: Past Influence and Present Challenge.* Edinburgh: Edinburgh University Press/New York: State University of New York Press art. 'The Art of Theology: Islamic and Christian Reflections', pp. 276-295.

1980 Kateregga, B D and Shenk, D W: *Islam and Christianity. A Muslim and a Christian in Dialogue.* Nairobi: Uzima Press (rev.ed. Grand Rapids, Michigan: Eerdmans, 1981) Foreword II by Kenneth Cragg, pp. xiii-xvi .

1980 ed. Johns, J H: *The Study of the Qur'an.* Canberra: art. 'The Qur'an in the Interfaith Future', pp. 157-81.

1981 ed. Stott, J R W and Coote, R: *Down to Earth. Studies in Christianity and Culture.* London: Hodder: art. 'Conversion and Convertibility—with special reference to Muslims', pp. 193-208.

1981 *Christian Presence and Witness in Relation to Muslim Neighbours.* World Council of Churches: Geneva: art. Bible Studies: 'God and Man', pp. 6-16 [reprinted in Encounter 82 (February 1982), pp. 1-16].

1981 ed. Jaegar, D-M A: *Christianity in the Holy Land.* Tantur: art. 'Muslim-Christian Relations at Large and the Focus of the Holy Land', pp. 301-14.

1982 ed. Berkey, R F and Edwards, S A: *Christological Perspectives: Essays in Honour of Harvey K McAthur.* New York: art. 'Doing the New Testament right: Synoptic reflections of a layperson', pp. 24-41.

1984 ed. Green, A H: *In Quest of an Islamic Humanism: Arabic and Islamic Studies in memory of Mohamed al-Nowaihi.* Cairo: American University in Cairo Press art. 'Tadabbur al-Qur'an: reading and meaning', pp. 181-195.

1985 Rahbar, Daud: *Memories and Meanings.* Privately pub. Boston, USA, Foreword by Kenneth Cragg, pp. i-vi.

1985 ed. Appleton, George: *The Oxford Book of Prayer.* Oxford: OUP, pp. 329-344 (section on Muslim prayers selected and partly translated by Kenneth Cragg).

1990 Mojzes, P and Swidler, L: *Christian Mission and Interreligious Dialogue.* Lewiston, Queenstown and Lampeter; art. 'Holding Faith and conceding Pluralism: a Christian Position', pp. 174-86.

1993 ed. Berkey, R F and Edwards, SA: *Christology in Dialogue* Cleveland: art. 'The Singer and the Song: Christology in the Context of World Religions', pp. 185-200.

1995 ed. Haddad, Y Y and Haddad, W Z: *Muslim-Christian Encounters.* Gainesville: art. 'Isma'il al-Faruqi in the Field of Dialogue', pp. 399-410.

2000 ed. Prior, M: *They Came and They Saw.* London: Melisende, art. 'The Will and the Dream', pp. 241-53.

2009 "Islam Hostage to Itself" in *World Christianity in Encounter, Essays in Memory of David Kerr* Volume 2, Edited by Stephen R Goodwin, London: Continuum, pp. 128-144.

MAJOR ARTICLES AND REVIEWS

1952 *The Muslim World* vol. 42 Jan, Apr, July and October art. 'The Christian Church and Islam Today', pp. 11-22, 112-123, 207-217, 277-287.

1953 *The Muslim World* vol. 43:2 April art. '"That Somehow may be This-how" A plea for constructive Muslim-Christian theological relations today', pp. 118-129 (under the name 'Abd al-Tafahum).

1953 *The International Review of Missions* XLII art. 'The Arab World and the Christian Debt', pp. 151-161.

1953 *The Muslim World* vol. 43:3 July art. 'Persons, Situations and Books: Christian Literature for the Contemporary Muslim', pp. 197-207.

1954 *Middle East Journal* 8:2 Spring art. 'The Intellectual Impact of Communism upon Contemporary Islam', pp. 127-138.

1954 *East and West Review. An Anglican Overseas Quarterly* XX July art. '"The Genius of Christ"—A Muslim Estimate', pp. 88-96.

1954 *The Muslim World* vol. 44:3 and 4 July and October art. 'A Cairo Debate on Islam', pp. 236-252 (under the name 'Abd al-Tafahum).

1955 *Middle East Journal* 9:1 Winter art. 'Then and Now in Egypt. The Reflections of Ahmad Amin, 1886-1954', pp. 28-40.

1955 *The Muslim World* vol. 45:2 April art. '"Each Other's Face": Some Thoughts on Muslim-Christian Colloquy Today', pp. 172-182.

1955 *The Muslim World* vol. 45:3 July art. 'Pilgrimage Prayers' (Translation), pp. 267-280.

1956 *The Muslim World* vol. 46:1 January art. 'The Qur'an and the Christian Reader. I', pp. 61-68.

1956 *The Muslim World* vol. 46:2 and 3 April and July art. '"City of Wrong". A Muslim Studies the Cross' I and II, pp. 132-143, 224-236 (under the name 'Abd al-Tafahum).

1956 *The Muslim World* vol.46 art. 'The Qur'an and the Christian Reader. I', pp. 61-8.

1956 *Journal of World History* 3 art. 'Religious Developments of Islam in the Twentieth Century (with special reference to the pressures of the modern, secular world)', pp. 504-524.

1956 *Association of Professors of Missions and Related Fields* Third Biennial Meeting, June art. 'The Meeting of Muslim and Christian', pp. 46-56.

1956 *Religion in Life* Autumn art. 'Islam: Non-Christian Religions in the Contemporary World', pp. 483-493.

1957 *East and West Review* XXIII January art. 'Power and Suffering in the Arab World', pp. 3-11.

1957 *The N.E.S.T. Theological Review* vol 6:1 (Spring) art. 'Thoughts, Words, Pens, Deeds', pp. 7-12.

1957 *The Muslim World* vol. 47:2 April art. 'Ramadan Prayers' (Translation), pp. 210-223.

1957 *International Review of Missions* XLVI, no. 183 (July) art. 'Hearing by the Word of God' (a review of Hendrik Kraemer: *Religion and the Christian Faith*), pp. 241-251.

1957 *The Muslim World* vol. 47:3 July art. 'Seek Forgiveness of God', pp. 239-247 (under the name 'Abd al-Tafahum).

1958 *Bulletin of the Hartford Seminary Foundation* no. 24 (June) art. 'The Holy Spirit and the Mission of the Church', pp. 24-35.

1958 *East and West Review* XXIV art. 'Archbishopric in Jerusalem', pp. 3-9.

1958 *Frontier* vol. 1:2 April art. 'The Christian Approach to Islam', pp. 128-132.

1958 *The Muslim World* vol. 48:3 July art. 'West African Catechism', pp. 237-247.

1959 *The Muslim World* vol. 49:1 January art. 'The Exodus: an Egyptian View' (translation with introduction from Md Kamil Husain), pp. 30-40.

1959 Bible studies: '"In Thy Light we see Light"—Ps 36:9' in The Christian Faith and the Contemporary Middle Eastern World, Report of study conference held at Asmara, April; pub. by United Presbyterian Church in the USA [Summary in Dutch by DC Mulder in De Heerbaan for 12.6.59, no 4, pp. 125-174].

1959 *Indian Journal of Theology* April-June art. 'The Sense of the Word', pp. 41-7.

1959 *The Muslim World* vol. 49:3 July art. 'The Meaning of Zulm in the Qur'an' (translation from Md Kamil Husain), pp. 196-212.

1959 do. art. 'The Qur'an and the Holy Communion', pp. 239-248 (under the Name 'Abd al-Tafahum).

1959 *The Student World* vol 52, art. 'The Divine Word in Human Trust', pp. 376-384.

1960 *Frontier* 3:3 Autumn art. 'Islam and the Political Order', pp. 194-200.

1960 *Bulletin of the Henry Martyn Institute of Islamic Studies* Hyderabad, India: a series of articles entitled 'Christian thoughts on Quranic themes' [reprinted editorials from *The Muslim World*—see further section of bibliography].

1961 *The Student World* vol 54 art. 'The Encounter of Christianity and Islam', pp. 126-136.

1961 *The International Review of Missions* 50 (July 1961) review of Constance Padwick: *Muslim Devotions*, pp. 344-346.

1962 *The Muslim World* vol. 52:1 January art. Review of Norman Daniel: *Islam and the West*, pp. 59-61.

1963 Bishop J C Jones Memorial Lecture (CMS) art. 'The Christian Ministry in the World of Islam'.

1964 *Union Seminary Quarterly Review* 19:4 May art. 'Encounter with non-Christian Faiths', pp. 299-309 [reprinted in *Religion and Society* 14:1 (March 1967), pp. 37-46].

1966 *Union Seminary Quarterly Review* 21 January art. 'This Cruciform World. A Study in Christian Universality', pp. 103-115.

1966 *Duke Divinity School Review* 31:2 Spring art. 'Islamic Reflections on Contemporary Theology', pp. 99-112.

1966 *Union Seminary Quarterly Review* 21 May art. 'Technology, Theology and Christian Faith' (review of AT van Leeuwen: *Christianity in World History*), pp. 433-437.

1966 *The Muslim World* vol. 56:3 October reviews of (ET) P. Hitti: *The Origins of the Islamic State*, pp. 321-322 and Zygon: *Journal of Religion and Science*, pp. 322-323.

1967 *Study Encounter* 3:2 art. 'The Credibility of Christianity', pp. 56-61 [reprinted in *Dialog* 8 Winter 1969, pp. 59-63].

1968 *Union Seminary Quarterly Review* 23:4 Summer art. 'Common Prayer (Among All Religions)', pp. 367-376.

1969 *International Review of Mission* 58 October art. '"The Tempter said …" Reflections on Christian Theology and Development', pp. 378-389.

1969 *The Muslim World* vol. 59:4 October art. 'Constance E Padwick 1886-1968', pp. 29-39.

1970 *United Theological College Magazine* (Bangalore) 36 (1969/1970) art. 'You Took Advantage of my Simplicity', pp. 26-36.

1971 *Bangalore Theological Forum* 3:2 July art. 'The Cross in the Qur'an', pp. 11-19.

1972 *The N.E.S.T. Theological Review* July-October art. 'The Contemporary Near East as a School of Theology', pp. 5-14.

1972 *Frontier* 15:4 November art. 'The Paradox of Israel', pp. 237-239.

1973 *Islam and the Modern Age* 4 (i) February art. 'In the Name of God …', pp. 1-10.

1973 *Frontier* 16:3 Autumn art. 'Paradox of Israel: A Reply', pp. 165-166.

1974 *Islam and the Modern Age* 5 (i) February art. 'An Imperative Path. Law and Religion in Relation', pp. 29-38.

1974 *Theology* 77 October art. 'Cathedral for a Bridge: with each other about God', pp. 518-526.

1974 *Journal of Ecumenical Studies* 11 Winter art. 'The Qur'an and the Contemporary Middle East', pp. 1-12.

1975 *Anglican Theological Review* 57 January art. 'Christian-Muslim Dialogue', pp. 109-120.

1976 *Christian Study Centre Series* (Rawalpindi) no. 13, 'The Christian in the World of Islam: In Spirit, in Thought, in Action'.

1976 *International Review of Mission* LXV 260 October Contributions *passim*, pp. 365-460.

1977 *International Review of Mission* LXVI 262 April art. 'Retrospect—Us and Ours', pp. 169-175.

1977 *Religious Studies* 13:4 art. 'How not Islam?', pp. 387-394.

1977 *Tantur Yearbook 1976-1977* art. 'Salvation Concepts in Islam: The Search for Authenticity', pp. 105-123 [reprinted as Concepts of Salvation in Living Faiths Jerusalem: Ecumenical Institute for Advanced Theological Study 1979].

1977 *Islamochristiana* 3 art. 'Legacies and Hopes in Muslim/Christian Theology', pp. 1-10 [reprinted in *Encounter* 41 (January 1978), pp. 1-10].

1978 *Religious Studies* 14:4 review of B C Ray: *African Religions* (1976), pp. 540-541.

1979 *Studies in Islam* 16 art. 'Discussion on tauhid', pp. 122-126.

1979 *Theology* LXXXII 688 July art. 'Buddhism and Baptism', pp. 259-265.

1980 *N.E.S.T. Theological Review* III:2 art. 'Christianity as a World Religion', pp. 10-19.

1980 *The Muslim World* vol. 70:2 April review of tr. and ed. Issa Boullata: *My life: The Autobiography of an Egyptian Scholar, Writer and Cultural Leader* (by Ahmad Amin) Leiden: E J Brill, 1978, pp. 146-147.

1980 *Studia Missionalia* vol 29 art. 'God and Salvation—An Islamic Study', pp. 155-166.

1980 *Religion* 10 Autumn art. 'Being Christian and Being Muslim: a personal debate', pp. 196-208.

1981 *The Muslim World* vol. 71:1 January art. '"Greater is God". Contemporary takbir: Muslim and Christian', pp. 27-39.

1981 *Middle East Journal* 35:1 review of Md Asad: *The Message of the Qur'an* (1980), pp. 88-89.

1981 *International Bulletin of Missionary Research* 5:4 October art. 'Temple Gairdner's Legacy', pp. 164-167.

1981 *Ecumenical Institute of Advanced Theological Study* 1978-1979 art. 'Aspects of Quranic Prayer', pp. 115-127.

1982 *The Expository Times* 93:11 review of Y Y Haddad: *Contemporary Islam and the Challenge of History* (1982), p. 350.

1983 *Studia Missionalia* vol. 32 art. 'Finality in Islam', pp. 219-230.

1983 *Vidyajyoti* 47:3 April art. 'Man on the Loose', pp. 126-134.

1983 *American-Arab Affairs* 4 art. 'By the fig and the olive: perspective round Jerusalem', pp. 135-145.

1983 *The Expository Times* 94:9 review of I R Netton: *Muslim Neo-Platonists. An Introduction to the thought of the Brethren of Purity* (1982), p. 285.

1984 *International Bulletin of Missionary Research* 8:4 October Review of Lesslie Newbigin: *The Other Side of 1984*, pp. 180-181.

1984 *The Expository Times* 95:12 review of W M Watt: *Islam and Christianity Today. A Contribution to Dialogue.* (1983), p. 380.

1985 *The Muslim World* vol. 75:1 January review of V E Makari: *Ibn Taymiyyah's Ethics—The Social Factor*, p. 53.

1986 *The Muslim World* vol. 76:2 April art. 'The Iron in the Soul: In Memoriam: Dr. Fa'iz Sayigh', pp. 67-79.

1986 *Studia Missionalia* vol. 35 art. 'Sainthood and Spirituality in Islam', pp. 179-198.

1986 *Bangalore Theological Forum* 18:2-3 (April-September) art. 'Fundamentals and Initiatives in Islamic Hermeneutics', pp. 97-106.

1986 *The Expository Times* 97:8 review of Md Zia Ullah: *The Islamic concept of God* (1984), p. 253.

1986 *The Expository Times* 97:10 review of Larry Ekin: *Enduring Witness. The Churches and the Palestinians.* vol. 2 (1985), p. 311.

1992 *Journal of the Institute of Muslim Minority Affairs* 13, art. 'Peace, Pacifism and Religious Faith', pp. 215-21.

1998 *The Muslim World* vol. 88 art. '"My tears into thy bottle": Prophethood and God', pp. 238-55.

2004 *Islam and Christian–Muslim Relations*, Vol 15, No. 3 (July) art. 'A Strange Half-absence: Reflections on A Faithful Presence', pp. 317-329.

OTHER PUBLICATIONS

Articles

1943 *Under Syrian Skies* April art. 'A Moslem Stronghold', pp. 44-45.

1948 The Trinity (pamphlet) London: Church Book Room Press.

1949 Revelation (pamphlet) London: Church Book Room Press.

1960 *The Listener* vol. 63 no. 1613, 25 February art. 'Jesus in Contemporary Islam', pp. 347-349.

1961 The News Bulletin of the Near East Christian Council, Beirut: art. 'Thou That Art Highly Favoured', pp. 15-17.

1973 Lectures at Near East Christian Council Summer School, Lebanon, 16-27 July: 'Atonement' and 'Messiah'.

1977 Sermon preached at All Saints Cathedral, Cairo, 16 January: 'Who is Jesus Christ?'.

1978 review of Gai Eaton: King of the Castle in *The Times Literary Supplement* 3992:1126.

1980 *One World* 59 August/September art. 'Testing the Reach of Faith and Fellowship', pp. 14-15.

1981 *Church News* March art. 'In a (W)hole', pp. 1-3.

1981 *Church News* September art. 'The Ayatollah and the Archbishop', pp. 5-6.

1982 Sermon preached at Great St Mary's Church, Cambridge, 14 Feb: '"Light breakes where no sun shines": Iran and revolutionary Islam' .

1982 Bible Lands Spring Review of Dow Marmur: *Beyond Survival*, pp. 24-26.

1982 *Church News* April art. 'Bread and Wine', pp. 4-5.

1982 Bible Lands Autumn Review of David Brown: *All Their Splendour*, p. 82.

1983 *Church News* April art. 'Blake in Jerusalem at Easter', pp. 9-10.

1984 *Church News* July art. 'Privy Counsel', pp. 11-12.

1985 *Church News* May art. 'The Potters and the King', pp. 1-3.

1985 *Interfaith News* 9 October art. 'The Church and Other Faiths' p 1.

1986 *Interfaith News* 10 February art. 'The Church and Other Faiths' (continued) p 5.

1986 *Church News* March art. 'Faith in Faith?', pp. 1-3.

1999 Centre for the Study of Islam and Christian-Muslim Relations *Occasional Paper no.5*: 'The Heart of Religion and the Heart of God'.

2002 'Give Us this Day Messiah's Bread', an address given to the USPG/CMS Consultation *Challenges and Opportunities in Islamic Contexts.*

2003 'The Excellences of Jerusalem', London, Altajir World of Islam Trust, 18, pp. Brochure with bibliography of books by Kenneth Cragg.

2003 '"Dum Spiro Spero": Hope for Muslim-Christian Relations?' Inaugural lecture at the Edinburgh Centre for Muslim-Christian Studies.

Pamphlet Series

September 1957—June 1962: *Operation Reach* (27 double issues) Near East Christian Council Study Program in Islam, Beirut, Lebanon.

September 1962—December 1964: *Emmaus Furlongs* (20 issues) Near East Christian Council Study Program, Beirut, Lebanon/Canterbury, UK.

Spring 1971—Autumn 1972: *The Mind of Christ* (4 issues) Near East Council of Churches Study Program, Beirut, Lebanon.

Epiphany 1979—All Saints' Tide 1983: *Grace Cup* (20 issues) Episcopal Church in Jerusalem and the Middle East Farnham, UK.

Editorials in The Muslim World

1953 43:1 'The All-Great … the All-Loving', pp. 1-2 (signed).

1953 43:2 'There is no God but God' p 79 (signed).

1953 43:3 *'Tawwil Balak'*, pp. 157-8 (signed).

1953 43:4 *'al-Rahman al-Rahim'*, pp. 235-6 (signed).

1954 44:1 *'Hayya 'ala 'l-Falah'*, pp. 1-2.

1954 44:2 'The "Perhaps" Within (La'allakum)', pp. 83-4.

1954 44:3 'The "Middle" East *(Kadhalika ja'alnakum ummatan wasatan)*', pp. 161-2.

1955 45:1 'The Pilgrim's Cry *(Labbayka Allahumma labbayka)*', pp. 1-3.

1955 45:2 'The Criterion *(al-Furqan)*', pp. 109-112.

1955 45:3 'I Repair unto God *(a'udhu bi-'llah)*', pp. 215-8 [reprinted in *The Bulletin of the Henry Martyn Institute* LVIII:2 (Apr-June 1960), pp. 16-19].

1955 45:4 'Unto God is the Becoming *(ila 'llahi 'l-masir)*', pp. 309-312.

1956 46:1 'Lord of the Worlds *(Rabb al-'Alamin)*', pp. 1-4.

1956 46:2 'There is no Compelling in Religion *(la ikraha fi 'l-din)*', pp. 95-8 [reprinted in *The Bulletin of the Henry Martyn Institute* ILVIII:1 (Jan-Mar 1960), pp. 14-17].

1956 46:3 'The Baptism of God *(Sibghat Allah)*', pp. 189-192.

1956 46:4 'God the Unwearied *(la ta'khudhuhu sinatun wa la nawm)*', pp. 291-4.

1957 47:1 'The Servant and the Son *(lan yastankifa 'l-Masih an yakuna 'abdan li-'llah)*', pp. 1-4 [reprinted in *The Bulletin of the Henry Martyn Institute* ILIX:1 (July-Sept 1960), pp. 8-11].

1957 47:2 'Right Thoughts of God *(ma qadaru 'llaha haqqa qadrihi)*', pp. 93-7.

1957 47:3 'What God hath joined together *(yaqta'una ma amara Allahu bihi an yusala)*', pp. 183-6 [reprinted in *The Bulletin of the Henry Martyn Institute* ILIX:2 (Oct-Dec 1960), pp. 6-9].

1957 47:4 'The Hinge and the Lock *(an 'ala qulubin aqfaluha)*', pp. 267-270 [reprinted in *The Bulletin of the Henry Martyn Institute* ILIX:3 (Jan. 1961), pp. 6-9]].

1958 48:1 'Man's Unruliness and God's Rule *(hatta la takuna fitnatun)*', pp. 1-5.

1958 48:2 'The Hijrah of the Soul *(la malja'a min Allah illa ilayhi)*', pp. 89-93.

1958 48:4 'Meeting with your Lord *(bi-liqa'i rabbikum tuqinun)*', pp. 269-273.

1959 49:1 'The Right Righteousness *(la tubtilu sadaqatikum)*', pp. 1-4.

1959 49:2 'A Jesting Creator? *(ma khalaqna al-samawat wa 'l-arda … la'ibin)*', pp. 91-5 [reprinted in *The Bulletin of the Henry Martyn Institute* April 1961].

1959 49:3 'These Imperialists *(ista'marakum Allah)*', pp. 179-182 [reprinted in *The Bulletin of the Henry Martyn Institute* July 1961].

1959 49:4 'What's wrong with Independence? *(an ra'ahu istaghna)*, pp. 271-4 [reprinted in *The Bulletin of the Henry Martyn Institute* October 1961].

1960 50:1 'God our Sufficiency *(hasbuna Allah)*', pp. 1-4.

1960 50:2 'The Days of our Lord *(yawma wulidtu wa yawma amutu wa yawma ub'athu hayyan)*', pp. 81-5.

UNPUBLISHED WORK

1937 The Place of Authority in Matters of Religious Belief

Ellerton Theological Essay Prize, Oxford University.

1947 Morality and Religion

T H Green Moral Philosophy Prize Essay, Oxford University.

1950 Islam in the 20th Century: The Relevance of Christian Theology and the Relation of the Christian Mission to its Problems

DPhil thesis, Oxford University.

INDEX